Once Upon a Time in
PALM BEACH

Karen Soven

Copyright © 2025 by Karen Soven

All rights reserved.
No part of this book may be reproduced in any form or by any electronic or mechanical means, including information storage and retrieval systems, without written permission from the author, except for the use of brief quotations in a book review.

ISBN: [978-1-968339-09-8] (ebook)

ISBN: [978-1-968339-10-4] (paperback)

ISBN: [978-1-968339-12-8] (hardcover)

Cover Photo
Model: Nina Scherer
Hair & Makeup: Deborah Koepper, DK Beauty
Photography: Lucien Capehart

This work is nonfiction and, as such, reflects the author's memory of her experiences. Some of the names and identifying characteristics of the individuals featured in this book have been changed to protect their privacy, and certain individuals are composites. Dialogue and events have been recreated; in some cases, conversations have been edited to convey their substance rather than written exactly as they occurred.

For more information about Karen Soven and
Once Upon a Time in Palm Beach, scan the QR code below:

For Leslie, who never met her prince

"Until the lion learns how to write, the story will always be told from the point of view of the hunter."

—African Proverb

Advance Praise

"In *Once Upon a Time in Palm Beach: Tales of Life & Love From the Land of Sunshine & Money*, Karen Soven spins a sparkling tale of fairy dust and grit. Like every heroine worth cheering for, she faces her villains with courage, wisdom and a fabulous pair of shoes. Readers will revel in this peek behind the curtain, soaring beside her on a magic carpet ride through heartbreak and triumph. With wit, warmth and style, Karen reminds us that happily ever after isn't found—it's made."

—Rochelle Weinstein, *USA Today* bestselling author of *We Are Made of Stars*

"Karen Soven writes an addictive, engaging take on the modern Cinderella story, only in her fairy tale, Cindy can pick out and pay for her own party shoes. Kudos!"

—Annabelle Gurwitch, *New York Times* bestselling author of *The End of My Life is Killing Me*

"*Once Upon a Time in Palm Beach* is a sultry, sun-drenched tale of a mother determined to rise above her struggles and claim her place among the glittering elite of Island life. Between charity galas and whispered scandals, she navigates desire and deception with stilettos sharp enough to draw blood and a wardrobe that speaks louder than her secrets. The story shimmers with temptation and triumph, capturing the intoxicating pull of ambition, luxury and love under the relentless Florida sun. It's racy, irresistible and as stylishly unapologetic as its heroine."

—Nicole Nicholas, author of *Made in Sin*

"In a fractured world yearning for connection, Karen Soven gives you an insider's glimpse into the glamorous enclave of Palm Beach. Claim your golden ticket to this invite-only soirée where you'll dazzle as your truest self. No gown? Karen and her squad of fairy godmothers will drape you in bespoke splendor ensuring you arrive not just invited but unforgettable!"

—Melissa C. Butterworth, author of *Clues*

"In the glitzy world of Palm Beach high society, secrets are as valuable as diamonds—and twice as dangerous. Karen has chosen to guard those of her neighbors, but her story could still unravel the curated lives of the elite residents of the Island. *Once Upon a Time in Palm Beach* is a stylish tale of power, betrayal, and the price of perfection."

—Sir Michael Honablue, founder of Global Billionaire Palm Beach

Table of Contents

PART I: A LIFE 1
A Place to Call Home 3
- Ballet and Ball Gowns 13
- The Winner Is the Highest Bidder 18
- Dances and Daughters 23
- Social Climbing or Climbing the Ladder to Prosperity 27
- You Can Take the Boy Out of Brooklyn, but You Can't Make Him Palm Beach 37
- M'mm M'mm Good or Not so Good 43
- Life, Lilly and the Pursuit of Happiness 48
- Thanks a Trillion 52
- Strangers Among Us 56
- Bachelor #1 60
- When You're Single You Mingle 67
- Takeover Target 70
- Bring Your Daughter to Work Day 74
- His (But Not Hers) in Highland Beach 82
- Two Kinds of Investments 85
- Cashmere & Castles 92
- Taking the Show on the Road 95
- No Box of Candy This Valentine's Day 106
- Bachelor # 2 110
- Prince Charming #1 119

Home for the Holidays 125
Buy In or Goodbye.. 130
PART II: A LIVING... **135**
Mother Knows Best 136
Stepping Up to the Plate or Stepping Down in Status....... 143
The Little Prince.. 151
Dating or Mating... 155
Prince Charming #2.. 161
Date 8: Would You Care for Dessert? 173
Training & Gaming... 179
When It Rains It Pours 186
Prince Charming #3.. 192
London Bridges Falling Down 199
A Happier Valentine's Day 202
Prince Charming #1 Returns 207
Spring Fling with Faith 211
Ring-a-Ding Daphne 213
No More Knights in Shining Armor.............................. 217
One Door Closes, Another Opens 221
There Goes Someone Pulling the Rug Again 228
Breaking Free From the Valentine's Curse.................... 231
Buyer's Remorse.. 238
Beware of the Black Swan 242
Gin and Toxic 250
Escape from Palm Beach 256
A Hobby Lends a Hand 259

Frog or Prince 270
Farewell to Fundraisers 274
Fleeing the Festival 278
Part III: A Legacy 280
A Prince, a Princess and a Castle 281
One Last Visit With Valerie 290
Back to Sweeping the Chimney 296
Trial Separation (Not the Kind You Think) 304
Second Time's the Charm 308
Pumpkin Carriage or Prince? 311
Another Door Closes 317
One Last Sweater Sighting 320
Hip-Hoppin' and Rockin' 327
A Valuable Lesson From Lana 337
Once Upon a Time in Miami 347
Once Upon a Time in Palm Beach 351
Acknowledgments 357
About the Author 359
About the Publisher 361

PART I:
A LIFE

A Place to Call Home

I missed the Island. Not "the islands," as people often referred to the ones in the Caribbean or the Greek Islands where my grandparents came from, but the Island of Palm Beach, Florida. I had worked there for a year in 1995 before I was fired. I may have lost an income, but I left with an important realization that hit me as soon as I was back on the mainland: I didn't want to just work on this Island; I wanted to live there.

Being out of work gave me the chance to observe my husband Scott's profession more closely and strategize how his career moves could get us where I wanted to be. Scott wasn't happy about this. Currently, he was a middle manager at a finance firm. It seemed to me the way to advance in this field was not on the administrative track, but as a wealth advisor. "The advisors have connections to rich people. That's how they attract clients," he protested. "I don't—I'm from Brooklyn; I'm 31—most money managers are older."

As I sat at the kitchen table in our small rental apartment in West Palm Beach, I pondered our situation. Living in Manhattan in my 20s, I fell into the fashion world as an apprentice to a menswear designer. The fast pace, the long days that turned into nights out on the town and the money that fed my appetite for adventure intrigued me. At the time, I thought this fast-paced life would be my forever. All that changed when my daughter Emmy was born.

A PLACE TO CALL HOME

I'd ditched my Saint Laurent suits and Manolo Blahnik pumps to care for my daughter. In Manhattan, I couldn't imagine how it would be possible to send her to the elite private schools my former colleagues' and clients' kids attended, assuming I knew someone who could help her get in. A tragic event from my past plagued me; living in the suburbs wasn't an option. When Emmy took her first step, I was ready to leap back into the luxury goods arena. Working in a market outside of New York would give me the work-life balance I needed. Once I broadened my search, it felt like more than luck that I landed a position as sales director for the handbag designer Lana Marks in Palm Beach.

Who better to help me further my dream of starting a fashion label one day than this Princess Diana look-alike who charmed her way to the pages of *Vogue*? And she did it while raising two tweens. The finance firm where Scott worked was opening a branch office in Florida, and a move would accelerate his career path. The timing was perfect.

Scott wasn't connected to people with money in New York, but we were in Palm Beach now. I set out to spend time in places the natives frequented to better understand this place so steeped in history. I first met Nina at the Recreation Center when she was walking barefoot with her son, who seemed to be about Emmy's age. When I asked her name, I almost expected her to say "Ariel" as her flaming ringlets of red hair and twinkling blue eyes immediately made me think of the Disney princess. She accepted the ride I offered, explaining she lived close by. She told me the bare feet were a product of growing up here when Palm Beach was a sleepy little beach town. That piqued my curiosity. I knew there were few people our age who could lay claim to being born here. The Island was a winter playground for the rich, not a place where people lived year-round.

"How was it, growing up here?" I asked. "I work nearby and I'm shopping for a house. The suburbs of West Palm or Palm Beach

Gardens don't appeal to me," I said, referring to the places where people our age were putting down roots. "They seem so removed from all the action."

"I loved it," Nina said. "I can't think of a better place to raise a family. Mine has been here for three generations. My father owns Kassatly's, a store that sells linens. It's the oldest shop on Worth Avenue. It was founded by my grandfather."

I assumed the Island was out of our price range, available only to those with old money. Then Nina described "the North End." Because this section was two miles away from town, it was considered far from everything and was therefore less expensive. The homes in this area were Bermuda-style beach houses, which meant they had one story with a split floor plan: a premier bedroom with an en-suite bathroom on one side and two bedrooms and bathrooms on the other. These homes were modest compared to the ones designed by the famous architects Addison Mizner and Maurice Fatio in the estate section and center of town. The commute from any suburb outside of New York City required boarding buses, trains and ferries along with millions of other people doing the same thing. By contrast, a scenic drive along the ocean seemed like a luxury, not an inconvenience. In this part of town, the houses displayed various styles of architecture, and the residents of each street socialized at beach cabanas that dotted the coastline. Maybe the North End was our place.

For as long as I could remember, my mind moved like pieces in a chess game—my thoughts racing ahead, calculating the next play before it was my turn. If Scott was going to manage money for high-net-worth individuals, wouldn't the best way to build relationships with them be to live among them? I relayed my plan to Carl, the managing director of the firm. He agreed. No one from the firm had settled on the Island. The cost of an entry-level home was the same as a two-bedroom apartment in Manhattan, and

Carl assured me we'd be able to afford one on a money manager's salary. He even offered to help.

"I'll give any leads that come in from the Island to Scott," he said, smiling. "In the beginning, I'll go to client meetings with him. He can do it; I know it. And you can network with him at charity events, Kari."

Carl had been a wealth advisor before he was given the position of managing them. He had confidence in Scott, and so did I. Scott was trustworthy and a trailblazer when it came to investing. Few guys could claim they owned a Manhattan co-op by age 30. After much discussion, my husband agreed to try it. I promised myself we would be living on the Island before Emmy started school. This gave me less than three years to do two things: find a house and save for the down payment to buy it.

When my mom came to visit, I took her to see these homes constructed in the 1940s, '50s and '60s. Most of them had been built as vacation cottages for northerners coming to Palm Beach for the winter. Many had maid's quarters off the kitchen, a throwback to the times when people traveled with staff. This space would be perfect for a nanny! The only downside was the musty smell that reminded me of the mudroom at our beach house when my sisters and I left wet bathing suits in a heap overnight. My mom thought it was ridiculous for us to shell out money to live like this.

"I can't believe this is ritzy Palm Beach," she said. "These homes are uninhabitable. And you are really going to do laundry in a garage?" she asked, referring to the location of the washing machine and dryer. "This isn't how you were raised, Kari. You're being foolish. Scott will never go for this. There are brand-new starter homes in West Palm Beach that are much less expensive."

My mom loved Scott. To her, he was the knight in shining armor who rode in on a white horse and rescued me when my previous boyfriend promised marriage then reneged, leaving me like a used dress someone attempts to return after wearing.

After seeing 30 or more of these homes, I was feeling discouraged as well. But something about the Island gripped me like the pull of the ocean during high tide. It seemed that once you settled here, doors to its refined way of life and old-world traditions would open. Nina invited us to some parties around town. The exchanges between the people we met seemed deeper and more intimate than the ones we had forged in Manhattan. The immensity of city life disappeared in this village. It seemed once you lived here, your name was added to its permanent guest list. All you had to do was RSVP. This was a world I wanted to belong to, one I wanted my daughter to be a part of. Nothing was going to stop me from getting our name on that list.

We met Drew and Bri at the apartment complex in West Palm Beach where we lived. From that day on we referred to them as our "first couple friends." Drew and Bri were 25, a bit younger than us, and didn't have any married friends. They'd moved from Drew's parents' house on the Island for the purpose of making some. I laughed when Bri told me that.

"You gave up a mansion on the ocean, free rent and live-in help to live here?" The apartment complex had a pool, a gym and racquetball courts, amenities that young people desired, but it didn't compare to a waterfront estate. Bri moved to West Palm Beach as a teenager, when her parents opened a restaurant here. The way she tied a silk scarf on her purse gave away her French background. She invited us over to sample her cooking. The Porsche Drew parked outside alluded to his privileged upbringing. Scott was afraid he'd be snobby, but Drew was the opposite, accepting of everyone, regardless of their background or status. The way he listened when I spoke made me feel like I mattered. Between Bri's many cousins and Drew's single friends, their extra bedroom was always full.

"How would we meet any couples our age on the Island when there are none?" Bri asked. "Besides, I wanted to 'play house' in my own house, not my in-laws. And if we hadn't moved out, we would never have met you and Scott." I admired her courage and independence.

Bri was right; we were lucky to find each other. I taught everyone how to play bridge, so we could all have game night. Bri and I hung out when the guys watched football on Sunday or went to a midnight movie. We bonded the way people sharing a stage of life do. Drew, like Scott, attended college in New York City and chose finance as a career. Bri, a chef by trade, taught me how to cook. Scott was delighted to save money on dining out. I, on the other hand, taught Bri about resourcefulness, which Drew admired. Bri was about to spend a small fortune on party favors until I showed her how a bit of tissue paper, cellophane and ribbon could turn the simplest item into one made by a party planner.

When their baby girl was born, Drew and Bri began their own house search. Drew's mom, a doctor, had the inside scoop on one a patient of hers was selling. Drew's mom possessed a European glamour that attracted the socialite set to her practice. Certainly a house fit for one of her patients would be appropriate for me. Bri felt this particular home was too small for her and Drew; they hoped for a large family. However, she thought it was perfect for Scott and me since two was our magic number when it came to kids.

As I drove down North Lake Way, I passed the bronze animal sculptures of the Phipps Estates. When I approached the house number Bri gave me, I was surprised to see a freshly painted pale yellow one-story contemporary home. My eyes were drawn to the colorful toucans in the etched glass of the double entry doors. Guessing the house was vacant, I checked to make sure no one was watching and snuck around to the backyard (Scott later informed me this was trespassing). I was awed by what I saw through a bay window that ran the width of the living room—white ceramic floors stretched out like cotton fields, and floor-to-ceiling glass invited the outdoors inside. Unlike the others I'd seen, this house had been renovated. It looked brand-new.

The grassy green yard I was standing in was enclosed by high ficus hedges and trees with the tops squared and rounded off so perfectly one might guess that Edward Scissorhands was the gardener. A row of palm trees planted across the length of the backyard gave it a secluded feeling. French doors off the kitchen led to a clay-tiled loggia where two large ceiling fans whooshed. There was a cool breeze coming from the ocean, one block to the east. Perfect. Emmy would have two playgrounds: the backyard and the beach. I wrote a letter expressing my desire to buy the house, addressed it to "Owner," and slid it into the envelope.

I will always remember the day when Darlene, the owner of that lovely yellow house, telephoned and invited us over to see it. We were greeted warmly at the front door by Darlene herself, dressed in palazzo pants and a Missoni print headwrap that kept her long hair off her face. Her lipstick color was the perfect combination of coral and pink. She and I bonded instantly when she told me she was a countess. I was obsessed with royals! She explained that her main home was a ranch in Loxahatchee, where she kept exotic pets like monkeys and llamas. She used this one when she came to town for luncheons and charity galas. That would explain why one room contained rolling racks of cocktail dresses, gowns and fancy skirt suits.

Darlene's sense of design was on display in every corner of the house. She led us from room to room carpeted with silk and wool Persian rugs that looked more like fine art than floor coverings. She offered to sell them to us along with the rest of the home's furnishings. I almost choked knowing that it would be a stretch for us to come up with a down payment, let alone her treasures. Her boyfriend, Beau, a banker type with a Boston accent, looked closely at me and Scott. I could tell he was skeptical we could afford this mini mansion they were selling.

"Let the boys work the numbers, Kari, that was never really my thing," Darlene said as she led me away from the men into the kitchen. Numbers may not have been her thing, but they were mine. I had already come up with one we could manage.

At some point in the negotiation Scott walked over to me and whispered, "Beau says the house is worth a lot more than what we are offering."

"Don't worry," I said. "Tell him you think it is too and wish we could pay more, but this is our first house, and this is the most we can afford."

We left with Scott loving the house as much as I did, but no deal. August turned to September, and we heard nothing. Scott was nervous; he knew the house was a good investment.

"Call Darlene, Kari. We'll give them their price. I don't want to lose it."

"The season doesn't start for another three months. The house isn't listed and they only have two options: put it on the market before buyers return to town or accept our offer." I was confident our phone would ring.

In early October, Darlene called and asked to meet again "to see if we could all get together and figure something out," as she put it. We offered a bit more and they accepted a bit less. Beau agreed to give us financing if we couldn't get it on our own.

In December, we waved goodbye to West Palm and drove over the bridge that transported us to the Island. A light rain cleared and the sun shone through—a rainbow of red, yellow, green, indigo and violet stretched out to greet us. I would need to work some magic to furnish this house that was three times the size of the apartment we left and larger than the house where I grew up in the suburbs. Once my dad was gone it haunted me, like a horror movie you start to watch and then shut off because you've seen it before and can't bear the ending. Once I turned 17, I chose a school as far away as possible and never looked back.

Once Upon a Time in Palm Beach

In Palm Beach, mailboxes are placed where property lines meet the street. One day, my next-door neighbor was getting her mail at the same time as I was.

"Hi, I'm Brenda Straus," she said, introducing herself. "Welcome to the neighborhood. Where did you move from?"

"Originally New York City," I said.

"How funny, me too," Brenda said. "My family owned stores there."

I knew her last name sounded familiar. "Do you mean Abraham and Straus?" I asked, referring to the iconic chain where my mom took me to get my prom dress.

"Yes, that's the one. Sadly, it closed," Brenda said.

"Really? I didn't know that. My family and I have been living in West Palm Beach and haven't been back to the city in a while."

"I didn't know people moved from West Palm Beach to Palm Beach," she said.

She didn't mean to disparage me. West Palm Beach and Palm Beach were close to each other on the map, but they were worlds apart. West Palm Beach was working class and Palm Beach was a bastion of old money. This divide was so entrenched, culturally and historically, that moves between the two rarely happened.

"I'm certain most don't," I said. "But I fell in love with the Island and knew I couldn't live anywhere else."

Months later, after we settled in, I bumped into Darlene lunching at Dempsey's. She told me the widow of Aldo Gucci, founder of the famed fashion house, had inquired about Darlene's house. She thought it would be ideal for her now that she no longer needed an oceanfront estate.

"I told her it was sold. Bruna is a dear friend, and she would have paid more, but I'm happy the house is yours, Kari. I know you will care for it the way I did."

Darlene was right; I would. It took three years of searching to find this house. But we arrived a year earlier than I planned—Emmy wouldn't begin school until fall!

"That's some starter home," my mom said when I sent her pictures. "I can't believe it was the same price as those decrepit ones you took me to."

"It was a bit more, Mom, but this one's not a starter—it's a starter and a finisher. It will be our first and last house. We're never leaving."

Or so I thought.

Ballet and Ball Gowns

Finding work in this lush Garden of Eden we called home proved to be as difficult as furnishing our new house. To give myself a reprieve from both, I socialized with Amanda, the wife of Scott's boss, Carl. Since Scott was Carl's right-hand guy, Amanda was determined to keep him happy. It was important for me to stay on good terms with Amanda for two reasons: one, because she was fond of Scott—she'd known him longer than me and thought of him as a brother. The second was because she was a pro in the corporate wife role, and I wasn't.

Amanda and I sat among the crowd of ladies who lunched at Ta-boo. This restaurant was the go-to for women who spent their days shopping. It was located in the middle block of Worth Avenue, nestled between upscale jewelry stores and designer boutiques. The bar at Ta-boo seemed busy for midday. I recognized men accompanied by women who appeared several decades younger—many of them were familiar to me from *The Shiny Sheet*. This was the nickname for *The Palm Beach Daily News,* which reported the comings and goings of the Island's inhabitants. It got its nickname from the smudge-proof high-end glossy paper it's printed on, but it dished out all the dirt on the locals.

As Amanda and I dug into our warm steak salads, she casually asked, "So did you get your gown yet?" I had no idea what she was talking about. When I didn't answer, she continued. "For Ballet Florida's anniversary gala at The Breakers Hotel? It's black tie. Carl told me the firm is the corporate benefactor."

BALLET AND BALL GOWNS

I was no stranger to formal affairs, but in the early '90s in Manhattan, that meant a fancy cocktail dress, a jeweled clutch and high-heeled shoes in silk or satin. Other than my wedding day or the high school prom, I had never worn a gown. The only women I knew of who did were beauty pageant contestants, and the only ball I was familiar with was the one Cinderella crashed. Amanda was British, 10 years older than I was and always had a way of making me feel that if I didn't heed her advice, I might make a disastrous blunder. I didn't want to appear naïve, so I said, "Scott hasn't mentioned it, but I'll make sure I come up with one."

Scott confirmed what Amanda said, that the firm had bought a table. That night I flipped through some *Vogue* magazines and discovered that evening gowns were quite expensive. I called my former college roommate, Celina, who lived in Texas, and relayed my dilemma.

"Don't worry, Kari. I've been doing the charity circuit here with Michael," she said, referring to her husband who also worked in finance. "There's no reason to be intimidated; since you're a guest and not chairing the event, wear something simple yet elegant, a dress that lets you fit in without standing out." She sounded more like a writer for a fashion magazine than a new mother tending house and hearth in Houston.

Celina was wise and knew what to do in any situation. She was the friend who always came up with an excuse for why we needed to exit a fraternity party before it turned wild. She and I both wore a size four and had shared clothes in college. This gave me an idea.

"Can I just borrow one of yours?" I asked. "I'm out of a job, I have a new house to decorate and I just can't fathom spending a few thousand dollars on a gown right now. If you send one to me, I'll pay for the shipping. And I promise, when I do buy a gown, I'll lend it to you."

So, long before two girls from Harvard came up with the idea for Rent the Runway, two wives trying to advance their husbands' careers discovered the value of trading designer dresses. The black silk charmeuse halter-neck gown Celina sent was perfect. It was slit up to my knee on one side. I'd splurged on a pair of crystal-embellished red satin shoes for Scott's firm's Christmas party. They would give Celina's gown the perfect pop of color.

Carl asked me to invite two couples from the Island to be our guests at the firm's table. The ideal guests should be ones interested in the arts that might become clients. This "table" was the price of a year's tuition for preschool, so I took this job seriously. Drew worked in finance like Scott, so he and Bri were out. Nina had a family commitment and couldn't come. My only other friends were the moms I'd met through Emmy's Montessori class. I chose two, Summer and Kate.

Summer was a teacher and a lounge singer in New York before she married a real estate developer and moved to Palm Beach to raise children. Her voice was as smooth as kittens' fur and everyone applauded when she broke out in song at a dinner party. The bright patterned tunics she wore over leggings made it seem as if she was ready to step onstage at any moment instead of carpooling our girls to dance class. Kate was graceful in a swanlike way; I couldn't decide if it came from her southern upbringing or her proper style of dressing in a crisp white blouse and flared skirt for the school pickup line. Both had much older husbands and lived on the Island, so I presumed they fit the criteria of potential clients. I was delighted when they accepted. This was my first real foray into navigating the social structure of Palm Beach fundraising—figuring out who could help whom by giving what or showing up where.

The week leading up to the ball, I began to panic. Scott resembled James Bond in the tuxedo he'd purchased. He had never owned one and had resisted buying it. I justified the cost as an investment in our future. However, I began to second-guess my selection of formal attire. I worried my borrowed gown looked more like one meant for the bedroom than a ballroom. I took the dress and shoes to Bri's to get a second opinion. Bri not only said yes to my dress, but as if I had a fairy godmother, she produced a pair of gold chandelier earrings with real rubies for me to borrow. "Just be careful with them, Kari. They were a gift from Drew's mother."

The formal entrance to The Breakers Hotel was different from the one we used to access their beach club where we had a summer membership. A uniformed doorman led us through the grand lobby and informed us that our party was in the Venetian Ballroom. As we walked down the long hallway, I noticed other ladies in evening attire. My gown and jewelry were perfect for my age, which was half that of most guests. My crystal shoes made me feel like a modern-day Cinderella.

I discovered that the main event at these balls was preceded by a cocktail hour in a more intimate setting that gave guests an opportunity to mingle. Waiters served a continuous stream of drinks and small bites. Across the room, Summer was engaged in conversation with a group from St. Edward's Church, and Kate sipped champagne surrounded by a circle of male admirers.

It wasn't long before a series of doors were opened and we were ushered from the cocktail hour to a space transformed by the Moroccan décor of genius event planner Bruce Sutka. Lanterns made of colored glass cast a sultry glow over the room. The silky golden fabric draped from the ceiling made it seem like we were in a sultan's tent. Scott rolled his eyes as I pointed out these details. He never understood why every party I organized for Emmy had to have a theme, beginning with the invitation and ending with a favor. That year I reserved a poolside cabana at The Breakers Beach Club and threw a *Little Mermaid* party. The year before that was a *Beauty-and-the-Beast*-themed event.

Music from a 10-piece band played. Male guests laughed as they were led onto the dance floor by dancers disguised as harem girls. A three-course dinner was served on mosaic-themed dinner plates as waiters poured both red and white wine. Dessert was presented on a table adorned with linens in bold blue and green hues that evoked the color of the Mediterranean Sea. No detail was spared to create this *Arabian Nights* fantasy. I imagined every woman present felt as I did—that no matter what had happened during her day, tonight she was a princess.

As the clock struck midnight, each couple was presented with a goodie bag. One item stood apart from the rest: a 14-carat gold ballet slipper charm. The note attached to it stated that it was donated by Helen Boehm, known as the "Princess of Porcelain," whose designs were sold at a boutique on Worth Avenue. The details in this piece were exquisite. When I got home, I slid the charm onto to a delicate gold chain and wore it as an everyday necklace.

A week later, I received a handwritten note from Summer and flowers from Kate as a thank-you for the invitation. Neither of them became clients, but Summer referred friends who did, and Kate became a benefactor of Ballet Florida. Despite my initial apprehension, the gala was a perfect evening out. How funny... Scott's firm springs for a table, I'm asked to dress like royalty, bring my friends and play hostess in a hotel built by oil baron Henry Flagler, and on top of that, unlike Cinderella who lost her glass slipper, I was given a gold one at the end of the evening. Had I stepped into the pages of a fairy tale?

The Winner Is the Highest Bidder

It was our first fall in our new home—we'd been here 10 months. Thus far, I'd had no luck finding a job. Admittedly, making friends and networking with Scott kept me so busy I hadn't given it much thought. Work would always be there, but Emmy starting kindergarten was a once-in-a-lifetime event. I got involved at her school and volunteered for two committees: lunch duty and the kindergarten class project. I relished the chance to be so present for her.

My mom called to see how Emmy's first week went. She was happy to learn that her granddaughter loved school and was learning more every day. She was much less pleased to hear that her ambitious eldest daughter was spending her days unpacking lunches and sticking straws in juice boxes.

"We're not from here. It's a great way for me to meet the other parents," I said defensively. "These families are going to be part of Emmy's life for the next nine years." I didn't dare confess I was enjoying it. My mother had always held the status of stay-at-home-mom in the highest regard, and my professional ambition clashed with her ideals. Now, with a child of my own, I found myself fanning the twin flames of motherhood and business achievement.

The class project presented more of a challenge. I was quickly filled in by the other moms about the concept behind the school's "live" and "silent" auctions. The class project was part of the former. Both auctions were held on the evening of the school's biggest fundraiser, "The Rose Bowl." As I tried to figure out why the event was named after the college football game that took place each year in Pasadena, California, I realized I had gotten it wrong. It was the Rose "Ball," not "Bowl," named after the school, Rosarian Academy.

Items for both auctions were gathered by parents through donations. The difference between the live and silent auctions was that the items in the live auction were high-ticket ones and bid on just like expensive pieces of art at a real auction. This auction offered things like a two-week stay at a home in Casa De Campo in the Dominican Republic with staff and airfare included, or the chance to play a leading character in a novel by local author James Patterson. The items in the silent auction were less pricey—things like wine or garden-themed gift baskets. Guests bid on these things by writing a number assigned to them and a dollar amount on a piece of paper next to the item they hoped to acquire. The highest bidder in each auction won the donated item.

There were two classes for each grade, and each class made a project that was bid on in the live auction. At the first meeting, I was told that the kindergarten class project would be a patchwork quilt made from squares of fabric with the faces of the children drawn on each square by the children themselves. I was amazed at how much Kate and the mothers from Palm Beach knew about quilting. Perhaps while I had been cheerleading in high school, these girls had been taking sewing lessons.

When it was complete, the kindergarten teachers couldn't wait to show us the final product. When the quilt was revealed, I smiled. Kate knew I planned to bid on the quilt at the auction. When she'd sewn all the squares together, she placed Emmy's face directly in the center. I saw the faces of the other children as it continued to unfold and those of the two teachers. However, in the bottom left-hand corner there was a sketch of a woman with an oddly shaped hat that covered most of her forehead. I looked closer and under the drawing of the face, it read "Sister Ann."

THE WINNER IS THE HIGHEST BIDDER

"Who is that?" I asked, pointing to the image of the elderly woman.

"That is Sister Ann, the school's principal," the head teacher explained.

When she could tell I was confused by her head covering she went on, "That's a habit she's wearing; she's a nun, one of the last remaining ones here. One of the children moved leaving an empty space in the quilt, so we added her."

I'd given Scott the lowdown on this quilt and told him we must bid on it. He wasn't privy to the news about Sister Ann being added. Scott wasn't a fan of organized religion. He would have preferred Emmy go to the Palm Beach Day School, a secular one. My friend Dinie, a rabbi's wife, had hoped I would pick the Jewish Day School, but few Island kids went there, and I wanted Emmy to attend school with the kids in town. I chose Rosarian for two reasons: I liked the discipline the religious component brought to education, and second, it focused on the arts. Emmy was taking tap and ballet classes, she loved singing with me in the car and she was a natural actress. The school's mission statement said it welcomed students from all ethnic and religious backgrounds. I was the parent who stayed home with Emmy. I knew what was best for her.

Dinie and I met the previous year while shopping at Pastel, a children's boutique. We had both grabbed a dress from a rack at the same time. I was shocked when she released her grip and said I could have it. Her accent was familiar, clearly New York. But this woman had an aura about her that made her stand out from the other shoppers. It wasn't her beauty, thick mane of chestnut hair or translucent complexion. Perhaps because it was December, and Christmas decorations graced every corner of the Island, she resembled an angel to me. When I mentioned that, she laughed and introduced herself. "Since the dress is blue, I'm guessing it's for Hanukkah?"

"It is," I said, trying not to sound surprised as the population of the Island skewed white, Anglo-Saxon and old-moneyed. The woman introduced herself as Dinie and asked if I belonged to a synagogue. When I said I didn't, she wanted to know why not. "Don't you want your child to grow up with religion?" she asked.

"Absolutely. I even enrolled my daughter in an elementary school with Christian roots because I was drawn to its emphasis on spiritual development."

"But what about Judaism? Isn't that your faith?"

"I observe its traditions, but my beliefs aren't very strong because of..." I trailed off. I didn't know this woman well enough to tell her about the death of my father, something that had fundamentally shaken my faith. What kind of higher power takes a dad from four young daughters? "Because of how I grew up," I said finally.

"My husband and I came here to help a temple that is struggling," she said. "We're starting a Sunday school program for kids. The first meeting is the day after Christmas; why don't you come and bring your daughter?" And so I did.

When Emmy and I arrived at the penthouse of the Palm Beach Hotel there were jelly donuts and games set up. Kids rushed to include Emmy in the fun. Dinie introduced me to the other parents, who were warm and welcoming, and to her husband, Rabbi Moshe. He mentioned the synagogue they were helping was Modern Orthodox—which meant the congregation was more devout than the Reform Judaism I'd been exposed to.

Rabbi Moshe persuaded me with almost messianic zeal of the importance of enrolling Emmy in Sunday school. He didn't care that I was a Sunday school dropout. "We welcome families from all levels of observance. But your daughter deserves to learn about her heritage," he said. I sensed that, although they were young and we came from completely different backgrounds, Rabbi Moshe and Dinie, like us, were determined to build their lives in this community. Dinie even invited us to her home for a Friday night dinner!

That morning on the rooftop ballroom of a hotel, something bigger than Emmy starting religious school happened: A miracle occurred. The son and daughter of Russian immigrants to this country made me believe in God again.

I laughed each time I walked by my girl's room and saw Sister Ann smiling at me from her corner. Between Sister Ann and the gold mezuzah Rabbi Moshe placed above the door post of our house, our family was blessed. Finally, I felt safe.

Dances and Daughters

The Recreation Center on Seaview Avenue became the go-to spot for me and Emmy after school. Even if Emmy didn't have a planned activity, she could always find kids there to play with. Each month, they published a newsletter that listed upcoming events. When I saw the announcement for Daddy-Daughter Date Night, I thought it was the cutest idea ever and rushed to register Emmy and Scott. Steph, who worked in the office, told me the dance took place around Valentine's Day. It was the one night of the year the dads on the Island could escort their daughters, not their wives, to a formal event.

I was paying for Emmy's tennis lessons when Steph mentioned the dance might be canceled because not enough people had signed up. This gave me an incentive to put my college marketing degree to use and promote it. I encouraged all my friends with daughters to go. Summer was reluctant to let her husband Ray attend.

"I don't want Ray out alone at night with all these other women, Kari. And I suggest you think twice about letting Scott go," she whispered to me as if she were a day trader passing on insider information.

"Summer, the only women going are the daughters. No wives will be there," I explained. I didn't blame her for being concerned; there was a group of women on the Island looking to "trade up" in the husband market. Their behavior was apparent at charity affairs and the private clubs, and it did reveal a darker, more competitive side to the social scene of the Island. But this dance would genuinely be innocent. I saw Summer questioning Steph, probably to make sure I had gotten my facts right, before registering her girls. Summer found me by the courts, where I was watching Emmy practice her backhand, and relayed the news that Ray and their daughters—Alex and Jax, would be going. The conversation quickly switched to deciding which shop on Worth Avenue—Cloud 10 or Spring Flowers—had a better selection of party dresses.

"Let's try Cloud 10. Emmy is constantly losing the white gloves she needs for the cotillion classes at the club, and Pearl, the owner, is kind enough to stash an extra pair in her size behind the counter for her. I'm sure she'd do the same for your girls. But be prepared to get a lesson on teaching kids to be responsible for their belongings."

As a girl who spent a large part of her life longing for love, it was no surprise that Valentine's Day was my favorite holiday. I decided the Daddy-Daughter Date Night was the perfect time to reciprocate for all the invitations we'd accepted. Palm Beach being Palm Beach, the dads had complained the previous year that no alcohol was served at the dance. Naturally, there wasn't. The dance took place at the town's Recreation Center; they didn't have a liquor license.

I came up with the perfect solution to that problem and decided to host a cocktail party for the girls and their fathers prior to the event. At cocktail parties, guests are standing, so I didn't have to think about seating. Due to Scott's resistance to buying furniture and our never-ending social schedule, which meant less time to shop for it, we were a little light on chairs. The dads in our circle liked to drink; they'd be more focused on top-shelf liquor than lounging on sofas. Because the guest list was made up of men and their daughters, I didn't have to worry about any pesky mothers inquiring why my home was still not properly furnished.

Emmy and I decorated the house with pink and red roses, streamers and heart-shaped helium balloons. My childhood friend, Matt, owned an accessories company. Recently, he'd added costume jewelry to his collection. When we were in our 20s, I gave him the courage he needed to start his own business; in return he promised to give me free products for life. Matt sent me a shipment of necklaces and bracelets. There must be something about jewelry that is embedded in the X chromosome. The girls were in awe as they gathered in front of the dressing table in my bathroom to play with the faux gemstone pieces. Scott stood behind the island in the kitchen and acted as bartender. I played waitress and walked around with a tray of Shirley Temples and hors d'oeuvres for the girls.

There was one glitch. The men's cocktails were served in crystal lowball glasses. When it was time to go, the dads started leaving with their drinks. This made me extremely nervous. I didn't want to be responsible if they were pulled over by the police with alcohol in their car, nor did I want them leaving with my good crystal! These were accomplished businessmen, 10 to 20 years older than I was. Did they need me to scold them like a schoolteacher? I had to act fast. It was our house, and we would be to blame if something bad happened. I approached Ray, an older dad and one that the others looked up to, and took the glass from his hand. I attempted to make a joke out of it by saying, "You're not trying to steal my good crystal, are you? These glasses were a wedding gift from my grandmother, they have sentimental value."

He gave me a mischievous smile, let me take the glass, then kissed me on the cheek and thanked me for hosting the party. I observed the other dads as they placed their glasses and cocktail napkins on the glass table in the entranceway before leaving.

Then next time I saw Steph at the Rec Center, she was anxious for my feedback on the dance. She laughed when I told her what had happened at my party but was grateful for my "input."

"Do you think we would get a better turnout if we moved the event to a place where the fathers could drink? Maybe one of the private clubs?"

I thought for a moment.

"I do, but there must be music and a DJ. The dads told me dancing with their daughters was the best part of the evening."

The following year the dance was moved to 251 Sunrise, a nightclub in town with a liquor license. This way, the dads could do most of their drinking there instead of at our house. We hosted the cocktail party again. The first time, I'd only invited the girls and fathers in our friend group. This year our friends asked if they could bring friends, which meant more dads and daughters were added to the list. Of course, I said yes to their requests. It was important I show everyone the same courtesy the natives had extended to me.

A decade later, when Emmy was too old to attend, I ran into people in town who told me Daddy-Daughter Date Night was still taking place. A new family was hosting the cocktail party, but everyone knew about the couple from North Lake Way who had come up with the idea. An invite to the pre-party had become another event to add to the social calendar—a rite of passage and a way to enter this close-knit Island community.

Social Climbing or Climbing the Ladder to Prosperity

I scored high on my hostess skills after Daddy-Daughter Date Night, but I was still a failure on the furniture front. Apart from two antique Persian rugs, one from my mom and the other from Drew's mom, most of our stuff was from Scott's bachelor pad in the city. My husband balked at the prices for dining room pieces. He said he'd rather never host anyone than waste money on a table and chairs we'd rarely use. And although it might sound silly, that highlighted a tension building between Scott and me. It wasn't really about the chairs. He didn't understand at all how entertaining at home would totally elevate his business!

Drew and Bri bought a house within biking distance from ours. One Sunday they came over with Drew's friends, Sascha and Dave. Scott and I loved meeting the boys Drew grew up with. They were eager to give us the inside scoop on this place we'd chosen to plant roots. As I showed everyone around the house, Dave pulled me aside and whispered, "Do you know your neighbor is a witch?" Before I could respond, he went on, "In the coral reef, just around the corner, you'll see the window of her house. It has metal bars on it. Walk by at night; if the moon is bright, you might see her."

I chose to keep this bit of folklore to myself. A wife who insisted her first home must be in Palm Beach was scary enough to Scott; there was no reason to frighten him further. I continued with the house tour. Bri pointed out the polished nickel bathroom fixtures.

Sascha liked the indoor/outdoor area with a wooden Japanese soaking tub. Scott showed them the high-gloss white crown molding that gave height to the ceilings which otherwise would have seemed low. None of this mattered—we had a house, our first. That's why I found it strange when Sascha said, "Wow! This is a real party house. Are your parents home?"

"Our parents are up north," I replied.

"When are they coming back?" he asked.

"Um...they've never been here. They plan on visiting in the spring."

"You mean this is your house?" Sascha seemed shocked. "I didn't know people our age could afford a house in Palm Beach. I'm still living with my folks in the one I grew up in on Everglade." He gestured toward an area south of us, closer to town.

The house on North Lake Way was a stretch for us—we'd put down every cent of our savings. Scott was establishing himself in his new position as a wealth manager, and I could tell it was causing him stress. His temper was a little shorter. He seemed distant. But he was building up his roster of clients, so I figured this was the hardest part. Meanwhile, Emmy was enrolled in kindergarten at a school that was a good fit for her. What definitely wasn't going according to plan was me finding work in fashion. The directory of wholesale businesses where I'd found my position with Lana was no longer in print. I pounded the pavement in the only two business districts that existed. It seemed that each one led to a dirt road, or since Palm Beach is an island, to the water. The founders and CEOs of fashion companies such as Lilly Pulitzer, Jones New York, Nine West and Sam & Libby Shoes lived here, but their headquarters were located elsewhere.

In the city I'd come from, people only cared about what others did for a living if it benefited them financially. Here, that didn't matter at all. Everyone was involved in volunteerism and philanthropy. In New York, I had never once been asked to donate time or money to a charity. I presumed that was the world of Vanderbilts and Astors. But the inhabitants of this Island had already made their fortunes. They were the scions of American business dynasties such as Kleenex, Wrigley's gum, Post cereal, Jell-O and Estée Lauder. Their stories inspired me and their civility appealed to me, but they were here to enjoy life. I'd come to make one.

In my 20s, my Greek-American mom was desperate to marry off her daughters. She urged me to get out of my office and into the world of available men. "Prince Charming won't come knocking on your door," she chided. Her advice led me to Scott, so I decided to apply her logic to finding work.

When we attended fundraisers for Scott's firm, I was focused on helping him cultivate clients. It didn't seem appropriate to ask about work for me. But there were a handful of events taking place each night and we could pick and choose which ones to attend. So Scott and I joined the social circuit—Young Friends of the Red Cross, The Heart Ball and so many more. I wish I could say I just wanted to give back, but my motive was gainful employment.

No sooner had we begun doing this than a connection to a job turned up in my backyard. My Scottish neighbors to the east—Masie and Will—had a daughter in Emmy's grade. Masie loved to entertain, and an invitation to one of her sit-down dinner parties was highly desirable. I learned this when I spoke to a disgruntled neighbor who'd never been invited to one and wasn't pleased to hear that Scott and I were.

There was always an eclectic group seated at Masie's table. Her guests included royalty, like the brother of the deposed Shah of Iran and a duke and duchess from England, as well as the great-granddaughter of Henry Phipps, heiress to the Carnegie Steel fortune. But the person I met at the cocktail hour was neither European nor American royalty, but the Scottish knitwear designer Valerie Louthan. Before the guests moved to the dining room, I scooped up her place card and switched it with another one so I could sit next to her. At that time, I knew she'd be an interesting person to meet, but I could never have guessed this gutsy woman with fiery red hair and a passion for pheasant shooting would give me the opportunity of a lifetime.

Valerie had porcelain skin and spoke the Queen's English. She designed cashmere sweaters for men and women that were made in Scotland. Over a main course of quail breast, she explained to me that she had previously sold her collection in department stores and high-end boutiques. Because of the affluent clientele she had cultivated over the years, she changed her business model to a direct-to-consumer one. This gave her more control over her brand and her profits. The menswear company I'd worked for in New York, The House of Bijan, operated the same way, I told her. Valerie's eyes lit up when I mentioned I was eager to return to work. We arranged to meet at her shop for "tea and a chat." I couldn't wait.

Valerie's store was in the Paramount Building, which housed specialty shops, unlike the posh Worth Avenue where locals and tourists spent their money, old and new, on well-known designer brands. The entrance to this two-story stuccoed landmark had the same arched logo as Paramount Pictures, a throwback to the era when the movie theater at its center was an entertainment venue for residents. Valerie's shop was on the street level. When I stepped inside, she was there to greet me. I tried to hide my disappointment as I observed my surroundings. A banquette the length of a bay window was upholstered in a faded tartan fabric that Valerie brought from her home in Scotland. The slate blue carpet was stained in spots. I couldn't believe that the society clientele she spoke of felt comfortable here. No wonder I had never noticed the store the many times I passed by it.

Toward the back, behind the dressing rooms, was a stockroom. When Valerie swung open the door, my heart raced like it did when I bought my first Chanel bag. Cashmere sweaters in the most dazzling turquoise blue, tomato red and dusty pink were stacked on shelves from the floor to the ceiling. Each one was wrapped in a clear plastic bag. But it wasn't just the array of colors or the surplus of goods that got my heart thumping. The spreadsheet of monthly revenue was shocking—how could Valerie sell so much cashmere in the sweltering summer months?

"Ah," Valerie said, her eyes glistening, "that is where the trunk shows come in."

I knew all about trunk shows—I'd done them with Lana at the Saks Fifth Avenue stores throughout the Southeast. A trunk show is a personal appearance by a designer, or an employee of the designer, in a store where the brand is sold. The store sends invitations to its best customers in order to increase the sales of the designer's brand.

"But if you don't sell your product in stores, where do you have the shows?" I asked.

She explained that after Memorial Day, she closed the shop for a month. The first two weeks were a vacation, a reprieve from the long hectic season. After that, she traveled to Scotland to design the new collection. Beginning in July through the end of August she held ten shows at hotels or clients' homes in resort towns across the northeast, like Nantucket and Southampton.

"Kari, these shows bring in as much business as the shop does the entire season. If you can get away, we could tackle the larger markets together."

When she asked me about my hiatus from work, I explained about being alone in a new town with a toddler and the struggle to find help with childcare.

"But now that my daughter is in school, I'm ready to jump-start my career again," I said with certainty. She said she understood. She'd raised four children, also taking time off when they were young. She said I reminded her of her second daughter. What she didn't say was that the girl I was replacing had quit and was leaving for England the next week. Valerie was happy to hear I had experience in both production and sales. If I came on board, I'd be responsible for both. She offered me a reasonable base salary plus two percent commission on the merchandise I sold.

"The hours are Monday through Friday from 9:30 to 5:30, except for the months during Season when you will need to work on a Saturday. You can choose which weekday you would like to have off and my friend Harriet will take your place at the shop. And if you need me, I'm just up the road working from my home studio."

I was tempted to accept her offer, but I remembered my position with Lana. Traveling for work meant paying for babysitters. If this job required it, I would need help and help cost money. I described my unstoppable work ethic and promised Valerie she wouldn't be disappointed by my performance, but I needed a bonus structure to give me more of an incentive.

"Kari, how about in addition to what you sell on your own, I give you an equity stake equal to one percent of the total sales of the business?"

"Yes!" was all I could say. I'd be there on Monday to train for the sales manager position. So, just like that, after a three-year stint of full-time "wifedom" and mothering, I reentered the world of luxury goods. The keys in my hand were proof I was back in business.

Meanwhile, Scott was gradually building a client base through referrals from accountants and attorneys. To get the firm's name out in the community, we attended charity events with Carl and his wife, Amanda. Carl had charisma combined with an economic sensibility that made it easy for clients to trust him. He teased me about my ability to recognize the "big fish" at the galas, engage them in conversation and then toss them to him and Scott.

"It's not hard to figure out, Carl. Anyone who reads *The Shiny Sheet* knows who these people are."

Carl wasn't buying it.

"Are you sure you don't want to sit for the Series 7 test?" he often asked.

A passing score on this exam was a prerequisite for a position as a money manager. "Absolutely not," I always answered. "I can't work in a field where I don't understand the product."

I was flattered, but finance is a male-dominated field. I saw how hard it was for my female co-workers to get ahead at my first job in private equity. Apart from the fact that I didn't find finance interesting, I didn't believe clients would hand over large sums of money to an artsy girl like me who would rather invest in antiques than stocks. They were more likely to place their trust in guys like Carl and Scott with MBAs and securities licenses.

"Carl, the minimum amount to open an account is a half a million dollars, right?"

"Yes, that's correct."

"And most of the clients who give the firm this amount are men, I presume?"

"Mainly married couples," he answered, and I could tell he was wondering where I was going with my questions.

"I'm guessing the men are usually the decision-makers?"

"I would say so."

"Well, the only reason I could see a man giving me a half a million dollars would be so I could head to Neiman Marcus and go shopping."

Carl burst out in laughter. "You know, you may just be right, Kari."

On my first day of work, I was greeted by Elinor, the manager I was replacing. She was dressed in a frilly blouse and peasant skirt. This getup made her look more like Heidi the goat herder from the Swiss Alps than a young lady selling luxury goods. Valerie must have read my mind because when Elinor stepped out to smoke a cigarette, she said, "Due to the large amount of inventory we carry and the fact that my husband and I are only here six months of the year, we can't hire just anyone. The person we employ must be trustworthy; Elinor's parents are friends of ours from England."

"In that case, I'm flattered. Do you need references?" I asked.

"I trust you, but even if I didn't, I would know where to find you." I laughed, a little uneasily, understanding she meant it.

Valerie didn't know it then, but she had found in me the ideal person to run her business. From day one I treated it as if it were my own. If I was the perfect person to run the business, then Elinor was the least perfect. Other than the fact that Valerie trusted her not to abscond with the inventory, Elinor was not suited at all to deal with a clientele who consisted of America's ultra-rich, many of whom had inherited, not earned, their good fortune. Glancing at the client list, I told Elinor I felt like I was privy to a copy of *The Social Register*. Elinor frowned and said she was a socialist.

The first part of the training session was to become familiar with the styles of sweaters.

Valerie had made it easy by giving each one in the women's collection a feminine name and each one in the men's line a masculine name. I'd done my homework and studied the brochures and press kit Valerie had given me. Elinor showed me how each style of sweater was stacked in alphabetical order in the stockroom and displayed in cases on the selling floor.

When Donnelley Publishing heiress Naoma Haggin walked in with a friend, I recognized her from seeing her photo in *The Shiny Sheet*. Valerie had just left, so I introduced myself, and eager to please, I pulled out the tunic she'd requested.

"Kari, The Everglades Club has a 'no pants' policy for women that seems so outdated. I remember seeing a style with a wide leg. If I wear them with this tunic they may pass for a skirt." The palazzo pants weren't in stock in the colors she desired, so she placed an order for four pairs with matching tunics. She had never placed a special order before and questioned Valerie's policy of putting down a 50 percent deposit. However, when I explained she could put the deposit on her credit card and pay the balance when her order came in, she agreed. Her friend, whom I knew to be the wife of an oil company executive, bought some three-ply zip-up sweaters to wear in Newport.

I was excited to put my selling skills to use again. Just as I was getting into a groove and having fun, I noticed Elinor sitting at my desk and scowling. After the ladies left, she asked, "Doesn't it make you sick to see these women spending so much money on sweaters?"

"Why would I be upset?" Valerie's cashmeres were gorgeous. I owned a few cashmere sweaters from my days living in a colder climate, but mine were your basic pullovers, raglan-sleeve cardigans and shapeless crew necks. These were couture knits. The styles were shaped to fit the body. In addition to the cardigans and pullovers, there were shawls and shrugs that could be worn over ball gowns and evening sweaters trimmed with the finest silk and satin from Paris that looked elegant paired with floor-length taffeta skirts. I was thrilled to represent such a unique product and the designer who created it. There was a reason Valerie was referred to as the "Queen of Cashmere." Besides, I am someone who never liked boundaries; having direct access to the mills where the sweaters were made meant there was no limit to how much I could sell.

I knew this wouldn't resonate with Elinor so I said, "Yes, it is sometimes difficult to deal with demanding, entitled women, but if there weren't people like this in the world, people like you and me wouldn't be able to earn a living." And earning a living meant educating my daughter and decorating my dream house.

She shot me a bewildered look, picked up the "Closed" sign from the desk, walked to the front of the store, and hung it on the glass-paned door so it faced the outside.

"We're done for the day, Kari."

I looked at my watch and saw that it was 5:00 and said, "But it's only five. Aren't we supposed to stay until 5:30?"

"Yup, that's right." Elinor may not have physically left Valerie's employ, but her enthusasm clearly had.

"I'm exhausted and Valerie won't care," she said wearily.

Odd. I had never had so much energy in my life.

You Can Take the Boy Out of Brooklyn, but You Can't Make Him Palm Beach

Memorial Day arrived, and that meant the population of the Island dropped from 40,000 residents to 10,000 residents. This tony milieu transitioned from people scurrying between house parties, galas and restaurants to a tiny beach community practically overnight. Although the entire town was within walking distance to the beach and boasted more country clubs per square mile than any other place in the country, everyone left. Residents blamed the extreme heat for why they decamped to more moderate weather in Martha's Vineyard or Maine. Not me; I savored these months.

This was when I got to see who lived in this paradise all year round. Most folks were young families with kids, like us. Unlike most people who see Palm Beach as a winter vacation spot, to me, because of my career, summer was the only time it seemed like one. Scott and I joined a private country club at the end of our street called The Beach Club. They had a day camp where I dropped Emmy on my way to work. There she took part in traditional camp activities: tennis, arts and crafts, archery and swimming.

We met our friends Charlotte and Russell through Kate. Russell was a retired CEO, and Charlotte and I had chaired a gala for a children's charity together. Like us, they played bridge, and we had a standing card game every Tuesday night. Before they left for Portugal for the summer, they asked if Scott would watch their car for them—as in would he start it up and drive it occasionally? I agreed to babysit their car on Scott's behalf. I thought driving it on the weekends might get him to relax.

If you met Scott, you'd immediately think he was the kind of guy you'd trust with your money: He was grounded, conservative, and even-keeled. But despite the step-up in his compensation, perks of his new position, and the second income from my job, he seemed more stressed than ever. He was quiet and moody. Truthfully, I said yes to amuse myself. I could just imagine Scott's face when I told him their navy Rolls-Royce sedan would be his for the summer.

After I convinced my husband it would be fun, and he got over being nervous about the idea, he began driving the Rolls-Royce to and from the office on Fridays. In season, this car was unrecognizable as so many people drove one that it could well be a Honda Civic. But with the younger summer crowd, it was noticeable. I realized this when one of my friends asked if either my or Scott's trust fund had kicked in. Scott was shocked when I shared this with him. The fact that anyone assumed either Scott or I had any money from a source other than our hard work was unimaginable.

Scott didn't find that funny at all, because the only thing that "kicked in" were the repair bills to fix the damn thing.

"Well, at least you know you never want to own one," I said, trying to make light of it.

"Like I ever could, Kari."

"You could, but now you know you never would."

Scott rolled his eyes in my direction. "Really, Kari, sometimes I don't understand what planet you're living on."

The lazy days of summer wore on. Relaxing on a chaise lounge with a book and listening to the waves crash to the shore calmed my busy mind. I wondered if my fellow Island dwellers didn't have second, third or fourth homes, or if there wasn't a stigma attached to being here in the summer, they would have stayed and enjoyed the Island like we did. Palm Beach was never humid because of the gentle breeze coming from the ocean, plus restaurants were grateful for our business and then remembered us when reservations skyrocketed during the Season.

August was the month when our friends who'd moved away came to stay in their parents' homes while those parents were vacationing at their previously mentioned second, third or fourth homes. Nina lived in Wellington, a gated community west of the Island that catered to the equestrian set. She summered at a family home on North Lake Way. Our husbands met when Nina invited us to a charity event. A guest had mistaken Scott for Wes, which wasn't surprising since Scott and Wes looked alike. The guest initiated a conversation with Scott about the sport of polo. Wes was a professional polo player who had played with every member of the British monarchy. I can assure you that Scott, who grew up in Borough Park, Brooklyn, had never come within 50 miles of a horse, let alone a polo pony. Yes, he and Wes both had jet-black hair and wide boyish grins, but their backgrounds couldn't have been more different. When this happened, Scott and I forgot whatever it was we were fighting about, and I laughed so hard my chest hurt.

In the summer, our family spent weekends with Wes and Nina at The Sailfish Club—The Beach Club's reciprocal lakeside counterpart. By the end of August, I was exhausted from work. Last week, the air conditioning in the Paramount building broke down and I had orders from the July trunk shows that needed to be shipped; my clients didn't know and most likely didn't care that Florida's heat felt like a steam shower. Once the weekend rolled around, I could never seem to get into the relaxation mode, but Nina and Wes made it impossible not to. One Sunday, Wes called and said he was picking us up to go to the Sailfish Club.

"Thanks, Wes, but we'll have to pass. School begins next week, and I'm absorbed in a project for Emmy."

"What project could you have before school even starts, Kari?" he mumbled in his raspy movie star voice. I explained that the teacher had given out a list of supplies that the children were required to bring with them on the first day of class. Each item had to have Emmy's name on it. I borrowed Scott's P-touch machine from the office and was busy printing labels for every item, including each No. 2 pencil.

"That's ridiculous, Kari," Wes said. "Our son is in the same class, and I haven't seen any list. I'm on my way," he said.

I tossed the label maker into my beach bag and called out to Scott and Emmy, who were in the backyard, to get ready. Minutes later the three of us climbed into Wes' Range Rover next to their son, Nicholas.

By late afternoon I had caused quite a stir at the Sailfish Club, sitting yoga style on my lounge chair typing away on the P-touch. A group of parents had circled around me and offered to pay me for my label-printing proficiency. I gracefully turned down their requests. This was a tedious job, and I had performed another one all week. I did it as a labor of love for Emmy and Nicholas. But I did let the parents know where they could buy a P-Touch label maker so they could print the labels themselves. With school supplies off my list and our trip to get uniforms at Harris Prep Shop completed, it was time to shop for the house. Two seasons without furniture was too many. It was time to feather our nest.

Scott and I were at odds about how to decorate our house. He was convinced it was perfectly acceptable to furnish our new home from Rooms To Go. As far as he was concerned, any sum of money that wasn't making money was a waste of money.

In theory, what Scott said made sense, but I didn't want our decor to just "make sense." I hoped to layer our home with color and texture, choosing furniture and artwork we collected from our travels. I wanted it to represent us and to be a place we connected with friends, Scott's clients and the community. And I was tired of waiting—waiting to buy a house, waiting for Scott to be promoted to the advisor role, waiting for a job in fashion. Ultimately, we compromised: Scott agreed to let me purchase furniture from the Church Mouse if I promised to only buy secondhand pieces.

When I mentioned this to a client she said, "It's true. They have quality goods, but the best items get snatched up by regulars. Go to Antique Row in West Palm Beach just over the middle bridge. Don't let the name scare you, Kari. They have pre-owned furniture too, not just antiques." I was hopeful. At first, I was unsure of my taste and was afraid to buy anything. When a salesperson saw I was having trouble deciding, he made my mission easier, asking where I lived.

"On North Lake Way, on the Island."

"Fabulous, why don't we deliver these pieces on approval so you can see how they look in your home?" He didn't ask me for my driver's license or a credit card. This seemed to work in shop after shop. Unbeknownst to me, my address was proof of status in this part of town. I saw something I liked, gave the salesperson my address and phone number and slowly my home was filled with furniture: a marble-topped Louis XVI console table, an antique English bamboo chest, a mother-of-pearl game table from the Middle East.

Once I saw the pieces in my home and how perfectly they fit, how could I send anything back? Since Scott had never bought furniture, he had no idea what it cost. He would have been shocked to find out he was now a collector of rare antiques.

Although I was keeping other shops busy, foot traffic was slow at Valerie's. Mistakenly, I'd thought it would surge when September ended. Valerie told me this was because the core customers didn't return until mid-November. Throughout the summer, my job consisted of shipping orders from the trunk shows, getting the fall collection into production and filling phone requests. I was anxious to do more. Choosing furniture gave me an idea: If high-ticket items like game tables and armoires could sell on approval, think how much I could sell if I applied this strategy to sweaters. Valerie was reluctant, but I convinced her it would work.

"We already have the clients' credit card numbers on file. I'll only do it for the customers I know, I promise." Sales increased dramatically. Valerie had never seen numbers like this in the fall. To this day, when I look at my English bamboo chest and fruitwood game table, I smile as I remember how I acquired them and the valuable sales lesson they taught me. I will probably never play cards on a table previously owned by a Turkish sultan, but I was thrilled to see Emmy's love of cards blossom as she and my mom played canasta on it. Each time I look at the broken stretcher at its base now, I remember it got that way when Emmy and Nicholas were engaged in a game of checkers. They were so little, their legs didn't reach the floor and they had used the stretcher as a footrest.

At the time I had been afraid to tell Scott. There was no need to be. Many months passed and he never noticed it was damaged, the same way I had no idea that Scott and I, the couple our friends called "Barbie and Ken," weren't actually the picture-perfect pair featured in *The Shiny Sheet*.

M'mm M'mm Good or Not so Good

Valerie's most lucrative trunk show was the one in Northeast Harbor, Maine. I learned about this vacation enclave long before I met Valerie. Many Island residents owned homes there that they used during August. Since Scott and I could barely manage to maintain one residence, I couldn't understand why anyone would go through the trouble of owning a house they used only one month of the year. But Ian told me the Northeast Harbor trunk show boasted our highest sales, so off I went.

Valerie would be arriving from her vacation home in Camden, so I had to lug a duffle bag of sweaters along with my own luggage to the airport and across the tarmac to my little prop plane. When I finally plopped down in my seat, I looked up and saw Candy Van Alen standing in the aisle next to me. Candy was a client and a Newport and Palm Beach socialite. She had recently chaired the International Red Cross Ball—the highlight of the Island's social season due to the presence of ambassadors and foreign diplomats. As I watched this small-boned woman hoist her bag into the overhead compartment, I promised myself I would never complain about prop planes, walking across a tarmac or hauling luggage onto a little prop plane again. If this 80-something-year-old woman could do it, so could I.

I greeted Candy, and it didn't take long for the conversation to turn to cashmere. She inquired about Valerie's fall collection. I dug into my carry-on and pulled out a piece of taffeta with black-and-white polka dots that could be made into a ballroom skirt. I explained how the same trim could be sewn around the neckline and cuffs of a black cashmere sweater to create an outfit. Candy ordered it on the *spot.* I promised her I wouldn't sell another like it to any other clients from Palm Beach until after she was photographed in it.

"I'm so glad I bumped into you, Kari. I'll pop by during the week to order some pieces for the winter season," Candy said. She drove away, and I was left admiring her spunk and zest for life. After I arrived and checked in at the hotel, Valerie and I set up on the large wraparound screened porch. We had the preparation down to a science, and the weather was delicious. There was a constant breeze from Penobscot Bay that smelled of fresh rain. The view was of mountains and forests. Could this be why people spend the entire month here?

Valerie told me that dinner that night would be a dressy affair with clients at the hotel, so I couldn't fathom why she turned white when I stepped out of my room in a form-fitting knit dress in a floral pattern and high-heeled sandals.

"Kari, what on earth are you wearing?" she asked.

"A dress; it's from Franceska Paris on Worth Avenue," I said, a little defensively. I thought this town would be a northern version of Palm Beach. I couldn't have been more wrong.

"Kari, that will not do," she said as she looked me up and down with disapproval. "You look like a tart. What else did you bring?"

The fashionista in me proudly pulled out the other dresses I'd brought. Both were patterned in bright colors. They were made of nylon, a fabric that didn't wrinkle when packed, and were reasonably priced—even before the discount the owner gave me for referring customers. Her shop was a staple for someone like me who was short on time and long on places to go.

"Dressy here is not the same as dressy on the Island," Valerie clarified. "Choose an evening sweater and pair of slacks from the collection, and please hurry up. Diana Wister, whose grandfather founded Campbell's Soup, is hosting us tonight." I changed into a pair of cream-colored raw silk pants and a single-ply scoopneck elbow-length sweater in a leafy green color. I slipped on a pair of espadrilles and ran to catch up with Valerie and Ian as they trekked down the hill to the dining room. I was embarrassed. I thought I knew how to dress for any occasion. This was unfamiliar territory for me. I needed a cocktail. Luckily, this group drank a lot, and the cool weather was a reprieve from the heat of Florida. I managed to converse comfortably with everyone in attendance, moving quickly past my almost-fashion mishap.

I awoke early feeling refreshed and ready to sell. The show started at 10 am, but by 11:30 there were still no customers. What if nobody showed up? Valerie reached into her handbag, pulled out her jade green worry stone and rubbed it for good luck.

In each market, business marched to a distinct rhythm. Here, it seemed shoppers arrived after their morning hike. Being first a city girl, then an Island girl, I didn't even know that hiking was something anyone other than a forest ranger did, let alone the ladies from Palm Beach. Evidence proved otherwise, as I noticed the canteens and hiking sticks clients stashed in the foyer before shopping. And if trying to imagine these women using these items was difficult, their appearance was more shocking. They looked so disheveled; I told Valerie that if I saw them on the street, I would offer them a dollar. She burst out in a robust laugh.

"Believe me, Kari, that look is contrived. That is why they vacation here; so, they can be outdoors and connect with the rugged beauty all around them, a complete escape from how they're expected to behave in Palm Beach." As Valerie predicted, things picked up. We couldn't write orders fast enough to keep up with the cashmere flying out the door of the screened porch.

During the last hour, a customer so desperately wanted the ribbed two-ply lilac mock turtleneck I was wearing, I took it off and sold it to her.

M'MM M'MM GOOD OR NOT SO GOOD

My mom was always impressed by my generosity. "Kari, you'd give someone the shirt off your back," I recalled her telling me ever since I was a little kid. I don't think she would have imagined "the shirt" as a pricey cashmere sweater or the "someone" as a Palm Beach heiress. It seemed I could never please my mother, yet I was reluctant to give up trying.

After three days of constant standing, running down the hill to access the computer at the main hotel to send emails to Scotland and the continual companionship of clients—day and night—I was exhausted. However, the show was a success. Our numbers beat last year's. The hotel penciled us in for next summer.

On that final day of the show, Diana invited us for afternoon tea. She served the tea in Campbell's "Mushroom Barley" and "Chicken Noodle" cups. How cute! The conversation turned toward hiking. Diana's husband made it sound like a hunt for buried treasure, the treasure being the breathtaking scenic view at the end of the trail. I decided I had to see what all the hype was about.

The next morning, while it was still dark, I rose early, put on my Keds, and set out into the wilderness to try and understand what all the fuss with hiking up here was about. I ventured onto a marked trail in the wooded area near the hotel. As I got deeper and deeper into the forest, the sun came up. I went to check the time on my cell phone and realized I'd forgotten to bring it. I turned around and an animal I recognized as a moose was staring into my eyes. I was terrified. I hadn't told Valerie or Ian what I was up to.

Ian always teased me about how responsible I was. "Didn't you ever have a night where you drank too much and wound up at some bloke's house with a hangover?" he asked. I was never late and never called in sick. They would never imagine I ventured off on a hike. They would have no idea where I was. I certainly didn't. What would happen to Emmy if I never found my way back? How would Scott manage? If I made it out of these woods alive, I vowed to never attempt this again on my own. I continued on, found a trail marker and ran all the way back to the hotel.

I couldn't wait to get home. I called a bellman to bring the trunks to the main lobby of the hotel. Valerie and Ian had headed back to their vacation house in Camden, and Valerie had arranged a car service to take me to the airport. I was restless. It seemed like the car service was taking forever to arrive. I kept getting up from the chair in the lobby to see if it was in the driveway. I was afraid I'd miss my flight. I called Valerie and explained the situation. She panicked, which didn't take much, and hung up. She called me back immediately.

"Kari, the car service has been waiting in front of the hotel for 45 minutes."

I walked to the driveway and saw a peculiar old lady open the hatchback of a "woody" station wagon. I hadn't seen one of these since I left the suburbs after high school. The woman began waving at me and it clicked. This was my car service. No wonder I hadn't seen it. In my world, a car service was a black town car with a uniformed driver. I hopped in the back and asked the man driving, who happened to be the woman's husband, to step on the gas. My annoyance turned to appreciation when the woman opened a small cooler and offered me a drink and a sandwich. I chided myself for being so narrow-minded. Despite the initial confusion, I arrived at the airport on time. I gave them a hundred-dollar bill as a tip, which I knew I couldn't expense, to thank them for their kindness.

Life, Lilly and the Pursuit of Happiness

Despite all the designer boutiques on Worth Avenue, it was rare that a customer would ever get to meet an actual designer. Palm Beach was more of a place to have a presence than a place to live and work for New York's fashion elite. That's why I jumped when given the chance to meet the designer Lilly Pulitzer. She put preppy Palm Beach fashion on the map. Her husband Peter, of the Pulitzer family known for the prize, owned a citrus-growing business. As a new wife, to keep herself busy, Lilly opened a juice stand. When she spilled orange juice on herself at work, the idea of a bright-colored cotton shift dress was born.

It was pre-season on the Island, and that meant another round of fundraising for Emmy's school. I realized the school held their affair in October so as not to compete with the events on the charity circuit that took place during "high season," which ran from January through Easter. After my experience with the quilt, I decided my talents would be of better use requesting gifts than giving art lessons. Last year, when I joined the committee responsible for gathering kids' things for the silent auction, I learned that since I was a regular customer at all the children's boutiques in town, these stores were glad to grant my request for a donation. These items, along with the kids' stuff from Trendsetters, Matt's company, gave me a head start on the task of gift gathering.

Kate and I became close friends after the quilt project. Since we worked well together, we volunteered to co-chair the committee called the Children's Corner. It was customary for chairpersons to host a breakfast or luncheon for their category. Each mother who came brought an item that would be bid on at either the live or silent auction. The Palm Beach homes got the best turnout, thus the most gifts, because everyone wanted a chance to see them. However, year after year, the promise of viewing a house and eating a muffin gets a little stale, pun intended!

Kate and I brainstormed about how we could revamp this formula to get more mothers to come and thus collect more gifts for our corner. Kate grew up on the Island and her mother knew Lilly Pulitzer. It was Kate who came up with the idea to have her husband build a dollhouse and use Lilly fabrics on the furniture and drapes inside it. The breakfast would be held at my house, since I was new to town and few people had seen it. I suggested we call the event for 8:15 am—just after drop-off. This time slot would encourage more moms to come before they headed to the tennis courts or country clubs.

"Kate, wouldn't it be great if we could say that Lilly will be at the breakfast in person to sign the dollhouse? Will you invite her?"

Kate loved my idea. Lilly said yes, and that's how I got to meet one of my idols, a debutante turned designer, a woman who came from a New York society family. who married into an even more prestigious one, who didn't let that stop her from creating a global fashion dynasty.

Having grown up with a mother and grandmother who loved to bake, I had nostalgia for anything made from scratch. A random taste of a home-baked cookie or cake transported me back to my childhood kitchen with my mom and grandma. But my time in the kitchens of these Palm Beach domestic divas was limited to watching and tasting, not baking. Luckily, Kate made up for the skills I lacked.

LIFE, LILLY AND THE PURSUIT OF HAPPINESS

In honor of Lilly, I bought fresh-squeezed orange juice and poured it into crystal pitchers. I placed the pastries on Herend porcelain platters given to me by my mom and placed pink and green linen cocktail napkins on the round glass table in my foyer. Lilly was a character as vibrant as her fabrics, even in her sixties. She strolled through the entranceway of my Bermuda-style house and the first thing she said was, "Oh my, I love your front doors." They were solid mahogany with toucans and palm trees etched onto the glass that set the tone for the coastal theme of the house. I was flattered, but I doubted my modest home compared to her sprawling compound she called "The Jungle."

She complimented me on my hostess skills and signed the dollhouse as the other mothers looked on. Kate was more than delighted to make banana bread and a variety of muffins: blueberry, corn and bran. The whole affair came together more perfectly than I could have imagined. When the breakfast ended, I escorted Lilly to the front door and thanked her for coming. She kissed me on the cheek and said: "Kari, you're a girl who thinks with her heart—you will go far in this town." Then she whispered in my ear, "And never forget, a Palm Beach address gets the world's attention."

My analytical mind wanted to decipher what Lilly meant by "going far." But this was no time for daydreams. The only "far" on my mind was how far my house was from the shop, and how to avoid the procession of moms in SUVs who would be headed down County Road in that same direction—it was almost 10:00 and I had a store to open.

When I got to the shop it struck me that the colors of Valerie's sweaters were similar to the ones Lilly used in her playful patterns. I chose a one-ply tunic with bracelet-length sleeves in aqua and had it delivered to her house along with a thank-you note for attending the breakfast. I enclosed a picture of me and Emmy dressed in matching pink and yellow dresses from her mother-daughter collection. I also included my business card and invited her to visit the boutique. She called to thank me and said she'd stop by when she had errands in town. I looked forward to having a private audience with her and learning how she'd built her brand without a bunch of moms in the background vying for her attention.

Thanks a Trillion

As autumn returned to the Island, my mind turned to Halloween. If you were to think of the perfect place to trick-or-treat on Halloween, it would be hard to imagine a better location than Worth Avenue in Palm Beach. The entire street, from the ocean to the lake, dedicated the day to dressing up. The avenue was home to the most iconic designer brands in the world. Behind the stores were landscaped vias and courtyards. Tucked inside the vias were one-of-a-kind boutiques.

In keeping with the street's upscale image, each shop offered the best candy imaginable: oversized Swiss chocolate bars and gourmet lollipops. Because the stores were situated next to each other, a kid could collect lots of candy without doing a lot of walking. Each year, the couple who owned much of Worth Avenue's real estate, Burt and Honey, hosted a costume contest that took place in the Gucci courtyard. Later in the night, kids trick-or-treated on the "sea" streets—Sea View, Sea Breeze and Sea Spray—where the houses were closer together. Summer and Ray hosted everyone for pizza.

Although it was unlike me not to devote time to Emmy's costume, last year was our first fall on the Island; my mind had been focused on finding work, not on pumpkins and witches. Emmy went dressed as Princess Jasmine from Aladdin in a costume I ordered from a catalogue. The silky turquoise outfit didn't get her a prize in the costume contest.

Emmy was competitive. This year she was out for a win. My sewing skills didn't measure up to those of the women on the Island, but I knew someone who was an expert seamstress: my Aunt Irena in Virginia. I called and asked her if she could make a costume for Emmy. She was happy to help. Irena would be forever grateful to my Grandpa Michel, her brother, who provided the dowry to bring her and her siblings to America from Greece.

This year Emmy wanted to dress up as Dorothy from *The Wizard of Oz*. Aunt Irena sent a blue-and-white gingham pinafore dress with a full skirt. Emmy wore it over her white puffed-sleeved school uniform blouse. I found ballet flats with red crystals to resemble Dorothy's ruby slippers at The Purple Turtle, a children's boutique in The Esplanade. This costume, combined with Emmy's idea to carry a wicker basket with a stuffed dog inside and my instructions to skip, not walk, down the runway, made her a shoo-in for a win in the "cutest" category.

The following year, the hand-sewn bumble-bee costume along with a jar of honey and a dictionary turned Emmy into a "spelling bee." For this she won "most original." The prizes were what Emmy liked best: a cashmere bunny from Kassatly's one year, a Madame Alexander doll from Cloud 10 the next.

It didn't hurt that the color photographs of Emmy winning, with Scott standing in the background, were published in *Palm Beach Society Magazine* for all his clients to see. This was proof that Scott was an insider in this intimate seaside enclave. There were never many pictures of me; I didn't photograph well and avoided the camera.

Scott was convinced the judges, many who owned or managed shops, were partial to me because of the amount of money I spent in their stores. He was wrong. Palm Beachers tend to have big families and therefore purchase a lot more children's clothing than I did. Despite the high prices, moms frequented Worth Avenue for their kids' wardrobes because we were too busy to leave the Island to drive to Old Navy.

There was another reason I enjoyed this event. Designer brands were beyond my reach at the moment. Halloween gave me the chance to walk into these stores and view the latest collections without the nasty gaze of a commissioned salesperson looking me up and down and deciding I wasn't a buyer and therefore didn't exist. This was the one day I was free to mix with the other shoppers and stroll in and out of the shops under no pressure to purchase anything. This year, I was on a mission. I wanted to see these salespeople in action and learn what my customers were spending money on when it wasn't cashmere.

The staff in the stores knew they wouldn't be making much money on Halloween. It was a gift from Worth Avenue to the kids of Palm Beach and the ones who came from near and far to partake in the festivities and collect candy. It was also a way for Scott and me to bond with other families in the community. The weather was heavenly this time of year. It was so cute to see all the little witches, ghosts and goblins parading up and down the avenue with sacks of candy, instead of the "ladies who lunch" crowd with their miniature dogs and designer shopping bags.

Several boutiques sold cashmere. I walked into one called Trillion. As I turned a corner near the back of the shop, I noticed a box with a packing slip taped on top. I recognized the logo of N Peal, the same factory that made our goods. Inside were men's cable-knit crew necks. I saw one displayed on a shelf and glanced at the price tag. The price was almost double what we sold ours for. I knew why. The rents on Worth Avenue were much higher than those in the part of town where Valerie's shop was located. I couldn't wait to share this news with my customers. Armed with this knowledge, I was already thinking how much product I could sell. I thanked the store owner and exited the shop so I could catch up with my husband and Emmy; I spotted them in front of a jeweler's.

A mom friend dressed as a witch must have cast a spell on Scott because why else would he have offered to buy me a ring displayed in the window of Greenleaf & Crosby? Scott's gesture surprised me. Jewelry was another thing he felt had no return on investment. I had better cash in now before the spell was reversed. Maybe this was Scott making some effort to show me appreciation for hosting a dinner for his college alumni association and give me some attention; lately we seemed more like roommates than husband and wife.

I couldn't wait to show Valerie my new lapis heart ring. We often joked that the gifts we gave each other were better than those our husbands bought us. Her last gift from Ian had been a kayak; she had hoped for a thoroughbred horse. She relished mine—a red leather Hermés address book that put access to our clients at her fingertips. I loved Scott's gift of a framed family photo, but it couldn't compete with the cashmere wrap with a ruffled edge Valerie designed and named the "Kari" cape after me.

Strangers Among Us

The Royal Poinciana Shopping District, home to Valerie Louthan Designs, was less imposing than Worth Avenue. The courtyard of the Paramount Building evoked a storybook setting with its lush greenery and white flower boxes blossoming with color. The shop oozed charm, especially after I persuaded Valerie to refurbish it. The worn carpet had been replaced with a plush heather blue one and the banquette featured a vintage floral fabric. Evening sweaters hung from satin hangers on freshly painted warm vanilla walls. This setting inspired me to do my best work.

And this work was important to me; it gave me a renewed sense of purpose. To meet my sales goal, every minute of the day mattered. The business phone traveled with me wherever I went: the bank to make deposits, Fedco to get office supplies and even the restroom, which was located outside the store in the courtyard. Linda, our accountant, was focused on how the business was growing. "This is no longer a hobby," she told Valerie and Ian. "It's not just something for you to do between meals anymore."

Valerie had sold her home on the Island and was finalizing plans for one she was building in the Bahamas. She intended to spend the season there instead of in Palm Beach. For this to happen, she needed me to take over her responsibilities. Now our collaborations would be even more infrequent. "You've done a fabulous job writing copy for the trunk show invitations and choosing which sweaters to advertise in *The Shiny Sheet*, so that task is yours now, Kari. Since this puts a lot more on your plate,

Anabelle will help with shipping so you can focus on production, sourcing materials and merchandising." Anabelle was the daughter of our seamstress. Her English was poor, but when I gave her silk and satin trims for her mom to sew on sweaters, she brought them back in a timely manner. I was excited to have an assistant!

Ian often dropped off sketches of new designs en route to his office. Valerie confessed her first two husbands married her for money and never again would she allow a man to live off her. Prior to keeping the books for her business, Ian served as an officer at The Royal Military Academy at Sandhurst. Each month, I provided him with our sales figures so he could send the proper taxes to the state of Florida. Valerie suspected he was an alcoholic, but this was Palm Beach, and it seemed many people here could fall into that category.

Although the shop's entrance was visible from the road, there was rarely any walk-in traffic. People who came to the store were regulars who knew of our location. Because we were a small business, the customers felt like family: The boutique was our gathering spot. My days at work seemed more like time spent with friends dropping by to catch up than clouds of cashmere going out the door or credit cards being rung up in the double-digit thousands.

That's why, when an unruly man barged through the front door and demanded to speak to the owner, I was shocked. Our male customers were genteel and exuded sophistication. This one wore wire-rimmed glasses, smelled of tobacco and carried a tattered brown briefcase. He introduced himself and said he was an IRS auditor and demanded I provide him with proof that we actually shipped the volume of merchandise out of state as our tax returns claimed we did.

"One moment, sir. The owner is here; I'll ask him to come over."

I called Ian and informed him about the man and the reason for his visit. Often, retail businesses are accused of falsifying shipping records. This occurs when merchants say they are sending a client's goods to another state, don't charge tax and then let the client walk out with their purchase. This practice is illegal. However, it is common in the luxury industry because customers don't like to pay sales tax and businesses like to keep customers happy.

When Ian arrived, his breath smelled of alcohol. Ian used alcohol to soothe himself when he felt overwhelmed. In a fast-paced environment like fashion, that was often. I pulled the shipping records from the file. There were copies of the labels for every order that was shipped. On each label was a sales order number. The trunk shows' receipts accounted for half the revenues of the business. They were proof that although the orders were taken outside of Florida, they were shipped from this location. Whew... we were in the clear.

"Great work, Kari," Ian said. "That was smart thinking to include the invoice number on each shipping label. You can leave early today."

It had taken the man hours to sort through the records. I was grateful for the compliment and glad for a chance to skip out and get a head start on preparing dinner. But this party wasn't over. As I was leaving, another unlikely guest walked into the shop. This time my guard was up.

This woman looked frazzled—her hair was unkempt and her shirt was only partially tucked in, but she was fidgeting with it nervously.

"Hi, I'm Kari. Are you shopping for yourself or for a gift?"

Her behavior was strange. She didn't act like someone shopping would; she didn't really look at the sweaters but glanced casually around the store before focusing in on me. Odder still was her barrage of questions:

"How long have you worked here? Do you live near the store? Are you married?" Valerie had instructed me to never give out personal information to customers. When this woman refused to let me show her a red sweater for Christmas, I redirected the questions she was asking me toward her.

She revealed she had a daughter my age who was an attorney. This daughter had three kids who attended the same school as Emmy. "What's your daughter's favorite color? Maybe she'd like a scarf or some gloves in her stocking?" Again, the woman changed the subject and began quizzing me about life in Palm Beach.

When I wasn't with a customer, I was getting orders into production or creating marketing strategies. I had no time to waste making small talk with this strange bird. I'm certain she would have stayed longer, but Mrs. Benson called to check on her order. Each Christmas, Mrs. Benson gave each of her daughters and daughters-in-law three sweaters with matching silk taffeta skirts or pants. I assured her all 36 pieces would be gift wrapped and shipped to her home in Ohio by December 21st. When I stopped to catch my breath, I noticed the strange woman had left the shop without saying goodbye or thanking me for my time.

I didn't think about her again until I was writing in my journal at bedtime. It had been a grueling day dealing with the IRS agent on top of all my other responsibilities. I replayed the interaction with the woman over and over in my mind. It struck me that something wasn't quite right, but I couldn't pinpoint what.

Bachelor #1

When my neighbors Masie and Will moved back to England, a tall guy with a toothy grin named Todd and his breezy girlfriend Erin rented their house. Like many newcomers to Palm Beach, Todd had made a killing from the dot-com boom of the late 1990s. He was leading a life of leisure until he made his next move. Erin was a teacher. She didn't think a guy in his 30s should spend his days relaxing by the pool. She encouraged him to return to the workforce. He accepted a job as a day trader at a firm where his cousin worked. When Todd described the firm, it sounded just a bit too familiar.

"Is this company called Magnum Securities by any chance?" I asked.

"Yeah, how did you know?" Todd asked, looking surprised.

"Because the guy who started that firm was my first boyfriend in Manhattan."

"Are you serious? *Seth?*"

"Yes, Seth."

How could I forget the name of his firm? Seth and I had come up with it when we ordered a bottle of champagne that size to celebrate our one-year anniversary. The sitcom *Sex and the City* was the hottest show on television. Todd, Erin and I were obsessed with it. I told Todd that Seth had been my "Mr. Big," as Carrie Bradshaw, the character played by Sarah Jessica Parker, referred to her on-again-off-again boyfriend, who also worked in finance.

"Seth started the firm when we were a couple," I said. What I didn't say was that to me he would always be "the one who got away." We had a tumultuous courtship for most of my single days in the city. We both had oversized ambitions and dreams of conquering the world. He was the opposite of most men in his field who possessed the toxic masculinity inspired by the movie *Wall Street*. He was more than a math genius—he had compassion for others. I had fallen for him when he canceled a date because he needed to help a friend who suffered from addiction.

Seth knew I wanted marriage and children. He said he did too, but like his doppelgänger in *Sex and the City*, he was afraid to commit. To my frustration, he would reel me in, woo me like a wife in training and then break it off because he didn't want to waste my time. Before I'd managed to get over him, he would come back, beg for another chance and the same pattern would repeat.

Now, he was 41, single and had never married; not that every husband-hungry girl in Manhattan hadn't tried to change that. At first, I told Todd not to mention we were neighbors. Scott was aware of my history with Seth. He didn't need to relive it in his own backyard. But Todd couldn't resist. I was shocked to hear Seth's voice on the other end of my cell phone one afternoon. It was the same soft-spoken one that had made my heart skip a beat 12 years ago.

"Hi, Kari. It's Seth."

"I know," I said. He asked about Emmy, and we made small talk until he changed the subject to that of my work.

"I can't believe you're in the cashmere business," he said. "I love cashmere. I buy a lot of my stuff on Worth Avenue."

This didn't surprise me. I had exposed him to the finer things in life early on. He had been an A student, curious and eager to learn. I remembered how grateful he was that I had studs and a pair of cufflinks on hand when we attended a black-tie event together. We were getting ready at my place when he discovered his

BACHELOR #1

white dress shirt had buttonholes but no buttons. He'd packed a bow tie but had never heard of studs and cufflinks. Luckily, I had a set left behind by a previous boyfriend.

"I come to Palm Beach a lot; I'd love to see your men's things."

Hmm...something didn't add up. I hadn't spoken to this man in 10 years. For most of my 20s he occupied every inch of space in my heart and my head. Now, he was asking to see my sweaters. Scott and I were navigating rough terrain in our marriage. It seemed like we couldn't agree on anything, even which charities to support. We were seeing less and less of each other at home and just going through the motions when we attended events side by side. Scott knew who Seth was—his rapid rise to the Forbes list was legendary in the world of finance. But I knew Scott; a billionaire ex-boyfriend back in the picture would only add to our problems. Nonetheless, there was no reason I should let a potential client of this caliber slip away.

"Do you still play golf?" I asked, thinking of the large array of V-neck slipover vests that had just come in from Scotland and needed homes.

"Of course," he said. I recalled all the mornings he had left me lingering in bed alone so he could get on the course with the guys.

"Good. I have something you'll love. I'll send some pieces to your office with Todd," I said, like it was the most natural thing in the world for us to be having a business conversation.

"That would be great, Kari." He sounded so sincere, not like the "wolves," or men who dominate Wall Street and are known for preying on unsuspecting women. I asked him his size and color preferences and told him to expect a package on Monday.

A simple exchange of goods. That was how Seth came back into my life. Todd brought back the pieces Seth wasn't taking. His personal assistant, Dana, called to pay for the pieces he kept. Seth didn't ask for a discount, nor did I offer one.

In the winter months, Seth traveled between his homes in New York and South Florida. Every so often he called to talk. Once, he took it a step further and asked if he could see me. "If your husband wouldn't mind…just a casual dinner," he said. I declined and made up a reason why I couldn't. I didn't want to let on that my relationship with my husband was on fragile ground. I wondered if Todd had mentioned anything.

And "trouble" was putting it lightly. After supper, while I helped Emmy with homework, Scott retreated to the guest room, where he now slept. He said my habit of jotting down work-related items in the middle of the night disrupted his sleep. Our fights were always the same: I'd suggest things we could do together, like a walk on the beach, a bike ride or a stroll through the gardens at The Four Arts. He'd say he wasn't interested. He was obsessed with money—keeping what he'd made already and making more. He lived in fear that one wrong move could land him back in Borough Park, living in a crowded apartment with four roommates. He criticized my career. He complained that I was being taken advantage of and not compensated fairly for my efforts. Meanwhile, work was the area I felt I was succeeding in.

A month later, when Seth called to invite me to dinner, I said yes. I decided not to mention it to Scott. Instead, I chose a night Scott played racquetball, asked my babysitter to stay late and told Seth I'd meet him near his office.

"Can you please pick a place where I won't run into anyone I know?" I asked.

"Anything you want, Kari. And…Kari?"

"What?" There was silence on the other end of the phone as I waited for his reply.

"I can't wait to see you."

"Just give me a day and time and I'll be there," I said, as my spine tingled with guilt.

BACHELOR #1

Seth called midweek and asked me to join him at the Sea Grille restaurant. En route to meet him, I expressed that meeting him may not be a good idea. "Don't worry, it will be fine, Kari. I've got it covered." That's how it was with Seth. He made me feel protected, like a full-length mink coat in below-zero weather. Being married to Scott never made me feel safe the way I thought it would.

Seth arrived first. The hostess led me to his table. Seth stood up to greet me and pulled out my chair. He had less hair than I remembered, but his blue eyes still sparkled the same way. His smile made me melt like a girl who's asked to a middle school dance by the boy she has a crush on.

"Is it always so quiet here on a weekday?" I asked as I sat down and looked around. Before he could say anything, I noticed we were the only people in the restaurant. He had closed the entire place so we could be alone. The waiter poured Cristal champagne and we dined on caviar, oysters and grilled snapper. Unlike the girl I'd been in my 20s, I didn't care that he had shut the place down for me or consider how much it cost to do so. We reminisced about our shared past. He admired my courage in securing an equity stake in a business. I told him I was more impressed by his philanthropy than his fortune.

We discussed our mutual friends and what they were doing. I laughed when he told me that Glenn, the former maître d' at Peter Luger's, was still at his firm—I was dining with Seth when he plucked him from the famous steakhouse. Seth thought that if Glenn could manage the clientele there, the traders and investors would be a cakewalk.

He smiled when I told him Arianna Mills and her daughters were my clients. The Millses were friends of his parents. Like me, Seth felt very at ease around older people. He played golf with Mr. Mills at Piping Rock Country Club. When Seth joined his poker game, Mr. Mills became a friend and one of the first investors in Seth's firm.

Most importantly, Seth was the same: modest, funny and warm. Money hadn't changed him. He said the same was true for me. Before those feelings could take us to a place I wasn't prepared to go, I thanked him for a wonderful evening and got up to leave. He signed the bill and walked me to the valet.

"Thanks for coming, Kari," he said as the valet retrieved my white Mercedes sedan. His convertible sports model followed. He tipped the valet for both cars.

"It was great to catch up," I said, trying to pretend that what had taken place was nothing more than a dinner between old friends. I stepped into my car and drove away. I had a feeling this wasn't the last I'd be seeing of Seth.

My situation with Scott only got worse. He questioned the effort I was giving my work relative to the income it was bringing to our family. In a way, he was right; giving eight hours of my day to work did take time away from maintaining the house. We'd been fined by the town for having a dead tree in our front yard and the hedges on our property were infested with whiteflies and had to be replaced. In the past, I would have been more focused on these things. Our life was definitely more complicated now that the two of us were building careers. So that we could have some private time, I arranged a playdate for Emmy and made a list of fun things we could do together. Scott said no to all of them.

"Then let's have a 'sexcapade,'" I suggested. Physical affection was the way we rekindled intimacy in our relationship when the flame was temporarily extinguished. He declined, saying he needed to go to the office. Now that I thought about it, he had been spending a lot of Sundays there in recent months. I couldn't remember the last time we made love.

On Valentine's weekend, after the Daddy-Daughter dance, Scott surprised me not with his usual gift of breakfast in bed, but by telling me he was leaving. He had found an apartment nearby and asked if I would help him pack his things. Blindsided, I agreed. I knew he wasn't happy, but I didn't understand why, and I certainly didn't think he was this close to leaving. No counseling? No deep discussion to work things out? Perhaps time apart would make him appreciate the life we'd worked so hard for. We told Emmy her dad needed to have a place of his own for a while and that it had nothing to do with her. He would see her on Wednesday nights and every other weekend.

Emmy seemed okay with the new arrangement, but it was much harder for me to accept. How did we get here? I took my marriage vows seriously. Having come from a single-parent home, I'd promised myself I would never raise my children in one. I never imagined that I may not have a choice.

When You're Single You Mingle

Erin and Todd had become fast friends with both me and Scott. They were regulars at our holiday get-togethers. That's why it wasn't unusual that they were willing to help me when Scott moved out: Todd with car repairs and Erin tutoring Emmy in math. Perhaps because of this, it didn't faze me when Todd asked me to arrange a dinner with his new boss.

"It would mean a lot for me to sit down with Seth away from the trading desk and really learn about this business." Todd knew how to get to me. Helping people further their career ambitions was a cause I could never say no to. I caved in and told him I'd arrange a date on a Wednesday night.

Seth had been calling me a lot recently. I'd been reluctant to see him again after our first meeting. He was surprised when I phoned to make dinner plans and asked if Todd and his girlfriend could join us.

"That would be great! Where do you want to go?"

"Can we go to Ta-boo?" I picked this restaurant because it was not somewhere Scott or any locals would go on a Wednesday night.

"Sounds good. I'll pick you up…if you want me to."

I hesitated. Part of me really wanted him to see my house and the part of town where the young families lived. I agreed and told him to come at 6:30. I purposely had Seth drive down North Lake Way to get to my house. I wanted him to see the beauty of this street, the leaves of the treetops as they dusted the high hedges like the silk fringe on a pashmina and how the road curved past the gates of the estates of families named Ford and Fisher, one who invented an automobile, another the seat belt. "Do you want to come in?" I asked as I opened the door and let him kiss me gently on my cheek.

"I would love to see where you are when you're talking to me on the phone," he replied. What was it about this guy that he always knew the perfect thing to say? I led him through the kitchen and pointed to the covered loggia.

"Right there." I pointed to a chaise lounge upholstered in a coral cotton fabric patterned with palm fronds. Next to it sat my antique English bamboo accent table with my house phone perched on top. He laughed when I opened the door that led to the garage and saw two bicycles.

"I can't believe you ride a bike, Kari." I laughed too. The Kari he knew was a city girl whose means of transportation was chauffeur-driven cars—paid for by the private equity shop she worked at. Back then, I had been so career-driven, my love for the outdoors had been placed on the layaway plan along with travel, my other passion.

When Seth and I entered Ta-boo, the staff greeted me by name.

"You really are Miss Palm Beach, aren't you, Kari?"

"I don't know about that."

I could certainly name a lot of women much more deserving of that title. Come to think of it, they were competing in the evening gown competition every night. My thighs would have never made it past the swimsuit round. When I saw Todd in a sports jacket, I remembered I'd forgotten to tell Seth he was required to wear one. Seth was wearing one of the V-neck sweaters he'd bought from me. I felt bad when the maître d' brought him a much-too-big jacket and insisted he slip it on. He did so without complaining. His much younger self had behaved equally well when we were invited to Doubles, a private supper club in Manhattan.

"Do you remember when that happened in the city?" I teased.

"How could I forget?" he quipped back. "It was around my birthday. Afterward you bought me a Brioni sports jacket and wool dress pants from Bergdorf Goodman. It's still the nicest gift any girl has ever given me."

I laughed; I had always been generous. Sharing my discerning taste for luxury goods with those I felt close to gives me pleasure.

Todd was glad when I steered the conversation toward commerce. He wanted to hear about the trading strategies that made his boss so successful, not relive our romantic history. We enjoyed a delicious meal that ended with me insisting we all share two of Ta-boo's best desserts—the famous cappuccino and the Worth Avenue Sundae. When the evening ended, Erin said Todd would give me a ride home.

"There's no need for Seth to drive north when he's heading south," she said.

Seth smiled. I thanked him for coming and said goodbye. I think Todd sensed why it was best that he, not Seth, take me home.

Takeover Target

In the weeks that followed, Seth continued to call. I was in no rush to see him. Funny, he never asked about Scott. What wasn't funny was that a mom friend saw Scott in a restaurant. He was kissing a woman she recognized from our kids' school. My friend didn't know this woman well, but she was able to tell me three things about her: She had three children, her name was Lauren and she was a lawyer. My theory that Scott would miss me and come running back home had clearly backfired. Still, I held out hope that this friend was mistaken. We were separated, but part of me believed we'd come back together.

So when Scott asked if he could take Emmy skiing over spring break, I was shocked. We never traveled during this time. When I learned this woman and her kids were going, I cried. I thought of all the time I'd spent trying (and failing) to get Scott on board about an activity—any activity—with me. I also thought back to Christmas and remembered the odd lady who came to the boutique and peppered me with questions. Her daughter was a lawyer who had three kids enrolled at Emmy's school, I recalled her saying. This seemed like more than a coincidence. Was it possible that her daughter was the one Scott was kissing? If so, I was certain this woman was sent to the shop to spy on her daughter's competition. I recalled the woman mentioning her daughter's name. My journal entry dated December 19 proved I was right. Her daughter's name was Lauren.

I felt preyed upon. How dare this woman send her mother to my workplace? My brief stint in private equity gave me a primer on mergers and acquisitions. In this industry, Scott was what's known as a takeover target—a good candidate for a business interested in acquiring another one. And this was not a hostile takeover, where a CEO was forced to step down. Scott walked away from our marriage of his own free will, and I was required to step down from my position as wife. I didn't know where to direct the level of anger I was experiencing—toward Lauren or Scott? I chose Lauren. Scott probably had no idea about her mother and her role as a mystery shopper.

Shortly after I put two and two together, Seth called and invited me to have dinner with him on a Friday night. This time, I said yes. Dana called to ask if I had any requests for dinner. I debated what it means when a man's assistant calls you to arrange a date, but he was inviting me to his home and that was worth something.

"I'm not fussy. Just make sure there's a yummy dessert." When I dined alone, I often skipped the main course and went straight for something sweet. I chose my outfit carefully. I wasn't expecting anything more than a casual dinner with an ex-boyfriend, but Seth was a very eligible bachelor, and I was flattered he chose to spend his Friday night with me. I pulled out a periwinkle blue cashmere dress. A cinch belt would bring it in at the waist. The silk slip I discovered in my lingerie drawer would feel good against the softness of the dress.

When I got to the black wrought iron gates of Seth's house in Highland Beach, I buzzed to be let in. After walking up two flights of steps, I rang the doorbell of his sprawling Beaux Arts mansion. I almost expected a butler to open the door, like Mr. French in *Family Affair*, but Seth opened it himself. He led me through the foyer to an alcove near the kitchen where an elaborate meal had been laid out. The table was set for two.

"And you did all this?" I asked.

"Let's just say I planned it, and my chef cooked it," he said, grinning.

I smiled back. One of the perks of working at a private equity firm was a chef that prepared lunch for the employees. Seth had promised me when he made it big, he would hire one. His success didn't surprise me. Even as a new trader, he made money in the stock market crash of '87. I knew then there was no limit to where his wicked smarts would take him. After a few too many sips of champagne, I let it slip that Scott had moved out and that another woman was involved.

"Wow, that's heavy; did you have any idea?"

"Funny you should ask…no, I didn't. He wasn't happy, but I couldn't figure out why. I guess he found someone better."

Seth took my hand, held it firmly, looked into my eyes and said, "There's nobody better than you, Kari. I would know. I wouldn't still be single if there was. No girl I've dated even comes close to you." He inched toward me on the banquette. At first, he brushed his full lips on my mouth before kissing me long and hard. Then he stood up, grabbed my hand, and led me to his bedroom. He beamed when he unzipped my dress and saw the silk slip. Then, as he took in the sight of me, he asked me to take off my wedding band.

"I don't need to be reminded that you're not mine," he said as he undid my bra and let it fall to the floor along with my dress.

I tried not to think about all the girls he must have undressed to get so good at this. His lovemaking was exactly as I remembered, tender but not timid. I loved the contrast between his strength in business and the gentleness he exuded in the bedroom. The pima cotton sheets caressed my skin like a lush body crème. He grinned when I recognized the pattern as Pratesi. After all, I was the girl who exposed him to these luxuries and the kind of money it took to acquire them.

Before the sun rose and reminded us we had important things to accomplish, we held each other tightly, attempting to eliminate any space between our bodies. Then he was off to the golf course, and I was off to work, just like old times. My body was so warm, I didn't notice how cold the gilded bedroom felt. I could hear men's voices in the kitchen. Quietly, I walked barefoot toward the foyer, heels in one hand, and slipped out the front door.

That's how it began again for Seth and me. He flew back and forth between New York and Palm Beach in his G5, another perk he had promised to achieve back when I mentioned I'd flown on one for business. For the rest of the season, we saw each other when he was in town and I was without my daughter.

Bring Your Daughter to Work Day

I was celebrating Bring Your Daughter to Work Day long before it ever became a Hallmark holiday. It wasn't because I wanted to show my eight-year-old how I earned a living each day but because when a sitter canceled at the last minute or there was a half day of school, Emmy went where I went. During those years when Emmy was little, I was so grateful to Valerie for starting a business that afforded me both a chance to run an apparel company and the flexibility to have my daughter in tow from time to time.

I set up a small table and chairs for Emmy in the stockroom away from the sweaters. I gave her paper and colored pencils and prayed a client wouldn't follow me in there and call Child Protective Services. On sunny days, I had her sit outside at a table in the courtyard. This way, I could look up and see her through the large horizontal window above my desk. Arlene, who owned the adjacent shop, Couture & More, sometimes brought her daughter to work too. The girls skipped rope in the courtyard or played dress-up with the gowns and shoes from Arlene's store, which made for a much more spacious playroom than Valerie's.

The day it all went wrong was when a group of four hedge-fund wives came in. I got so excited by the numbers adding up on the sales slips, I lost track of where Emmy was. When the women left, the shop was covered in cascades of cashmere from all the trying on. I looked outside...no Emmy. I checked the dressing room and stockroom...no Emmy. I called Arlene and explained how the hedge-fund wives had distracted me. I asked her to please check her store and see if Emmy was there. I checked the restroom in the courtyard. Empty. Arlene called back to say Emmy wasn't anywhere in sight.

My heart raced until I saw a small hand peeking out from beneath one of the pistachio and cotton candy pink heaps of cashmere on the floor. I dug through all the sweaters in a panic until I uncovered Emmy sitting on her knees in a child's pose. She was giggling, thinking it was all very funny.

"You scared me to death! Don't ever do that to me again."

In a rush to get us home—I still had to prepare dinner, check homework and get Emmy to bed—I showed her the correct way to fold the sweaters. Four hands would be quicker than two to return everything to the proper shelves.

On the way home, we stopped at Herbert's Market to pick up chicken breasts. I added a split of champagne and some goose liver pâté to celebrate my accomplishment. Just from the day's total, I'd made our sales goal for the month.

"Someone had a good day," Errol, the cook, said, smiling at me from behind the counter.

"Yup, four hedgehogs came in and spent a lot of money," Emmy piped up. I realized she must have overheard me talking on the phone to Arlene about the hedge-fund wives.

"It's hedge fund, not hedgehog," I said.

"Hedgehog sounds better," Emmy said. "They were hogging all the sweaters."

She was right; they were. From then on this became our nickname for these men and their wives. It crossed my mind to tell Emmy that if things progressed with Seth, I might become one of them. I decided against it. Scott and I had only recently separated. He could do as he wished, but it was too soon for me to tell my daughter I'd started dating.

Although everyone at school was gossiping about Scott and Lauren, I chose to keep my relationship with Seth to myself.

With the specter of divorce looming, I knew Scott would be more amicable if he thought I was alone. That meant my dates with Seth took place in Highland Beach. His house was an all-boys' club, full of traders. The guys enjoyed poker, pool and fine dining—courtesy of Seth.

Before our next date, Seth, not Dana, called to make the arrangements. He seemed excited to share his plans with me. I secretly wondered if having sex with him had earned me the courtesy of speaking with the man himself instead of his assistant.

"I can't stop thinking about you, Kari," he said. "I had a dream about you in a pink bikini." I felt inspired to make his dream come true. I called Sylvia, who owned my favorite shop, Franceska Paris, and told her I'd drop in after work. I scoured the swimsuit rack until I found a string bikini in cherry blossom pink. Like any good salesperson, she tried to show me the latest things she'd brought from St. Tropez. She couldn't tempt me. My thoughts were on Seth, not shopping. The night of our date, I pulled a Pucci dress from my closet. In place of lingerie, I wore the pink two-piece. I traded my flat closed-toe mules for sling-back high-heeled sandals.

When I arrived at Seth's house the gate outside was open and the front door was ajar. I let myself in and noticed that a card game was taking place in the den. I stood in the entranceway until Seth looked up and motioned for me to come in. I walked around the table and stood behind him. I glanced at his cards, careful not to reveal any clues to what his hand held. He'd taught me to do this when I watched him play poker in the men's card room at his country club. He was good at this game. I suspected these same skills were what led him to excel in the stock market. Although the guys tried to be discreet, they eyed me like another trophy being awarded to their billionaire boss.

Their behavior didn't upset me. I was familiar with the dynamic between these types of men and the kind of women who surround them. Besides, they didn't know my history with Seth, that we had dated when we were young, way before he had money or any of them had walked through the doors of his proprietary trading firm. I smiled as Seth moved the chips toward him, declaring victory.

"The guys are going to have dinner here," he said as Dana and a second assistant scurried about, helping the staff set out a feast for the traders. "I made a reservation for us at Il Mulino."

"Like the one in New York?" I asked.

Seth smiled. "Yes, I know it's a favorite of yours." Il Mulino was an Italian restaurant in Greenwich Village we'd frequented in the city. I didn't even know there was one in Florida. I couldn't believe he remembered how much I liked it. Before I could ask, he gazed at me approvingly and said, "Nice outfit." Scott never noticed what I was wearing. Each time I modeled a new evening gown or cocktail dress for him, the only thing he cared about was how much it cost. It was nice to be with a man who made me feel desired. And that desire went both ways.

"Are you hungry, Kari?" he asked.

I was, but more so for him than a meal. "I kinda am," I said, not wanting to let on what I was really thinking. "Can we just eat here instead?"

"Of course," he said as he instructed his chef to serve us in the dining room. He called Il Mulino to apologize for cancelling on such short notice. He was so polite—another thing I loved about him. That night Seth and I dined on grilled veal chops, sautéed spinach and vintage wine, surrounded by Flemish silk tapestries that came from a castle. Throughout the meal, he gently touched my hand or rubbed my thigh underneath my dress. I was so enthralled, I didn't notice that our plates had been cleared away. I thought about all the dinners I cooked for Scott. I never got as much as a thank-you when I cleared the plates. It was as if meal preparation and cleanup were my job, despite the fact I spent eight hours a day at my own 9 to 5, plus evenings and weekends networking for Scott's.

BRING YOUR DAUGHTER TO WORK DAY

"I hope you saved room for dessert," Seth said, grinning like a little boy who just received his first train set. He was such a kid at heart. It was the perfect contrast to his intellect and take-charge attitude. With him, I felt like I could be feminine yet playful; strong, not bossy.

Two large goblets of strawberry ice cream topped with fresh fruit and whipped cream were placed in front of us. I dipped my spoon in, took a bite, and let it melt in my mouth. Seth leaned toward me, teasing me with a spoonful that had more whipped cream than ice cream. He pulled me close and kissed me. I slipped the high heels off my feet as he pulled me onto his lap to face him, my legs wrapped around his back, my feet against the soft velvet of the oversized dining chair. I could hear the television and the houseguests talking in the family room near the kitchen.

Seth led the way to the bedroom, gripping my hand tightly as I followed behind him. I wondered if he instructed the architect to design the house this way—the premier suite on the first floor, far away from the five bedrooms upstairs. Seth grabbed the overnight bag I'd left in the foyer and placed it on a nightstand. Then he pulled the silk dress over my head. He beamed when he saw the pink bikini. He gently untied the strings of the two pieces and let them fall to the floor. We made love for hours. When it ended, he held me, stroking my long hair as I lay with my back nestled up against his chest. I was so comfortable that I didn't feel him crawl toward his side of the bed to get the sleep he needed before a stressful day of trading. Hundreds of millions of dollars, mainly his, were at stake.

When I woke up Seth was gone. I wasn't surprised. He had a disciplined morning routine. His trainer came at 6 am. After he worked out, he showered and read a stack of newspapers while eating breakfast. He got to his office at 9 am, half an hour before the stock market opened. I wandered into the kitchen hoping to find someone who might know where my shoes had walked off to.

The kitchen was empty except for a distinguished older man who was seated at a table drinking a cup of coffee.

"Good morning," I said, feeling embarrassed. I had not seen this gentleman last night. "Are any of the staff around?" I asked, trying not to appear anxious.

"They are. I don't know where, but I can buzz them if you like," he said, as if there was nothing odd about a barefoot woman walking into Seth's kitchen and inquiring where the help was.

"Can I pour you a cup of coffee?" he asked, stirring sugar into his.

"No thanks, I have to get to work."

I knew I had never met this man before, but he was looking at me with vague recognition. As I contemplated leaving this crime scene without my shoes—$900 Jimmy Choos, to be specific—the man introduced himself.

"By the way, I'm Lowell Zinn."

Well, there it was. He was Todd's father; the one Todd was estranged from over a business deal gone bad. Suddenly, I remembered that Todd told me his dad knew Seth. I thought back to the card game. There had been a guy there who resembled Todd—he must have been his cousin. This cousin must have told his dad who I was and that I was spending the night. Todd and his father weren't speaking, but Todd and his cousin sat next to each other at the trading desk. My thoughts whirred. I didn't want Todd to know about our sleepover; he might tell Scott. If Scott knew I was intimate with another man, it would give him more leverage if we divorced. If he knew the man was Seth, I was doomed.

"It's a pleasure to meet you, Lowell," I said. "Seth has told me wonderful things about you. I'm Kari. I live next door to your son Todd in Palm Beach."

"Yeah, some son he is to sue his own father," Lowell blurted.

"I'm sorry you two had a falling-out, but your son is a stand-up guy. I know you'll smooth things over."

BRING YOUR DAUGHTER TO WORK DAY

I could tell he wanted to talk more. Just then, a woman in a uniform handed me a small cloth bag with my shoes in it. Before I could wonder if retrieving women's shoes was part of her job description, I addressed Lowell. "If you could do me a favor and not tell your son I was here, I would be most grateful," I said.

"What, you married?" he asked in an accent I now recognized as New Jersey, specifically Bergen County.

"I'm separated, but yes, still married. I would prefer my husband not to know I was here. I'm sure you understand."

"I have nothing to gain by saying I ran into you," he said gruffly.

"I'm glad, Lowell, because I have everything to lose."

I was anxious to leave. Seth's housekeeper had opened the French doors to the patio off his bedroom because the weather had turned cool. There would be a long line of ladies waiting for cashmere when I arrived at the shop, and I had to get home to shower and change first. Without putting my shoes on, I bolted out the front door.

For the rest of the Season this is how it went. Seth would call me during the week to arrange the next date. This was exactly how it was when we dated 12 years ago. As with trading, he stayed in control. A date never turned into a weekend; Sundays never rolled over into Monday morning. I wondered if this was how it was with all the women since me. Part of me believed I was the only one he was seeing, but I wasn't naïve enough to think that my wish was the truth. How could I say anything? I was married.

If I were like many of the women in Palm Beach, I would have set my sights on Seth to move up in the marriage game, but games were never my thing; the only person I was in competition with was me. I rationalized that since I dated Seth before Scott, I wasn't really being unfaithful. Seth was my "hall pass," the way I saw it. If Scott came back to me he would understand. Part of me still couldn't let go of our marriage. Scott was the guy who boarded the express train I was steering without ever questioning where it was headed. I still loved him. The question was: Did Scott still love me?

His (But Not Hers) in Highland Beach

Seth asked me to fly to New York with him on his G5. He was excited to show me his Fifth Avenue apartment and how far his company had come since his mom and I decorated its offices. All I could think about was something terrible happening, and the newspaper headlines the next day: "Wife of Palm Beach Money Manager and Bachelor Financier Die in the Air." This was not the legacy I wanted to leave. I promised Seth I would come when the Season ended—I would fly commercial and buy my own ticket.

For the time being, I was enjoying our romance. I had no expectations. I was well aware of Seth's commitment issues. Scott was the man who had placed that Harry Winston diamond on my finger and promised me a future. He'd spent way too much; I cringed when he told me it had no flaws. "But Kari, any stone less than perfect is no way to start a marriage."

Seth had made no such promise, but he continued to buy cashmere sweaters for himself and his employees. He bought so many I told Valerie we should name one after him. At first, she was hesitant. She thought his name sounded odd compared to the others in the collection—"Seth" isn't a name you hear in the Scottish Highlands. However, it took all of one conversation for Seth to charm her and change her mind. Our one-ply men's crew neck sweater was named after our client Sean Connery, the film star. I decided the new V-neck style should be named after Seth, since he practically designed it. He told me the regular crew neck pulled at the neck. He pointed out that if it had a small V-neck, it would fit better, and he could wear a white T-shirt under it.

I had yet to tell Valerie about my separation. When she asked the identity of the new client who was buying up our men's line, I explained Seth was an old boyfriend who wanted to support my career. Valerie was a major worrier. I was constantly reassuring her that our bank account was flush, the clients were happy and our shelves were stacked with merchandise. I didn't want her to worry that on top of everything else, my messy personal life would affect my performance.

Although Seth loved shopping, he was never good about buying gifts for girlfriends. Even when we first dated, his gifts were practical —a hand-knit mohair sweater or the latest-model cell phone. I'm sure it had to do with his fear of giving of himself. It didn't matter; he gave me something better—he made me feel valued.

When he was in Florida, he preferred to entertain me on his turf. That meant our dates took place in Highland Beach. Just like old times, we laughed and teased each other like teenagers. I wasn't auditioning for the role of wife; I didn't even know if one had been written into the script. What I wrote, though, was an inscription that read: "To Jay, Love Daisy," on the flyleaf of our favorite novel, *The Great Gatsby*. Each time I was with him it felt like a roller coaster climbing higher and higher toward the top. Until it didn't.

One Sunday, I woke up early and found myself in bed alone. Seth was most likely teeing off on the golf course. His housekeeper knocked on the door with a freshly brewed pot of coffee and a basket of pastries. "Can I cook up something for you in the kitchen, Mrs. Kari?" she asked. Was this part of her training, to memorize the names of the women who made it past the velvet ropes to Seth's bedroom? Why was she calling me Mrs.? Had Seth told her I was married? Suddenly I felt slutty. Why did Seth have to leave me on a Sunday? Why was there no morning cuddling? Nothing had changed in 10 years.

"No, this is good," I said as I motioned for her to place the tray on the bed, eager to sip the piping hot coffee.

Seth asked me to leave clothes at his house, but I didn't. Part of me couldn't admit these sleepovers were premeditated. I showered and pulled out lavender capri pants and a cropped cashmere sweater in the same color. Monochromatic dressing was trending; wearing all one shade made the task of getting dressed so much simpler. Out of curiosity, I peeked into the "his" walk-in closet. It was filled with clothes, all color coordinated with each item hung perfectly. I gently nudged open the door to the "hers" closet and saw that it was completely empty, not even a bathrobe hanging on one of the hooks. I had a strong hunch it wasn't going to be filled anytime soon. Not by me or any other woman.

Two Kinds of Investments

The Season ended and Valerie's business had the highest sales volume on record, to the tune of over a million dollars. Valerie asked me to accompany her to Scotland to visit the textile mills and learn how the sweaters were made. She planned to introduce me to the senior staff—the people I corresponded with daily. I was flattered and excited.

More importantly, Valerie was making an investment in me. She said my work ethic reminded her of her own when she was my age. She hinted that if I continued to perform the way I did this year, she would pass the company down to me in the future. "None of my offspring are interested in my business, Kari. That means you're the next in line to inherit it." This was all the incentive I needed to up my game. Owning an apparel business had been my dream since I first discovered the thrill of seeing sketches come to life while working for a menswear designer. There was only one problem. I no longer had a husband to help with childcare. Fortunately, Scott said he'd take Emmy as long as he could pick her up after work. One problem was solved, but there was still a lot to do.

When I told Seth I'd be leaving for Europe in June, he begged me to come to the city to be his date at the birthday party he was throwing for himself at Cipriani. Michael Jackson was performing. How could I resist the "King of Pop"? The store would be closed, and school would be over. When Erin volunteered to stay with Emmy, I agreed to go.

TWO KINDS OF INVESTMENTS

Upon arriving in New York, Seth sent his driver to meet me at the airport and take me to his apartment on Fifth Avenue. I recognized the building right away; Bellini used to be there. Now, another famous eatery was on the ground level. Leave it to Seth to have the best food in New York City at his doorstep. The doorman escorted me to the elevator and pressed the button to the penthouse. The door to Seth's apartment was open. After kissing him hello, my eyes moved to a polished ebony wood table with a large vase of purple peonies placed in the center. Beyond it was a formal living room furnished with French art deco furniture that faced Central Park. He could tell I was impressed.

"Do you want a tour?"

"Lead the way."

He proceeded to show me the family room, circular dining room and a kitchen with a butler's pantry. There was a den adjacent to the formal living room. A premier suite and three guestrooms with en suite baths occupied the other side. The apartment was decorated to perfection, down to the white Frette duvet cover trimmed with beige satin stripes. Lalique crystal lions gazed out from a shelf waiting to greet the king who slumbered here.

My favorite flowers, bedding and crystal—I taught him well. The only thing that prevented this apartment from being on the front cover of *Architectural Digest* was the vinyl card tables set up in the living room.

Seth hung my garment bag in the closet in the premier bedroom and placed my matching duffle bag beneath it on the carpeted floor.

"We have reservations at 8:00," he said. "Is there anything you need to do in the city before then?" Well, there was one thing. My hairstylist from Palm Beach rented space at a salon nearby in the off season. I'd booked an appointment for highlights and a blow-out before Seth's party on Monday.

"I hope you don't mind," I said.

"Of course not. I love that you take such good care of yourself."

"Get your nails done too and buy anything else you need for the party. I know it was a big deal for you to come, Kari." He opened the top drawer of his nightstand and took out a wad of hundred-dollar bills.

Seth had never given me money. Before I could decide if this meant he was more serious about me or less, he slipped the cash into my hand and closed my fingers around it. He led me to the elevator and pushed *L* for lobby. A doorman offered to hail a cab for me. I said no. I wanted to walk the streets of my old neighborhood and reminisce—me and my Mr. Big—back where it all started. It was beginning to feel more like reality than fiction.

It was dusk when I returned to the apartment. Seth was showered and dressed for the evening. Coincidently, my sister Leslie was dating a friend of Seth's named Derek. Seth was fond of Leslie—he met her when she was a teenager. Seth was from a family of all boys; Leslie filled the role of the sister he never had. I was excited for our double date.

I drew a bath in the luxurious soaking tub. When I finished, I wrapped myself in a fluffy white towel. I put on a slinky silk jersey dress that fell just above my knee and ankle-strap high heeled sandals. I pulled my Fendi Baguette purse out of my bag.

The four of us laughed all night at Le Bilboquet like it was the late 80s again. Leslie was the sister I was closest to. We were both bookworms and pop-culture buffs. Seth and Derek went way back, so the conversation flowed easily.

Seth had plans to golf at his country club on Sunday and asked me to come along. I declined. I wanted to pay a visit to my three best friends in Manhattan: Bergdorf's, Barney's and Bendel's, who I dearly missed since moving to Florida. I strolled past the Lalique store on Madison Avenue and saw a crystal figurine of a lion and lioness snuggled close to each other. It would complement the ones Seth owned. Maybe it would remind him of us. I wrote out a card, gave the salesperson his address and told her to deliver it on Monday, his birthday.

The Chinese food we ordered on Sunday night was lukewarm when it arrived. Seth fumbled with a built-in microwave he had never learned how to use. How is it that these super smart guys can never figure out the simplest household appliances?

"Just let me do it," I said as I heated up the food and served it. After dinner, the conversation turned to his party. As he named the guests, I began to feel on edge. The list included his traders, his friends, his mom and dad and his brothers. These were people who had been fixtures in my life over a decade ago. What was I thinking? Accompanying him to this extravaganza at Cipriani on his 42nd birthday would be like a "coming out" for us all over again. I was a married woman with a little girl. That night his lovemaking was deliberate and passionate, but he could tell something wasn't right.

"Kari, what is it?"

"Nothing," I lied.

I rolled the scenario of this party over and over in my head. When I woke up in the morning, I knew this was one celebration I wouldn't be attending. Seth was already at his office. Normally, I would never call him during trading hours, but it was only fair to let him know. He was furious. When it became clear he couldn't get me to change my mind, he became vindictive.

"Well, I hope you know I'm not going alone, Kari."

"Do what you need to, Seth. I'll be at my friend Melissa's."

Melissa and I met when she hired me to work at The House of Bijan. Her calm demeanor and background as a classical ballet dancer, combined with the intensity I brought as a former competitive cheerleader, made for a perfect marriage at a boutique that boasted the highest retail sales per square foot of any store in the country. She understood my reasons for backing out of the party. Melissa invited me to dinner with her boyfriend—her own Mr. Big from the restaurant world.

"Thanks, Melis, I think I will." This was just the distraction I needed to keep me from thinking about Seth and the woman who wasn't me who would be his date for the party.

The next morning, I was getting a Brazilian bikini wax when Seth called to ask where I was. How fitting that he was calling while my legs were wide open, as the aesthetician spread the thick, hot wax. I loved this part of the procedure; it felt so erotic. I was never ready for the next step, when she ripped the hair off with one quick swoop.

Sometimes I wondered what kind of masochist decided this was the new normal in women's grooming. The smooth feeling afterwards was well worth the pain. Better yet, it was as if removing the hair down there made me feel lighter, as if I'd lost five pounds. Much easier than any diet. "I slept at Melissa's," I said. "It was late, and I didn't know how to get into the apartment."

"I always leave the door unlocked, and I left your name with the doorman." I smiled, thinking only he would be so trusting to do that. "Are we on for dinner tonight?" he asked.

"Sure, I'll meet you back home after work." I caught myself after that last sentence. *Home? Really, Kari? His penthouse on Fifth Avenue is not your home. Your home is a house in Palm Beach where, up until a few months ago, you lived happily with your husband and daughter.* The truth was, I felt adrift. The life I worked so hard to create had fallen apart, and instead of mourning it, I was playing house with Seth. I knew I was avoiding the feelings of loss, but I couldn't stand to face them. Instead, I stayed constantly in motion. My next stop was Matt's showroom. My sister, Michele, was the company's sales manager. She showed me different products that could mix with the theme of Emmy's school's auction. When I got back to Seth's, I showered and dressed for the evening. Seth told me how sorry he was that I missed his party. Michael Jackson dedicated a song to him. I didn't dare ask Seth who he took in my place.

"There'll be other parties," I said. "I'm just happy to be with you, Seth." Back on Fifth Avenue we sipped tea in the den and watched *The Family Man*, a movie we both loved. As we climbed into bed, my Rolex watch felt bulky on my wrist. I removed it and was about to place it on the nightstand when I saw it—a single diamond stud earring. It wasn't mine and it hadn't been there when I left on Monday. I'd have seen it. The nightstands were mirrored; not a speck of dust marred their surface.

It must have belonged to his date from the party. I was furious. I couldn't believe Seth let another woman sleep in the same bed we'd shared for the last two nights. It was one thing for him not to attend the party alone, but did his "date" have to include a sleepover? My makeup was in his bathroom. Did she not even notice or care?

Seth felt me pull away. "Kari, what's the matter?" I showed him the earring. He said he didn't know whose it was. It must have been there a long time. My instincts told me otherwise. It was after midnight. I couldn't bother Melissa at this hour, nor could I think of anyone else who would be interested in hosting a late-night visitor. I grabbed a robe, walked to the guest room and locked the door behind me. I could hear Seth knocking on the door, asking me to come back to bed. I pulled the goose-down duvet cover over my head and attempted to sleep. I was too old for these games.

I couldn't blame Seth. We hadn't committed to being exclusive. Seth hadn't changed. His funds were the only thing he could be faithful to, not me or any other girl. I awoke before dawn and took a cab to the airport. In the cab, tears ran down my face. I had known what I was walking into, but that didn't make it less painful to walk away from a guy I had so much history with. I remembered he hadn't mentioned my gift. When I landed, I called the store and discovered it was never sent. The manager apologized and offered to give me a refund; she knew the recipient's birthday had passed. I asked her to deliver it. Seth needed to have it as a reminder that once upon a time, there was a girl who loved him. She did right now, like she did back then, when he lived in Queens and traded penny stocks for a living.

Cashmere & Castles

Seth continued to call me, but I wasn't ready to talk. There was a long list of things to do before I left for Scotland. After Seth left so many messages that my voicemail was full, I called him and said I'd reach out when I returned. The past few months had been a whirlwind. I needed time alone to make sense of it all.

The rolling green farmland and dramatic cliffs of the English countryside were just the change of scenery I needed after a season in Palm Beach. I was speechless when Valerie told me we'd be staying at Mindrum, the castle owned by her friends Lord and Lady Fairfax. "It's only one and a half miles from the Scottish border, Kari; it just makes sense to stay here as it's near the mills," she told me. When Lady Fairfax insisted I call her and her husband by their first names—Ginny and Perry—I almost pinched myself. This was completely different from talking to Lady Fairfax (well, Ginny) on the phone about sweaters. That night, we were her guests of honor at a dinner she was hosting.

I was nervous to be mixing with the crowd Valerie knew since birth, but as I mingled over cocktails and foie gras, I felt myself slowly get more comfortable. *Nobility—they're just like us,* I thought. Amid the chatter, I heard one of the guests ask Valerie about the succession plan for her company. I froze. To my surprise, Valerie announced to all 12 guests that she would be passing the business down to me.

I could barely contain my excitement as the main course was served. I took a bite of the meat that had a slightly sweet flavor but

I couldn't determine what it was. Ginny explained that it was roe deer (baby deer). Images of Bambi filled my mind and caused me to lose my appetite. So as not to insult Ginny, I pretended to eat it, but instead pushed it under a pile of mashed potatoes.

Later that night, I was tucked into bed and wondering why it was so cold when Valerie knocked on my door. "Don't be fooled by the museum-quality paintings and gilded furniture. These castles have no electricity," she said. "And there's only enough hot water for one bath; I'll take mine now—yours will be tomorrow. And I'm leaving these for you," she said, and placed two sleeping pills on the bedside table. "I know sleep doesn't come easy to you in unfamiliar places."

Despite the pills, I was restless. My thoughts kept drifting back to Seth. How did I get myself into this situation? How foolish to think an ex-boyfriend who had never managed to commit to any woman would want something serious! It was too much to think about, and my future was at stake. I needed to save every ounce of energy I had to visit the factories and learn how these cashmere sweaters were made.

The next few days I did just that, even helping Valerie come up with designs for the new collection. When all our work was done, Valerie showed me Scotland—the house where she grew up, the one where she raised her kids and all the castles. But the biggest treat of all was called Manderston House. The castle was open to the public, but the family it was built for still lived in a section of it. Valerie knew this family—they used to share the same groundskeeper—which is how I ended up having tea in Lady Palmer's private quarters at the castle that afternoon. As we sipped our tea, Lady Palmer asked about the nature of our trip and about my first impressions of Scotland. I told her that truth—that I was completely taken with the landscape, the people I'd met and the experience of seeing our cashmere at the source.

"I'm so glad. It sounds like you'll be back to see us again, Kari," Lady Palmer said.

"She absolutely will," Valerie chimed in. "Kari knows the template of how to succeed in this business." I beamed, thinking of my future trips to Scotland and all the sweaters I'd design. But it was more than that. I felt so welcome here, so on the *inside*. Based on my lineage, I didn't technically belong in castles or on country estates. Even the factories in Hawick, Scotland are staffed by centuries of people in this business, and here I was, the granddaughter of Greek immigrants, feeling welcomed and poised to take over from Valerie in the not-too-distant future. This was my world now. Part of me didn't believe it was real.

When I returned from Scotland, Seth called and demanded to see me. But who was he to say I had to slide right back into the same pattern? I used the upcoming trunk show in Maine as the reason I couldn't meet up with him. Then, I was on the road again.

Taking the Show on the Road

The summer before, I traveled to Camden, Maine to help Valerie with shows in the Northeast. The Hamptons were familiar to me, but I had never been to Maine. To me, the whole state seemed like a giant ad for L.L. Bean. Everywhere you looked there were kids and parents dressed in earth tones, lugging backpacks and duffle bags. We had a loyal client named Julie whose husband's bank hosted a retreat for its top performers at a resort in Camden. Julie loved Valerie's designs so much, she wanted to give the other executives' wives a chance to own them.

The show we did the previous year was such a success that we were invited back. I looked forward to seeing the women who'd become regular clients. Many of them were my age and spent a lot of money on cashmere. The average order was as much as my monthly mortgage. I asked Valerie if my mom and Emmy could come along. It would be the perfect blend of work and relaxation—spending evenings with my family sounded much better than passing the time with Valerie and Ian, whose idea of a fun time was boiling lobsters (gross) and watching British television (boring).

"That's a smashing idea, Kari."

I had another reason for wanting to bring Emmy along. Kids her age were spending their summers at vacation homes or sleep-away camps. Our chance for a vacation home had walked out the door with Scott, so sleepaway camp seemed the only choice for a working mom who traveled all summer. My former boss, Lana, and the moms in Palm Beach concurred that the summer camps in

Maine were the best, "like country clubs for kids," they said. Since Camden, Maine was near these fancy camps, I thought I might as well see what all the hoopla was about in person before I sent my daughter all the way up north for the summer. The kids I grew up with went to camp in the Poconos or upstate New York, places they traveled to by bus so their parents could come for visiting day. I was never a camp kid myself and didn't understand the need to go so far, but I didn't want Emmy to miss out.

The first day in Camden, I gave my mom a list of activities the hotel offered for kids. She could drop Emmy there if she needed a break. I assumed my post in the ballroom for the show and worked my way through the crowd of ladies who came in droves to order cashmere. Everything was going fine until late in the afternoon when I looked up from my invoice book and noticed my mom in her orange and embarrassingly sheer pool cover-up walking toward me. Emmy trudged along behind her, scowling. I tried to motion to mom to exit the room but she either didn't understand or, more likely, pretended not to.

"You can't come in here. I'm working," I whispered when she got close enough to hear me. I turned back to the women shopping. "I'll be right with you," I said before turning again to look pleadingly at my mother.

"It's too cold," she said matter-of-factly. "Emmy won't even swim in the heated pool."

"Mom, you need to figure something out; you can't traipse in here in that get-up." I should have known this was not the time to play fashion critic because she immediately got defensive.

"Are you criticizing your Aunt Irena?" she asked, referring to my Greek aunt. "She made this for me."

"No, Mom. I'm not, but please go back to the room." I had to give her a little push to let her know I was serious. "I'll be back at the end of the day." I noticed Valerie peering over the crowd from the other side of the room, trying to see what had distracted me. I rushed back to my customers.

When the show ended, I raced to our room. I was relieved to find Emmy and my mom absorbed in a puzzle I had packed.

"I'm sorry if I was rude to you, Mom, but I was under a lot of pressure."

"I don't know why you were so mad. It's only sweaters."

"That may be true for you, Mom, but selling those sweaters is how I earn a living. You may think fashion's frivolous, but to me it's everything. Fashion determines how you see the world and how the world sees you."

Once mom realized it was her job to keep Emmy occupied during the day, the three of us bonded over the next few nights. Walking along the water in the quaint town of Camden reminded me of summers spent at Grandma Margaret's beach house. We discovered a fudge shop and I found a toy store for Emmy that allowed kids to try the games and puzzles they sold before buying them.

The last night of the show, Julie and her husband invited Valerie, Ian and me out to dinner to celebrate the show's success. I politely explained to Mom that I would drop her and Emmy off at a restaurant next door and pick them up on my way back to the hotel.

"I don't understand why we can't go to the same restaurant as you," Mom protested.

"This is a business dinner, and we are their guests."

"We'll sit at a different table," she persisted.

"You can't do that. Our hosts will feel uncomfortable. They would feel obligated to ask you to join us."

I dropped my mom and Emmy off. I couldn't help but feel guilty. I had promised them I would be available in the evenings. As I headed to the bistro next door, I decided that it would be best to take Emmy on vacation without Mom and when I was not traveling for business. My mom clearly didn't understand the importance of my work.

I felt a little self-conscious as the maître d' led me to our table. I didn't have any shoes to wear to dinner. In my attempt to look stylish at the trunk show, I had worn a slip-on wedge in a raffia material, which turned out not to be the best choice in footwear for standing all day. The fabric had rubbed against my big toe and created a large purple blister. I couldn't get a real shoe on my foot, and I had to wear my white Keds. When Valerie commented on my choice of footwear, I told her about my toe.

"You never complain about anything, Kari, so it must be quite bad. Come to my room when we get back to the hotel and I'll treat it with Neosporin and give you a band-aid." I did as Valerie instructed, and the blister started to heal. Nonetheless, I wore sneakers for the next few days as we toured sleepaway camps.

"Why are there no boy campers?" Emmy asked. She was full of questions. She was too young to care about boys in anything except a puppy love way, but she was a social butterfly and wanted to befriend as many people as possible. "It's too cold to swim here, Mom. The ocean and pool are freezing. I like to go in the water when I feel hot, not when I'm cold. Will it get warmer?"

Maine was *cold* and I was grateful for the sweaters I'd packed.

I was looking forward to being back in Palm Beach and not just for the warm weather. The show in Camden had netted over $70,000—far more than the previous year. I needed to return to Palm Beach and get the special orders into production.

When Seth called and invited me to his house in Southampton, I said I was too busy with work. I wasn't ready to see him, and besides, I had to pack for the next trunk show. Once mid-August came around and my workload lightened, I agreed to see him. Finally, I had just a little bit of space to hear him out. We met in the parking lot of the Paramount Building. I let him do the talking. He brought up the incident in New York and tried to explain that his date slept over after the party because it was late, but nothing happened. It didn't matter; my heart didn't trust him.

"I don't want to rehash what happened, Seth, just tell me how you feel now." He wrapped his arms around me and held me tight.

"I'm sorry, Kari," he said. "I was sure I wasn't clicking with any of the girls I dated because no one measured up to you. And you know what? No one does."

"So what does that mean for us, Seth?"

"I'm still not ready for anything serious, and you are. You have been since we first met. If your husband isn't that guy, someone else will be."

"Do you think you'll ever be ready?"

"I don't know, Kari. It's tempting to think about us getting married and starting a family. I know our kids would be brilliant. But it's not fair for me to do that to you if I'm not all in. You deserve better. I know you're going to get everything you want. I sense it the same way I do when I'm picking the next hot stock."

This wasn't the first time I'd heard this excuse from Seth. This time, my heart wasn't breaking. It felt more like it was doing somersaults down a hill—it was uncomfortable and it was out of my control, but I knew I'd be okay once I landed. Part of me knew our romance wasn't going to have the happily-ever-after ending I hoped for. I questioned if one still existed. How was I any better than Scott? After all, I'd let this Wall Street man from my past sweet-talk me again before Scott and I ever brought up the word divorce.

Stop it. This line of thinking wasn't going to help. Scott and I didn't value our marriage enough to fight for it. He was no longer my prince and I wasn't his princess. Our fairy tale shattered as if Cinderella's glass slipper had fallen from the top shelf of my closet. I tried to glue the pieces back together; they didn't fit. And now, again, I had tried on the fancy ball gown of a billionaire only to end up back on my own. After the last show of the summer, I told Valerie that Scott and I had separated.

"That's no surprise. I didn't want to tell you, but I saw it coming. You're the star in your relationship, not him, and he resents it," she said. It's amazing when someone outside of your situation can see it more clearly than you can. I hated being the center of attention. When Scott and I met new people, I thought I did my best to divert the conversation toward Scott. Somehow Scott, like Valerie, saw things differently. As the scent of fall enveloped the Island, I reflected on the summer season. I'd learned so much in Scotland and from doing trunk shows on my own. I'd learned from Seth and Kari 2.0, too. Seth was certain I'd get everything I wanted. I couldn't trust him to commit, but I trusted his stock-picking ability. He was certain mine would only go up.

Labor Day loomed ahead and that meant a long weekend with Emmy, which I was excited to plan. Until Scott called me and said he would like to take her for the weekend. "Haven't you and Lauren done enough traveling?" I couldn't help but ask. Over the past six months, Scott had vacationed more with this woman than we had in our entire marriage.

"Not that it's any of your business, Kari, but Lauren's no longer in the picture."

"Really, why's that?"

"She's had it hard, Kari; her ex skipped town and left her with three kids. Her mother took them in and put a roof over their heads. Lauren needs security; that means a husband, not a boyfriend. She was happy I didn't have a lot of baggage, but as she put it, 'my bags aren't packed.'"

"It seems you could change that if you wanted to, Scott."

"I'm confused, Kari. I don't know what I want anymore."

Was this Scott's way of extending the olive branch? If he was, I was desperate to grab it. Before I let him walk away for good, maybe we could salvage our marriage. My friend Gwen was privy to what was going on in our relationship. Gwen and I met at a Mommy & Me class when we first moved here. Her husband was a doctor, and Gwen had given me the names of the best physicians in town. She referred me to a psychologist used by many Palm Beach couples.

"Why don't we talk to a professional, Scott? Maybe that will help," I ventured.

"All right, make an appointment for a session before work."

We started seeing Alice together and individually. She and I hit it off at once. When she asked if there was anything kinky going on, I volunteered that Scott was taking our daughter to spend weekends with three strange kids at his girlfriend's mother's house. Alice laughed and said that wasn't what she was getting at. Was Scott one of the men whose names had recently been published in *The Shiny Sheet* for hiring escorts on Dixie Highway, she wanted to know. Scott and I almost fell out of our seats and explained that what she was suggesting was not why Scott left.

Just as we were making progress, terrorists struck the World Trade Center on September 11. When Ian called to tell me what was happening, I ran to the bank across the street and watched the second tower fall on their TV. After checking on my sisters in New York, I returned to the shop but was just going through the motions.

For the first time ever, I couldn't focus on work. When customers called to check the status of their orders, it took every bit of strength I had to pull the files and give them an update. Planning a party for Emmy's birthday didn't seem right. The gift certificate for a pizza party at Amici we'd won at an auction served as her celebration. In the weeks that followed, the stock market went wild, and Scott was too busy calming clients to keep our therapy appointments.

All this chaos in the world made me feel more vulnerable than ever. My mom raised me to believe in "the happily-ever-after" ending that came when my prince swept me off my feet. The story I was living was playing out differently, but I decided I was going to do everything in my power to save my marriage. I continued to see Alice on my own. She helped me understand things about men and their desire to feel appreciated. Having been raised by a single mom, this was something that never occurred to me. I thought Scott would feel valued by everything I did for him: entertaining his clients, running his household, cooking his meals, buying him gifts and being the best mother I possibly could. Alice pointed out that none of these things made him feel that I *needed* him.

This sentiment was echoed by clients and friends I confided in. "You are choosing to work, Kari; you don't need to earn an income to put food on your table. Even if you're tired from your professional duties, have your husband's slippers waiting at the door," was the type of advice I received.

But this was Palm Beach; it was too hot for slippers. Instead, I bought Scott three pairs of Stubbs and Wootton loafers, a wardrobe staple for men on the Island. These moccasin-like slip-on shoes were made from fabric and could be worn in the day or evening. One pair was velvet and could be worn with a tuxedo. I had them monogrammed with Scott's initials. I hoped they would make him feel like royalty...they didn't. He hardly noticed the effort, and I continued to feel like we were drifting further apart.

"When did things first start getting rocky for you?" Alice asked at our next session. Looking back, it was easy to pinpoint how things changed when I returned to work and shifted my focus to rebuilding my career. When I learned that UPS had a second pickup instead of working late, I loaded my car with packages and arranged for them to be picked up from our house. Scott wasn't pleased to get home and fight his way through boxes in the foyer to get to the kitchen for supper. On nights he had business dinners, he hated coming home to find a group of moms at our dining table helping me address trunk-show invitations. I insisted that a standard printed label would land them right in the trash. The personal touch, I was sure, made a difference. Scott disagreed, and though he may have been right, I continued to enlist the help of friends to address the hundreds of invites for each show. It was impossible to get these women to work for a wage, but wine and adult conversation were sure to get them to leave their husbands and kids for an evening.

"Did your perspective change at all when you went back to work?" Alice asked.

"Funny you should mention that, Alice," I said.

"I always wanted the husband to be the breadwinner, especially since I'd grown up in a house without one. But I never operated from a scarcity mindset. I think Scott feared I'd lost the discipline of sticking to a budget. Maybe starting to lean more 'Palm Beach wife' than the practical Kari he married. But to me, we were a team and I didn't like it that he thought my opinion didn't hold as much weight as his just because I was the lesser earner."

"Hmmm, that could be true, but I'm sensing something else was at play," Alice said.

"Well, we were having trouble conceiving. We'd tried to get pregnant when I was on a hiatus from work, but when it didn't happen, Scott thought we should wait until we had a house before trying again. Once we got settled in Palm Beach, I desperately wanted a baby. After a year with no luck, Scott said he wasn't sure he wanted another child, so I threw myself into work."

"You not conceiving was another event that made Scott feel he was failing you."

"But we had tests done and nothing was wrong. He refused to investigate further and insisted that I go back to work."

TAKING THE SHOW ON THE ROAD

"That may be true, Kari, but he didn't count on you falling in love with it. And while you were falling in love with work, he fell for another woman." She had a point. I knew my commitment to work had contributed to the distance that widened between us, so I felt I could forgive Scott's infidelity (and bid farewell to Seth for good) for the sake of the commitment we'd made to each other and the life I'd carefully curated. But this other woman had decided she wasn't going to let Scott go so easily. Scott told me Lauren gave him an ultimatum: If he got a lawyer and began divorce proceedings, she would give him a second chance. Scott promised there would be no intimacy with either of us until he made his decision.

I felt like Alice falling down the rabbit hole. Scott spent Halloween with me and Emmy, and together we hosted a cocktail party for Young Friends of Palm Beach Opera. We attended the school's talent show, spaghetti dinner and back-to-school night as a couple. Lauren came alone and glared at me from across the room. Scott planned to spend Thanksgiving with us and Christmas with Lauren. How long could this go on? Part of me felt invested in winning this competition, but another part of me questioned it. *What was I really winning? Did I want Scott or the security of a husband?* I was so frazzled I couldn't think, yet it didn't really matter because he held all the cards.

The limbo period seemed like forever. Scott asked me to be his plus-one for The Ultimate Dinner Party. When I saw our picture in *Palm Beach Society Magazine*, the vacant look on my face was obvious. I didn't look like myself; I looked like a ghost haunting a marriage that had died some time ago. This time, I brought up the "D" word. I mean, really, what were we doing? Maybe a divorce had been inevitable all along. But Scott was in no hurry to move forward. He, it seemed, got to stay in limbo for as long as he wanted. I felt stuck and Lauren was outraged. When she saw the photo of us in the magazine, she demanded he choose between us, and soon.

By Christmas Scott dropped me like a stock that had just plummeted in value. He chose to invest in Lauren instead. I recalled Rabbi Moshe's sermon about "kashrut" and "shechita," the slaughter method in Judaism. At first, it sounded inhumane. Now I understood why an animal must be killed with a single cut to the throat to be deemed kosher; a slow death, or in this case a divorce, was much more painful. A year after Scott and I initially separated, our marriage was officially over for good.

No Box of Candy This Valentine's Day

In the weeks before our divorce, I felt guilty for speaking to my lawyer during work hours, so I made up for the lost time by bringing my client list home. At night, when Emmy was asleep, I played a game I called "Dialing for Dollars." Due to the time difference, I was able to call clients on the West Coast to ask if they needed sweaters. Ironically, no one ever asked why I was calling at midnight East Coast time. When I got to work the next morning, I rang up the sales. I consistently reached our weekly sales goal before the "Open" sign was hung on the front door of the shop. Keeping myself this busy also distracted me from my depressing Valentine's Day plans.

Why did it have to be Valentine's Day? I thought as I got dressed to go to the courthouse. *Of all days for a divorce hearing...*

Gwen offered to go with me, but I said no. This was something I needed to do on my own. Scott was seated with his lawyer when I arrived. Jay, my attorney, motioned for me to sit beside him. The logistical part was easy; a judge just had to sign off on the paperwork. It was no surprise we wanted different things: Scott insisted on keeping the funds in our investment account; my priority was keeping our house, although it meant I would have to buy out Scott's share.

Luckily, he gave me three years to come up with the money. My wedding day was one of the happiest days of my life. Walking out of that courthouse was one of the saddest. When you break up with a boyfriend, you say goodbye to a future you imagined. In a divorce, you divide a family in half and are forced to divvy up the very real pieces: children, holidays, friends and possessions. The loss is tangible. It has names, faces, shape and weight.

Jay said he never saw a client show the resolve I did during the time I was separated. He wanted to conduct more discovery, to see if Scott was hiding any money. I told him not to bother. Our assets were in three places: our house, an investment account and a joint checking account. We weren't married long enough for me to merit much alimony. Because I had a career, the system felt I could take care of myself. Jay walked me to my car. "Call me if you need anything, Kari, I'm here."

The tears came when I got to my car. Usher's "U Remind Me" played on the radio. Usually hip-hop music soothed my soul, but I didn't want to be reminded of anything to do with this day. I fiddled with the tuner until I found a pop station playing a melody I'd never heard before. It had a catchy beat, but it seemed to consist of no more than seven words that the artist repeated over and over. "Do you think you're better off alone?" I couldn't help but think of my situation.

Scott called me a few weeks later to ask if he could have Emmy for spring break.

"Emmy wants to swim with the dolphins, so I rented a room in the Keys."

"A room?" I asked. "What about Lauren and her kids?"

"Lauren got tired of waiting for me to commit and moved on. She's engaged to an old boyfriend. It looks like we're both alone now, Kari." Scott was right; we were. Whether or not we were better off remained to be seen.

Somehow, I found myself in a position I never imagined: that of a single mother with a little girl to support. My mother raised me to believe I would never be responsible for anyone but myself, that I would get married and finances would be my spouse's job. Now I had a house, no husband and a child that needed to be fed and clothed. My modest stipend from Scott was not enough to pay the bills. I was shocked when tax time came and my accountant told me I needed to check the "Head of Household" box on my return. It was an "a ha!" moment, and I realized I was expected to maintain our lifestyle without a breadwinner income.

Shortly after Mother's Day, Jay asked me to meet him at The Grill to see how I was managing. Two glasses of champagne were waiting at the bar when I arrived. "Let's toast to the hottest woman on the Island," he said as we raised our glasses. I told him I'd have to learn how to survive on my own before my temperature went up. He tried to convince me another husband was the answer. I still wasn't over my divorce. Another man wasn't the solution. When Jay asked if I'd met anyone, I mentioned my handyman.

"I meant for romance, Kari, not repairs."

"That is where you're wrong, Jay. A handyman is the best man a divorced woman can ask for. My ex couldn't care less about my broken hot water heater." When we moved into our house, everything was new. After Scott left, things began to fall apart. First, the hot water heater went, the roof leaked and the AC broke. The cost was untenable. Bri finally caved in and gave me her handyman's number. As with reliable housekeepers and babysitters, friends were reluctant to share these people with friends lest they become less available.

"A handyman is a gift that keeps on giving, unlike husbands, who easily forget what you've done for them," I continued. "And speaking of gifts, I have one for you." Jay had charged me a reasonable fee. To thank him, I'd wrapped up a V-neck slipover golf vest.

"Wow, Kari, you shouldn't have, but that color is great." It was burgundy, the same color as the wines he collected. I knew he would appreciate the quality of the cashmere. Jay called to order three more vests and said he would send some friends to the store. He was a great lawyer; he could be an even better customer.

The golf vest had no name. I made a note to ask Valerie if we could name it Jay, after him. That reminded me—my friend Beth's mom had ordered the same piece for her husband. She would be glad to hear my shipment had come in. As it turned out, Beth's mom had an idea that was much more exciting than her husband's birthday gift.

Bachelor # 2

When my college bestie Beth, told her mom I was single, her mom insisted on setting me up with her newest client, Sam. Beth's mom Iris was a realtor, and she had the listing for Sam's house. Like any good Jewish mother, she didn't want to see a successful single guy get away, especially a radiologist. Sam recently accepted a staff position at a hospital in my area. I hadn't connected with anyone since Seth, so I gave Iris the okay to have this Sam call me.

Conversation came easily between us. Like me, Sam had just ended a long-term relationship. I mentioned that I hadn't been away since last summer. Sam asked if I would like to take a drive to Surfside and see his house before he moved. It was June and that meant a lull in business. I was eager to leave the Island. Palm Beach is bliss, but 10 months of the same people, places and parties had made me feel stifled, like I'd put on too many layers of clothes on a cold day only to remove some once I was indoors.

Driving south toward Dade County, listening to Notorious B.I.G.'s "One More Chance" made me excited about the prospect of a new romance. I exited at the Broad Causeway, which was the most scenic route to get from the mainland to the ocean side. Crystal blue water sparkled on both sides of the bridge that transported me to Surfside, but only after glimpsing the estates of Indian Creek Island to my right and the Morris Lapidus designed Bal Harbour shops on the left. I pulled up to a two-story mid-century modern style house and knocked on the door. Sam was everything Iris said and then some—not too tall, lean build and dark hair that begged me to run my hands through it. His curious dark brown puppy-dog eyes gazed into mine. *Where were guys like this when I was in my 20s?*

What Iris didn't say was that Sam owned six (six!) cats and a dog. Dogs are cute, but not only do I dislike cats, I am highly allergic to them. This should have been my cue to exit, but how could I when this slightly shy man was giving off vibes of strength and vulnerability all at once? Palm Beach was small. The men I interacted with felt familiar to me. They sat on the same charity boards as Scott, were the fathers of Emmy's friends or the ex-husbands of clients. This man was new. I took a deep breath and prayed I wouldn't start sneezing.

After giving me a tour of the house and admiring his collection of Meissen ivory figurines, he introduced me to his "family"—all seven members.

"And I thought I was the one with baggage," I whispered under my breath.

He explained they were rescue animals. Each was named after characters in his favorite novels. He named his dog Angie after Frank McCourt's character in *Angela's Ashes. He was literary too! Without the cats, he'd be too perfect.* He asked if I'd like to go for lunch at a place he frequented. The place Sam chose was Indian, a favorite cuisine of mine and, as I learned, his. As we sipped tea from a samovar, we talked about art and foreign films. This guy was curious about me as a person. He was interested in what made me tick. The men in Palm Beach seemed to talk about two things: their money and their status. This conversation felt refreshing, like a glass of lemonade on a scorching hot day.

The attraction was mutual. On nights he had to work the late shift at the hospital, Sam stayed at my place. When he came for the weekend, he brought Angie, his Border Collie mix. It was just us: no double dates, no galas, no pretenses. He was six years younger than me and respectful of my role as a mother. He was happy to

BACHELOR # 2

stay in the guest room with Angie, which I insisted on, if Emmy was home. We shared a love for nature and bike riding. Together, we discovered parts of the Island I never knew about—hidden trails and estates that had their own private beaches.

Due to the distance between us, our courtship became intimate much faster than usual for me. In that area Sam didn't disappoint either. The physical part with him was always novel. He laughed when I said as much. "You're just used to married sex." It was as if I had been on a diet and now found myself at a feast. When I visited him in Surfside, I was so satisfied after each lovemaking encounter, I barely noticed I was in bed with a dog and two cats. Angie slept near Sam and two of the cats snuggled near the bottom of the king-size bed. God must have known this was what I needed in my life at this time because I never experienced any allergy symptoms.

Sam rented an apartment in Palm Beach to be closer; he enjoyed tagging along as I dropped Emmy off at playdates. He brought her stuffed animals and other thoughtful gifts. He found it fascinating that I had the responsibility of raising a child along with that of running a home and a business. He begged his boss at the hospital to let him leave at lunchtime to walk Angie, so he thought it was "cool" that Valerie paid for me to have an English nanny live with us for the summer.

Sam invited Emmy to join us for dinner and a movie. I let my nanny babysit instead. I was afraid to bring Emmy into a situation that might not last. Sam and I had not yet talked about a future. I was still raw from the breakup of my marriage. My rekindled romance with Seth sent me reeling. For those first few months I enjoyed Sam's company so much, the lack of conversation about where our relationship was headed never seemed to matter. Until it did. My friends teased me about my "mystery man," as they called him. They demanded I bring him to one of the pre-parties in town. Season was just a few months away. They joked that they didn't want their first encounter with him to be via a picture in *The Shiny*

Sheet. This made me laugh. Sam was private to the extent of being reclusive.

"Would you be open to going to a formal event to benefit a charity?" I asked him.

"You mean one of those stuffy affairs where people are forced to sit at tables and talk to strangers?"

"It wouldn't be strangers; we'd be with my friends."

"Not a chance, Kari. I'm not a people person, that's why I have pets."

I tried to explain his position to my peers, but no one understood. Living in Palm Beach was like belonging to an exclusive country club. If you didn't want to socialize, you wouldn't join. I may have been a "member," but Sam would never be. He told me that he wasn't sold on living in South Florida. He asked me if I would move to another city with him if things got serious. I told him yes. I wanted a fresh start, not to have someone step into the shoes Scott left behind in our closet. Sam and I talked about the lack of good Chinese food in Florida, and while I fantasized about what it might be like to live with him somewhere more exotic, I also wanted to make the most of where we were. The Sailfish Club hosted "family nights" in August with international themes. I invited Sam for Chinese Night, my treat.

Drew and Bri were bringing their kids along with Drew's Aunt Meme. Meme was the matriarch of a third-generation jewelry business and a regular guest at Bri's. We bonded over the plight of being left for another woman. When hers moved on after 40 years of marriage, she declared the male species extinct. When I asked why, she said, "Men my age only want a nurse or a purse, and I'm neither." Their loss was my gain. I was after laughter and engaging conversation—not endless chit-chat about how to meet men and keeping one eye constantly peeled for an eligible suitor. Meme genuinely enjoyed our time out.

BACHELOR # 2

Sam drove us to The Sailfish Club. After leaving his car with the valet, we stepped into the bar area. Friends rushed over to me and asked where I'd been all summer. They pounced on Sam the way his dog jumped on me during our first meeting. I could feel Sam's discomfort as my friends bombarded him with questions. The room was loud due to all the kids present for Family Night. When we finally sat down for dinner, Bri's son Jordan hid under the table and started kicking Sam in the shins. I feared I'd made a mistake by bringing him here.

Sam had never married. He did not socialize with couples and certainly not entire families. He described his own family as dysfunctional, which is why, in addition to his more introverted nature, he made his own little family of felines. To me, my chaotic little chosen family of (admittedly) nosy friends and rambunctious kids was one of the best parts of Island living, but maybe it was too much for Sam. When we got to my house, Angie was vomiting. It was a school night and Emmy had a test. Sam kept asking me questions, oblivious to the fact that Emmy needed my attention. I was torn between helping him care for Angie and quizzing Emmy. I volunteered to call a veterinarian I knew of on the Island.

"I'm sorry, Kari, I have to get her to my vet in Surfside; he knows her." He threw himself, his dog and his bag in his car and left. Emmy felt betrayed that he cared more about his dog than about us. Maybe she was right. Were Sam and I too different?

While I was debating this topic, Sam asked me to join him for a long weekend in Washington, D.C. to celebrate his birthday. He'd done his residency there and wanted to show me the city. He felt we needed a weekend alone without our kids, his being the seven four-legged ones. Work was about to get busy. That meant no travel for me until June. It is said that 40 percent of the world's wealth passes through the town of Palm Beach in Season. I needed to be here to help these people satisfy their yearning for cashmere. An out-of-town getaway was just what I needed.

Valerie was a romantic like me. She was convinced that I would not only marry again, but three times, as she had. I winced when she said that. *Please, God, no.* She thought Sam was fun and of course she preferred younger men and shared his love of dogs. She agreed to work in the shop so he and I could travel together.

Sam showed me the city's museums, took me to a concert and we hiked in Rock Creek Park. I was glad I threw some of Valerie's two- and three-ply cashmeres in my suitcase. It was cold. Wearing the cashmere in this weather made me realize why they were so popular. They were not just stylish; they were warmer than wool ones and they didn't itch. As we walked around hand in hand, talking about art and history, I began to think Sam could be husband material. Even if I was wrong, I felt happy to have come this far and excited for what lay ahead. This five-month investment was worthwhile.

Gwen's daughter Dani was in D.C. visiting colleges. She'd decided to apply early to George Washington University. As a favor to Gwen, I offered to take her to lunch while I was in town. Sam was happy to join us and found a Lebanese restaurant frequented by students. He seemed to fare much better with kids in this age group than he had with Bri's four-year-old.

"That's some expensive school you picked," he said to Dani over lunch.

"Yeah, I know," Dani said. "My parents call it 'Israel on the Potomac' because of the large percentage of Jewish kids. They don't mind the steep tuition because of the strong academics and its location in a big city."

When we got back to the hotel, Sam said he was surprised my friend would pay so much for college. This seemed like an odd statement from a guy who was a doctor. He was springing for one of the most expensive hotels in town, the Four Seasons. I defended my friend and said she and her husband had saved for their kids' education since birth.

"Well, I'm glad I'll never be in that position," Sam said defensively.

"What position is that?" I pressed. "Paying for college? Didn't your parents pay for yours?"

"Yes, but I'm glad I won't ever have that responsibility." I was clearly missing something.

"Wouldn't you want your child to go to the best school possible?"

"Kari," he said, and I could tell by the tone of his voice I did not want to hear what he would say next. "I will never have to make that call because I never plan on having kids." I was silent for a moment.

"Can you say that again?" I finally asked. He repeated what he told me. I was shocked. In my world, a guy his age would only date an older woman with a child because he was ready to have a family.

"Well, why are you dating me then?"

His response was calm and deliberate.

"I thought because you already have a child, you'd be okay with it. I felt that, with your daughter and Angie and the cats, if things worked out, our family would be complete."

"But, Sam, you asked me if I would move to another city with you."

"I know I did. And I meant it! What's changed?" I was beginning to feel that Sam was a stranger instead of the boyfriend I was planning a future with.

"So you think it's okay for me to uproot my child, leave my work and my place in the community to be with you and not have a family?"

"Kari, you could find other work. And we would have a family. With Emmy and my brood, that's eight kids to care for. The way I see it, that's a big family." I couldn't believe what he was saying. I was glad we were leaving tomorrow. We barely talked on the flight home. Once we were back in Florida, I let his calls go unanswered. I placed the charcoal gray sweater I planned to give him for his birthday back in the stockroom. When he asked if I could come for the weekend, I said no, and that I was never coming again. He was surprised when I told him it was because of the "no kids" policy.

"Wow, Kari, I thought we had something. You seemed to take to Angie and the cats."

"I like them, Sam, but they can't replace the children and the family I plan to have."

I realized that I needed to get really clear on what I wanted from here on. I was an ambitious working mother who wanted to grow my family with a husband. No more Scotts (who didn't share my vision), Seths (who couldn't commit) or Sams (who were happy with a pack of fur babies). Come to think of it, maybe I should stop dating men whose names started with "S."

The holidays were around the corner. Each year, I hosted a Thanksgiving dinner that included my sisters, my neighbors and friends from town who had nowhere to go. Although we'd broken up, I invited Sam. He declined. It was for the best. Sam's love helped me through my first summer as a single woman. Autumn was backstage, waiting to make an entrance. Emmy was trying out for cheerleading and the school play. I was prepared to set my goals for the season. Last year Valerie and I surpassed the sales plan for the business. For the coming year, I was formulating a strategy to increase not just our sales but our profits.

My mom told me it takes as much time to get over a relationship as the length of time you were in it. I continued to date, but no one made it past date three. I constantly thought about Sam and how easy it was to be with him. I began going to temple on Saturday mornings. Sometimes I stayed for lunch afterward. It felt good to interact with people who were spiritual like me and step away from the deadlines and pressures of work. Rabbi Moshe said it

BACHELOR # 2

was okay to ask God for what you wanted. I prayed I would meet someone to share the life I'd created, which included Emmy, no pets and the people I called family. God must have been working overtime. My prayers were answered when a prince named Harry set foot in Palm Beach.

Prince Charming #1

Kyle was my allergist and my friend Lynn's brother. In our 20s, Lynn was my first pick for a friend to prowl the Manhattan hot spots with when we were in between boyfriends. Lynn swam in a gene pool unlike any other girl I knew—I never heard of a size 00 until we met. Her long blond locks fell away from her face like a fan was continuously blowing them. Her skin had the constant glow of great sex.

When Kyle entered the examination room, he noticed I was skimming through a magazine article about dating after divorce.

"I guess you've started dating again?" he asked. I told him I had but not with any luck. "If you really want to get married again, you should go for someone like Lynn's husband," Kyle advised. "I have a guy for you—my college roommate. He lives in Colorado but comes to Palm Beach in winter to see his parents."

"Does he have a good heart?"

"Of course, Kari. He's my friend, right?"

"I mean, is he kind and generous?"

"Harry's family is on the Forbes list of the wealthiest in the country. They give tons of money to charity. Giving is embedded in his DNA."

"Okay, have him call me," I said, a bit reluctantly.

When Harry called, we talked about the things newly divorced people discuss: our kids and the reasons why our marriages ended. He had two boys, both close in age to Emmy. Our first date was lunch at Cucina. Luckily, I knew the family who owned it. We were

PRINCE CHARMING #1

seated right away even though Harry hadn't thought of making a reservation. Kyle had shown him a picture of me, but I was seeing him for the first time. He was shorter than most men I dated, 5-foot 6 if I included his work boots. He had a laid-back Midwestern air that was unfamiliar to me. His green eyes gleamed with playfulness. It wasn't his height or his roots that concerned me, but his lack of confidence. He repeatedly said how gorgeous I was and how lucky he was to have been introduced to me by Kyle. I let it slide because he had old-school manners and seemed to be smitten with me! But I liked a man who carried himself with a little more self-assuredness.

After lunch, I invited Harry back to my house. While we nibbled on Rice Krispy treats, Harry asked if I would be open to moving to Aspen, where he lived, if we got serious. I found this an odd question to ask a girl on a first date and sidestepped the question.

A few weeks later, I asked Harry to be my plus-one for my friend Robin's 40th birthday party. I usually turned down these invitations because the guests were all in pairs and I had not found anyone fitting to bring. Avi, Robin's husband, was my internist and he squeezed me in whenever I needed an appointment. It would have been rude not to go, and Harry seemed like an appropriate escort.

Avi arranged a Hummer H2 limousine to take 10 couples to The Forge, a restaurant in Miami Beach. Harry was outgoing and able to hold his own in the group—everyone was charmed by him, including me—he was a world traveler. Robin loved my gift, a sleeveless shell in cobalt blue that matched her eyes. When we got back to Palm Beach, I invited him in for a cup of tea before he headed back to his parents' house. As we sat at my kitchen table, he asked, "Would you ever sign a premarital agreement?" Again, a strange question to ask a girl you've never even kissed.

"I don't know. I've only been divorced a year and haven't dated anyone long enough for that issue to come up. Why do you ask?"

"Because I really like you, Kari, but I can never get married without one. I just want to make sure you'd be willing to sign before anything gets too serious." I remembered Lynn telling me she had signed a premarital agreement because her husband's money came from a family business. She said it protected her and would be void when she had children. I made a mental note to call Lynn for advice if Harry and I became a couple.

"I'm sure we could figure it out if we needed to, Harry," I replied.

"Not really. The one you would need to sign is the same one my ex-wife signed. It spells out the terms clearly—$10,000 for each month we're married." I did a quick calculation in my head and added up what that number would be after 10 years. The value of my house was double this sum. It's not like I was trying to marry for the prenup payout, but since Harry introduced the topic, I couldn't help but realize this wasn't a particularly good deal considering his family's wealth. I didn't know if it was the topic of conversation or the lemon I had squeezed into my tea by mistake after adding milk and sugar, but my stomach was feeling uneasy.

"It's late, Harry. I think you should go," I said as I cleared the teacups and placed them in the sink. I walked him to the door. He kissed me on the forehead and said, "I had a great time tonight, Kari; your friends are good people. Think about the agreement, okay?"

Apparently, he wasn't the only one with marriage on his mind. I was admiring the tulips Harry sent for Valentine's Day when Scott called to say he was engaged. We had only been divorced for a year! When I asked him why the rush, he explained his fiancé, Candace, had never married and was determined to be by her 40th birthday. The wedding was set for that exact day in April. *How accommodating of you, Scott*, I thought, but I simply said, "Well, congratulations."

PRINCE CHARMING #1

When I called to thank Harry for the flowers, he asked if I had plans for the weekend. He was going boating with his dad and stepmom and invited me to come. They were regulars on the Palm Beach social scene. I knew them from the charity circuit but didn't know the story behind the Kent family fortune. Learning about it while lunching on a yacht sounded like a perfect way to relax. In place of a bikini, I pulled out a navy one-piece bathing suit for the occasion. His parents were in their 70s; I didn't want to look too risqué. It was a beautiful day to be out at sea. Harry's dad seemed to be as taken with me as his son. As I had predicted, the conversation turned to business. It was a subject the senior Mr. Kent and I couldn't get enough of.

Harry and his stepmom joined us for lunch on the main deck. Mr. Kent turned to Harry and said, "This girl's a keeper, son, she has the three B's: beauty, brains, and a body." I'd always thought the last item on that list was "bucks," but the fact that Mrs. Kent was a former swimsuit model led me to believe Mr. Kent may have changed the last "B" to reflect his own agenda. "Think of the offspring you could've had with her."

Right away I picked up that he had used the past tense. I was puzzled. I thought I looked much younger than my age, which was on the far side of 30. Did Mr. Kent think I was too old to have more children? Before I could ask, he turned to Harry and said, "I told you that vasectomy was a bad idea." I felt seasick and it had nothing to do with the waves.

I looked at Harry as if I were a young girl who just found out that the Tooth Fairy was make believe and asked, "You can't have any more children?"

"That's right," he said unapologetically. "Once I had my boys, I made sure of that."

"I told him not to do it," his father chimed in, "just in case he got divorced and met a woman who wanted kids."

Harry hadn't just ruined my afternoon but my dream of a future with a family as well. I was glad I had an excuse not to spend the evening with him. I'd committed to attending a black-tie fundraiser to benefit The Jewish Guild for the Blind. For the second year in a row, Jill, the chairperson, had given me a free ticket. In this town, a divorced woman's biggest fear is being banished from balls. Balls were never my thing, but each time I threw a cashmere shrug or shawl over my gown, sales of these items increased. Now, more than ever, I needed to advertise my product. When Mr. Kent's captain docked the boat, I couldn't get to my car fast enough.

"See you soon," Harry said as he waved goodbye. The marina was crowded with boaters exiting mega yachts as I made my way to the parking lot. I showered quickly but didn't have time to blow out my hair, so I pulled it into a loose bun. I slipped into a silver charmeuse gown that dipped down to my tailbone. The spaghetti straps reached over my shoulders and tied around my back like a string bikini. There had been no time to fetch my jewelry from the vault; my faux coral pieces would have to suffice. My face was glowing from the sun, so a brush of mascara and lip gloss took the place of a professional makeup application.

The cocktail hour was buzzing when I arrived. A waiter passed by with a tray of champagne. I anxiously reached for a glass before he could hand it to me. I was determined to have fun, despite the elder Mr. Kent's revelation.

When Harry called to arrange our next date, I told him there wouldn't be one but didn't feel it necessary to disclose why. Surprisingly, it wasn't the prenup but the "no kids" that was the deal-breaker for me. He continued to call to request a date. I politely declined, as this was the proper way to treat someone you'd met through a friend. When he invited me to his parents' house for Thanksgiving, I told him about my family from up north coming to town. It was the truth—I was hosting a large group of people this year.

PRINCE CHARMING #1

Valerie begged me to cater the dinner. Black Friday was one of our busiest days. She needed me to be focused and well rested. She feared my desire to entertain might interfere with my performance. Now that her new house was finished, she'd be flying to the Bahamas for the Season. Hopefully, she remembered to make cornbread and stuffing for my dinner like she did last year.

Home for the Holidays

I never enjoyed the holidays until I moved to Palm Beach. My Scrooge-like behavior began shortly after my father's death. My dad's sister, Connie, and my Uncle Ted stopped inviting us over to celebrate. The first time, my mom thought it was an oversight. When it happened again, it was clear that my mom and her girls were no longer welcome at their table.

When I questioned my mom as to why only her mom spent holidays with us, she said, "Sometimes a sibling doesn't feel the same connection to her brother's wife as she did to her brother." This was a complex concept for a 10-year-old girl to grasp. Especially since I had clashed with Aunt Connie before. Once, I dropped my fork during dinner. She cared more about food staining her carpet than the fact that my hair caught fire from a candle when I tried to retrieve the utensil. Deep down, I sensed there was another reason my aunt and uncle excluded us: They thought they were better than us. Their proper American mannerisms didn't mesh with those of Mom's Greek relatives. I saw the way they mocked Grandma Edie when she tucked the extra rolls in her purse after dinner at their tennis club.

My mom was an only child. Once her parents passed away, we were alone. My paternal grandmother, Margaret, split the holidays between our house and Aunt Connie's. My mom did what she could to make the holidays fun for us. When no one invited us, we traveled, mainly to Florida, where it was always sunny, people were happy and every day was a holiday.

HOME FOR THE HOLIDAYS

I promised my sisters when I grew up and had a family that they would always be welcome at my house. My sister Michele was the first to remind me of this. Shortly after we moved to Palm Beach, she called and said she and Leslie, our baby sister, were coming for Thanksgiving. Mom had sold the home we grew up in and would be spending the holiday with Jenn. Jenn was sister number three and the only one of us who'd married right after college. To Mom's delight, Jenn was a stay-at-home mom with two boys.

"Don't expect too much, Shell," I said. "I may have the house, but I've never hosted a holiday."

Until that year, Emmy, Scott and I had celebrated Thanksgiving at friends' homes or at The Beach Club. The first step on my to-do list was to get the tabletop items I needed. Worth Avenue had many shops that sold home goods. When I discovered one called Mary Mahoney, I felt like Alice stumbling into the Mad Hatter's tea party. I was drawn to its whimsical displays of tables draped in hand-woven cloths set with formal dinnerware, candelabras and crystal. The store had three levels. The third one was devoted exclusively to linens. Mary, the owner, gave me more than the items I needed; she gave me the confidence to pull off my dinner. It became my tradition to host the holiday each year. Emmy counted the days to Thanksgiving, knowing her aunts and *Yiayia*—Greek for "grandmother"—were coming to spoil her.

Late November was when the weather in Florida turned from humid and wet to cool and wonderful. Work was slow leading up to Thursday. The ladies of Palm Beach were busy preparing for guests, not shopping for clothing. Leslie was bringing a new boyfriend; I was excited to meet him. Bri, Drew, their kids and both sets of parents were coming. In college, Drew had been diagnosed with a spinal cord tumor. Up until now he'd been fine, but recently nerve fibers had wrapped around the tumor and were causing him pain. Because of the tumor's location at the base of his spine, surgery to remove it was impossible. Walking was more difficult for him, so he was wearing special sneakers with springs. We didn't talk about it much; he was still his upbeat self, but the truth was no one knew how much time he had. It made me especially thankful for the time with him. My mom would come too, along with Todd and Erin and friends from town.

Despite the fact that I thought of Bri as a sister, cooking for her always made me nervous. Given her training as a chef, no one could surpass her in the kitchen. Errol, the cook at Herbert's, walked me through the turkey roasting process as he did each year. I'd perfected my side dishes. Bri insisted on bringing the desserts.

The presentation was as important to me as the food. I pressed my long white cotton tablecloth and matching napkins. Each time I pulled out that tablecloth with the embroidered flowers, I thought of Mary. She'd found one exactly the size I needed at the right price point. As I rinsed my Baccarat wine glasses, I noticed a few were missing. I called Mary to replace them. "Do you need anything else, Kari?" she asked.

"Thanks! How about some hemstitch cocktail napkins with embroidered leaves and Manuel Canovas candles with the orange packaging?" These gave off a scent that was perfect for fall. Every year the table was set the night before and I began cooking on Thursday morning. Bri came early with her famous meringue cake and two pies—pecan and pumpkin—on silver-plated platters.

"I insist you keep the platters too, Kari; it's so generous of you to have all of us." As people began helping themselves, Leslie asked, "Kari, where is the pie I brought?" I had forgotten she came with one since there were so many desserts.

"It's in the fridge," Bri said, and I could tell by the expression on her face something was not right.

"I'll go get it," Leslie volunteered.

The next thing I knew, Leslie was walking into my living room with a box from Denny's fast-food restaurant with something in a mud-like brown color peeking out from beneath a crust. I was horrified. The desserts my guests brought had been baked with love. How dare Leslie serve what she called a "chocolate pie" from Denny's? Even the wax paper box stood out with its vulgar red and yellow logo. Bri quickly intercepted, took the pie back into the kitchen and brought it out on a crystal cake plate. It looked much better that way. But still!

"I would have brought an apple one," Leslie said. "But Denny's was the only place open today and this one was all they had."

"Of course it was. Even Denny's sells out of the most popular pies by Thanksgiving Day."

I knew Leslie had gotten to Florida on Tuesday. She could have picked up something more appropriate if she had given it any thought. I was tempted to ask her what she had been doing for two days. I decided against it. When all the guests had left and it was time to clean up, Bri and I glared at the Denny's pie. Bri stuck her finger in the chocolate pudding part and tasted it.

"It's actually not that bad," she said and laughed. I dipped a spoon in it and laughed along with Bri. I had to agree. I scolded myself for being so hard on my sister. Everything was not always going to go as planned. I couldn't expect people to do things the same way I would. In the case of the chocolate pie, the presentation saved the day. It was a good reminder not to lose my poise over something so trivial.

My mom told me how impressive it was that I was able to pull off the dinner in addition to raising a child and running a business. But of course she couldn't quit while she was ahead.

"The only thing missing from your life is a man, Kari. You were foolish to let Scott slip away. You need to find a husband before all the good ones get scooped up. You've had enough practice by now to spot a prince." *Sigh*.

The Friday after Thanksgiving was always busy, and my feet hurt from standing all day.

I went to bed dreaming about leftovers, which for me were the best part of the meal. Each year, I ate them alone in the shop, without the pressure of having to please anyone but myself.

I dozed off thinking about the upcoming season. Many things could go wrong that would be out of my control. I didn't want to spend another year swallowing sleeping pills to ward off dreams about shipments stuck in customs or worrying about finding a new factory to produce goods. Valerie certainly wasn't. So what if my Prince Charming hadn't panned out? My dreams for the future fueled my heart.

Buy In or Goodbye

Easter marked the end of five Seasons that I had run Valerie Louthan Designs. Each year, as more responsibilities were added to my job description, Valerie rewarded me with a 10 percent increase in my base salary. Once I was no longer helping Scott advance his career, I devoted all my time to my own. Last year, the company's sales increased by double digits due to my efforts. I established new markets for shows in California and Colorado. Therefore, I thought it was reasonable to request an increase in my commission or equity stake.

I asked around and learned that sales associates at designer boutiques on Worth Avenue were paid much higher commissions than what I was earning. Managers' salaries were in the six figures, and they got bonuses if their stores met specific sales targets. Shouldn't I be compensated relative to what the market was paying? Valerie's business was too small to provide me with benefits like health insurance or a 401K savings plan like these companies could. Therefore, I asked to have my equity stake raised from one to two percent or my commission rate increased from two to three percent. The small difference in either number would give me the necessary income to cover my mortgage payment.

Until Valerie was ready to relinquish the reins of the company, real estate was the only way I could invest in my future and in Emmy's. There was no cheaper house for sale on the Island. The cost of any house or apartment to rent would be more than my monthly mortgage payment. In old age, the home's equity would provide me with a large nest egg. I wasn't giving all that up to make someone else's business a success. My only choice was to stay in the home I owned. Plus, there was the emotional side of it. These four walls made me feel safe at the end of each day. And it was Emmy's childhood home—the place where she was growing up.

For three years, I treated Valerie's business like the second child I never had. It took a back seat to everything else in my life: dating, travel, friends and my hobby of making party favors. Ian delegated the job of managing the supply chain part of the business to me. He said I was more adept at this than Valerie. She had the ego most designers possess, a tendency to judge their self-worth by the demand for their product and therefore get stuck with too much merchandise. I optimized inventory analysis based on data of what was selling. This increased not just our revenue but our profits.

Valerie and Ian spent the Season in the Bahamas now. They kept a pied-à-terre in town for short visits. I was running a one-woman show with a part-time bookkeeper and shipping clerk. I worked six days a week and often seven if I counted the mornings I went in while Emmy was at Sunday school. Valerie wasn't here to cover for me. Harriet had retired. A friend of Erin's offered to fill in for me at the shop one day a week. The customers weren't willing to give her a chance. They were spoiled; I was the one who knew exactly what they wanted. They would walk in, realize it was my day off, turn around and walk out. Erin's friend grew frustrated and quit, as did a string of women I hired to replace her.

There was no such thing as a personal day or sick day. If I took one, the business would close for the day, there would be no sales and my wages would be docked from my paycheck. I didn't complain. I was doing what an *owner* would do, the job I aspired to, not the one I held. Valerie promised this level of accountability would prepare me for ownership. My eye was on that prize.

I assumed it would be in Valerie's best interest to keep me living near the shop. Who else would run over when the roof leaked

BUY IN OR GOODBYE

to place buckets in the stockroom to prevent the sweaters from getting ruined? Would anyone other than me hand-deliver orders to clients, meet them at the shop after hours or go in on Sunday to get a rush order to Scotland before the factories opened on Monday? Valerie taught me everything she knew about knitwear, but I was the one who took her business to the next level. In addition to my other duties, I learned product development. By researching the latest trends, I could have sweaters in production months before customers knew they even wanted them. Because I had their ear, I collaborated with clients to create new designs; many became top sellers. Was it that easy to replace someone who could do all these things?

Valerie didn't see it the same way. She thought I was asking for more money to sell the same amount of goods. She didn't care what the employees on Worth Avenue earned. After our conversation, Valerie ceased to show me the same respect as when I willingly accepted the pay she deemed fair. She proposed an idea—if I wanted a larger piece of the pie before she was ready to slice it, I needed to buy a stake in her company. For a girl who dreamed of owning an apparel business, this was my chance. I knew every aspect of how to make this product, market it and sell it. I had solid relationships with the factories in Scotland and a client list with over 1,000 names.

February 14 was 10 months away. It was the anniversary of my divorce and also the deadline to buy out Scott's share of the house. I'd calculated the amount I'd need to save to do this. If my sales this season equaled last year's, I would have the amount of money I owed Scott. Then the house would be mine. If, instead, I took that money to buy equity in Valerie's company, I would have more ownership over a business I felt confident I could grow—but as always in business, it was a risk.

If I took that money to buy equity in Valerie's company, I might not be able to buy Scott's share of the house. Did I risk my future for a business or Palm Beach real estate? It was one of the hardest decisions I'd ever faced. I considered selling my engagement ring to buy my stake. I'd gone so far as to have it appraised. Despite its coveted cut and clarity, its size—two carats—was considered small in the resale diamond market—it wouldn't net the amount Valerie requested. At night, I wrote letters to my father in my journal, which is something I'd done since childhood when I felt particularly alone. *Dear Dad, I hope you're having fun up there in heaven, but I could really use your help. Much love, Kari, your daughter down on Earth.*

I even considered calling Seth, but I'd heard he'd moved on to his next victim. Todd told me it was serious; this one had a shot at being his wife. Besides, I knew Seth well enough to know that becoming business partners with an ex-girlfriend would be of no interest to him.

After much deliberation, I decided to keep my house and pass on buying the equity stake. That meant not just losing a job, but what I considered my calling. Then I had second thoughts. I still had time to figure things out. Emmy was older now. Perhaps I could stay with Valerie and take on a second job at night to make ends meet? But Valerie had already decided my fate.

"I just don't think you'll be content with the same pay going forward, Kari, and I don't want someone here who isn't happy." Her tone was crisp, like lettuce in a salad just taken out of the fridge. Suddenly, it was as if she was a stranger instead of the woman who had been my travel companion throughout Europe and the States. I felt like a child who had been disinherited. I was no more than hired help, an employee who was too expensive to keep.

Most of my life I operated with a Plan B and C. This time I had neither. I trusted completely that Valerie would reward me for all my hard work. I truly believed that at some point that company would be mine. Now I didn't have a job at all—let alone my own company! Summer was slow on the Island. I had better find work soon, while Season was in full swing.

I was single and unemployed with a little girl to support. I had less than a year left of maintenance from Scott. Valerie gave me three months' severance pay, a letter of recommendation and an apology. "I'm sorry it didn't turn out how I intended, for the business to be passed down to you."

No one was sorrier than I was.

PART II: A LIVING

Mother Knows Best

It wasn't often that I took my mom's advice. She never understood the life I was trying to build. It seemed no matter which path I took, she was disappointed I hadn't chosen another, namely the safer route, the one she would have chosen. "You're so much like your father, Kari. You have his strength and free spirit, but those qualities won't help you land a husband." Emmy and I had just finished watching the Disney movie *Mulan*. Like Mulan, I didn't want to be disrespectful and tell my mother that those traits were exactly the ones I needed to attract the man best suited to me.

Each time we spoke, my mom's first order of business was my love life—not her granddaughter or my work. When she came to visit for Mother's Day, she was aghast that I had no romantic prospects. Things weren't panning out the way I'd hoped in finding a husband. "Kari, you need to be with a man who has been married before and has children. These guys you are dating are boys, not men," my mother said, referring to Seth and Sam. "Until a man has a family, he doesn't know what it means to put someone else first." I hadn't even mentioned Hapless Harry to her—she would have been too impressed by his pedigree.

My friend Beth agreed with my mom. She asked if she could give my number to a criminal defense lawyer she met at a party in her neighborhood in Miami. He was 13 years my senior and a father of three. Beth felt we were a match because he had a son who lived with him and was a year older than Emmy. She knew I longed for a second child, especially a boy.

"You're both in the same place, Kari...and Alan is spiritual like you."

"Sure, have him call me," I said. And one week later he did. His voice was soft and strong with a trace of South Shore Long Island—an accent that was very attractive. We both loved Broadway musicals and museums. I couldn't explain it, but speaking to Alan felt like a warm embrace and it had nothing to do with the cashmere blanket swaddled around me. Alan must have felt something too, because he continued to call me every night just to talk. During one of these conversations, he asked me to tell him something about how the dating scene was different from the one I had experienced before I married. I thought for a moment and recalled a conversation I had with a guy I met through my sister Leslie. He told me a story about a time he had a threesome with two women. I didn't know if I was more shocked that he did this or that he was telling *me*. Not knowing how to react, I said sarcastically:

"How did that turn out for you?"

"It was amazing. I satisfied myself and both girls," he said, as if to impress me.

Before I could tell Alan how disgusting I thought this was, he said, "The only reason two women would ever show up at my house would be to clean." I burst out laughing. "Hey, I'm coming to Palm Beach for a baseball game in two weeks. Can I take you out to dinner?" I didn't want to wait two weeks. A man who invites two women over to clean instead of for sex is one I needed to meet as soon as possible.

I was still brooding over losing my chance at owning a cashmere company. To keep a foot in the fashion world, I designed displays at the retail stores where my friend Matt's company Trendsetters' goods were sold. Two of the stores in my territory were in a shopping mall near Alan's house. When I mentioned I had business in Miami, we arranged to meet on Sunday afternoon, May 23.

I arrived at the Cheesecake Factory, the place he'd chosen, and did what I always did when I had a free moment: I took out my journal and started writing. Shortly after, I felt someone slide into the booth across from me. When I looked up, I knew immediately it was Alan. He had high cheekbones, a generous smile and strong shoulders. There was a star quality about him. It was as if he had walked off the set of a television show about defense lawyers instead of working as one in real life. As I put my journal away, a waiter came over and asked for our order.

"What would you like, Kari?" Alan asked. I wasn't hungry and was too nervous to look at the menu. I noticed that he was waiting for me to tell *him* what I wanted instead of the waiter.

"I'll have an iced tea," I said, trying not to stare too long at his hazel eyes.

"Two iced teas, please," he informed the waiter.

Alan and I started talking, and once we got past the initial questions of how long we'd been married and why our marriages failed, we realized we had a lot in common. Like me, he was born in New York and came from a big family. Both of our grandfathers emigrated to the States from Europe to chase the American dream. He was a young lawyer and I was a student when the TV show *Miami Vice* brought the glittering surfaces of Miami to the masses. It was the mid '80s, the decade when Miami became a destination for the international jet set. Neon lights, disco music, exotic cars and the drug trade were the currency that fueled the era. The price of admission was good looks and glamour. Anyone who experienced these times in Miami shares a bond that is hard for an outsider to imagine. Alan and I agreed that as exciting as Miami was back then, family life was far more of an adventure. I began to feel at ease with this man in a way that was new to me. We ordered two more iced teas.

Once Upon a Time in Palm Beach

As we were leaving, we bumped into my friend Meme from Palm Beach. She was with her two sons. Alan embraced them each with a hug. How did he know them? As it turned out, her son Charlie was part of his card game, and he coached soccer with Keith. If you are a believer in destiny, as I am, you know that this was no coincidence.

Alan walked me to my car and gave me a hug. "I can't wait to see you again, Kari," he whispered into my ear.

I could feel his full lips on my neck as he pulled away. I yearned for more, but something was different this time. I wasn't thinking about where this would lead or if he was "the one." Being with him felt like home, not the home I came from or the one I was forever trying to create. It felt the way a home should—one where I could be myself and feel safe and loved. I needed to be careful. Falling for Seth again, then Sam a year later and having everything unravel like a ball of yarn left my emotions in a tangled mess. But there was something familiar about Alan, like the old friend who shows up at a family function uninvited, yet everyone is glad he came.

"I had a wonderful time," he said. "And I want you to know this is a special day for me. Twenty-three is my lucky number." It didn't occur to me to ask him why. As I got into my car, I had a feeling my life was about to change in a big way.

A week later, Alan and his 12-year-old son, Noah, traveled to Palm Beach for a baseball tournament. After the last game, Alan arranged to leave Noah with the other parents so we could have dinner together.

"I picked a place that is special to me, Kari. I can't wait to share it with you," he said as I gave him directions to my house. Before I could process how he would even know of a restaurant on the Island, I saw his dark blue SUV pull into the half-circle part of my driveway that led to my front doors. I opened the one on the left and greeted him. I could see he was impressed by my house. It looked grand from the outside with the bright pink bougainvillea framing the arched entrance like an impressionist painting. Alan glanced at the wide-open spaces. Even with two large sofas, an oversized cocktail table and club chairs, the room looked remarkably empty.

"I'm guessing your ex took most of the furniture," he said.

"Just the things he wanted." I smiled, because the truth was we had never finished decorating this showpiece of a house, so there had been nothing to take. I was convinced the arguments Scott and I had over that exact issue contributed to the end of our relationship. However, I didn't think a second date was the time to let on that my husband and I had, at least in part, divorced over furniture—or a lack thereof.

I was surprised when we drove up to 264 The Grill in Phipps Plaza. Only locals knew about this spot; how did Alan? He explained that he'd lived and worked in Palm Beach early in his career. He pointed to the space that used to house his law firm. He almost moved here but decided to stay in Miami near his parents instead. We spoke about our first forays into New York City. Ironically, we both experienced our careers ending abruptly based on circumstances of the times.

Alan had worked in the garment district, dined out every night and had his suits made by a tailor until the oil crisis of 1974. He had used fossil fuels to manufacture women's polyester pants that were all the rage at that time. Without access to this commodity, he had no way to produce his clothing line and had to shutter his business.

My story took place in 1990 when I was a junior associate at a private equity firm. The owner was ousted by the board of directors. I was the youngest on the team and the first to be let go. Gone was the chauffeur-driven car, the chef who prepared my lunch and the stylist who dressed me in skirts cut at mid-thigh, form-fitting blazers with padded shoulders and four-inch-high heel pumps—the look that symbolized power dressing back then.

When you're in your mid-20s, as we were, you don't see how life could be better than that. We were alone, not knowing what to do or where to turn for help. We both landed on our feet: me as an apprentice to a famous menswear designer and he as a lawyer and the first professional in his family. Knowing he could overcome these obstacles and use them to better his life made me feel safe with this man in a way I had never experienced before.

The Grill was near the temple I belonged to, Palm Beach Synagogue. After we had sipped the last of our mint teas, I asked him to drive there. Another thing Alan and I shared was our deepening commitment to Judaism. We both attended services regularly now, not just on the holidays. I knew the back door of the building would be unlocked. As we entered, he kissed his fingers, touched the mezuzah on the doorframe. I found this appealing because a man's connection to religion shows he is in touch with his spiritual side.

For dessert, we went to Sprinkles, the only ice cream shop on the Island. After he placed our order at the counter, Alan pulled a chair out from one of the quaint white tables and motioned for me to sit down as he placed my cup of mint chip ice cream in front of me. I was trying to focus on his good manners and how it felt to have a man treat me like this. It was difficult; I could sense people I recognized from town glancing our way, trying to get my attention.

I smiled at Alan. "Can we just take the ice cream to go?" I asked. I was certain that if we stayed, some group from Emmy's school or The Beach Club would come over and I would have to introduce him. I didn't want a bunch of parents or kids joining us on our date. For just a bit longer, I wanted this man all to myself.

"Of course," he said as he picked up my cup and his cone and somehow still managed to hold the door open for me. We ate the ice cream in his car. I was in no rush to finish mine, as I was hoping to prolong this evening. He kissed me on the lips at my front door. Not a make-out kiss, but a beautiful, pure single kiss. For the first time ever, the 10-foot mahogany door felt heavy as I closed it behind me and made my way to the bedroom.

Stepping Up to the Plate or Stepping Down in Status

With my love life finally kicking into first gear, it was time to focus on my professional life. In the past, money was never my primary objective when job hunting. Now that my circumstances had changed, it needed to be. Research taught me that the role best suited to my talents that would increase my earnings was managing a designer boutique on Worth Avenue. It was well known that store managers make their money during the Season, then move on to other cities during summer when business slowed. After dropping off my resumé at two brands I respected—Dior and Chanel—I discovered no one was making an exit.

One Sunday, while reading *The Shiny Sheet*, I stumbled upon an ad that caught my eye: "High-Fashion House seeks self-starter with leadership skills." On Monday morning, I called and was put through to Liv, who seemed overly excited to meet me. She divulged the name of the shop, Valentino, and asked me to come in the next day. Naïvely, I thought I was interviewing for a management position. Liv informed me that she was the manager; the position that was open was the one *she* was moving up from, that of a salesperson. My resumé clearly said I had managed a business for five years. When I mentioned the wording in the ad, she explained that in high-end retail, leadership traits were needed because salespeople are expected to build their own base of clients.

STEPPING UP TO THE PLATE OR STEPPING DOWN IN STATUS

"Kari, the bulk of your income will come from a commission based on what you sell to these customers," she said.

Images of pushy gum-chewing dowagers filled my mind, the kind who would sell you the moon and stars just to pay their bills. I never held a job as a commissioned salesperson, not even during summers when I was a student. Before I could tell Liv that there had been a mistake, that I was not here to interview for a sales position, she asked if I had a book. Most days I carry a novel in my bag, but today I left my book at home. *Was this a trick question?*

"Not with me," I said. "However, I am reading *Anna Karenina,* and I'd be glad to lend it to you when I'm finished. It's not due back at the Four Arts Library for another month."

Liv's seriousness faded into a smile.

"I meant a *client* book," she said. She pulled out a small black vinyl three-ring binder and pointed to the tabs that divided her customers alphabetically by their names. I remembered being a page in one of these books years ago when I was a customer at Bergdorf's. Before I threw myself under a train and confessed I didn't, I tried to cover up my mistake.

"Oh, of course," I said. "Mine is in the form of a list."

"I knew you must have one, Kari. How else would you bring business with you?"

I could not believe this was where all my arduous work and experience had led me. My skill set was of no use here. This company was only interested in what customers I could bring. Although Valerie's shop was a mere two miles from the world-famous Worth Avenue, Liv had never heard of her sweaters or seen any of our ads. Sadder still, she didn't care. Liv carried herself with the poise of a socialite featured in *Palm Beach Society Magazine,* not a retail girl working the nine-to-five. Something didn't make sense. For me to understand a person or situation, I needed to know their back story. I decided to uncover Liv's by asking a question.

"I'm curious. How did you end up in retail?"

"I grew up here. I worked in sales at my Aunt Mary's store—Mary Mahoney—until I realized I would rather help women with their wardrobes than with what they dress their tables with."

Right away, I understood her background. Working for a Worth Avenue legacy like Mary gave Liv respect in the retail world most people entering the field wouldn't command. Residing here, among her affluent clients, rolled out the red carpet to a management job. Liv's enthusiasm for the Valentino brand was contagious. I began to think it might be fun to work with someone in my peer group on a day-to-day basis. There was an openness about Liv. It was more than her passion—she sparkled. Looking younger than my age was an advantage with her. I could tell she saw herself in me.

"I've been a customer of Mary's for years—she's mastered the concept of making a mom-and-pop store successful," I said warmly.

"She has. I am happy to hear you shop there. Many of my clients came from Mary's. If you come on board, I will be handing them over to you, as the corporate office has decided that the manager will no longer be selling. You may know some of these women." That's when Liv mentioned the magic word: money.

"You'll like this job, Kari. It pays much more than the store manager's job and carries less responsibility. I'm taking less money to advance my career. My plan is to move to New York and train to be a buyer."

I would be trading career growth for compensation, and she was doing the reverse. Perhaps we could help each other.

"What do you think, Kari? Are you interested? I'd like to hire you, but I don't have the final say. Your next interview will be with Jocelyn, the director of retail sales. If she says yes, you're in."

"I can't wait," I said, pretending to be more excited than I felt. As I left the store, I tried to make myself believe my words. This sales position didn't interest me, but the brand did. My first high-fashion purchase had been a skirt suit in the color the Italian designer made famous—Valentino red. I prayed I'd kept my client list; I had no idea where it was.

One week later I was surrounded by clothes that could have come from the closet of a Russian oligarch's girlfriend: sumptuous gowns in playful prints and skirts and knits with details that made dressing up for luncheons exciting again. I was impressed that the company was sending someone from New York to interview me. Despite my doubts about this position, I told myself I was going to go for it. I was excited to meet someone from my home turf. People who can succeed in New York are cut from the same cloth, no matter where the fabric comes from.

Jocelyn's demeanor was more chai tea latte than double espresso. Her vibe was much more Naomi Campbell than vice president of a famous fashion house. Liv gave me the scoop that Jocelyn came from the breed of women who prioritize career over everything else. She was not familiar with Valerie or her cashmeres, but she was clearly impressed by the sales volume of my former boss's business.

"Do you think these clients can become Valentino clients?" Jocelyn asked.

I didn't want to appear presumptuous, but I had worked in the luxury goods sector long enough to know that my clients trusted me. If I represented a designer, it was because I believed in the product, and my customers would buy it. Jocelyn seemed happy to hear this.

"Tell me about The House of Bijan," she prompted as she glanced at my resume. That was the name of the menswear company I'd worked for in Manhattan. This name was fashion-industry royalty. His stores were the only ones in the world where you needed an appointment just to walk through the door. As I was thinking about how to respond, she pressed:

"Did you get to meet Bijan, the designer? Is it true the Saudi princes shopped there?"

"Yes, I was an assistant to Mr. Bijan, and members of the Saudi royal family were clients, as well as heads of state from other countries, oil tycoons from Texas and American businessmen."

I was not here to name-drop. I was here to land a job. I wanted to convey how the unique skills I possessed would benefit the Valentino label, so I steered the interview in that direction.

"It was there that I learned how to build a luxury brand. I used to joke that the education Mr. Bijan gave me was better than an MBA from Harvard."

"Really...can you give me an example?" I relayed some of the lessons I had learned: how to diversify our supply chain so we had many sources to produce our varied product lines, his philosophy about the retail business—it wasn't the "fashion business," it was "show business"—which was how he explained why every detail from the flower boxes out front to the appearance of the store and its furnishings had to be perfect.

"Impressive." Jocelyn told me that an Italian textile company, Marzotto, had just bought Valentino. This company intended to revamp Valentino's image to attract a younger, more fashion-forward clientele. The current customers were aging and dying off.

"No more bows and buttons for Valentino," she said. "We need new blood. Do you think you can help accomplish this?" Usually, I was reserved when it came to my abilities, but this new owner seemed to be in start-up mode. Start-ups were my specialty. I made eye contact with Jocelyn.

"Nothing is more exciting to me than taking something that exists and making it better. I did it with Lana's bags, and I've done it with Valerie's cashmeres for the last five years." A huge smile spread across Jocelyn's mauve-tinted, bow-shaped lips.

"I'm sold. If you can sell Valentino the way you just sold yourself to me, you will be successful." This retail job was starting to sound more promising. "Is there anything you want to ask me, Kari?"

STEPPING UP TO THE PLATE OR STEPPING DOWN IN STATUS

"Can I have two Saturdays off each month to be with my daughter?" Jocelyn assured me that wouldn't be an issue since Liv was required to work every Saturday and the other salesperson, Cedric, a single man, preferred to work that day as it was one of the busiest.

"Anything else?"

Trying to appear nonchalant, I asked about the dress code. I couldn't shake the image of the saleswomen that helped me in New York, haughty spinsters outfitted in all black. Everyday life was my fashion show; how I displayed my style was directly related to my job performance. I couldn't work in this town, which resembled a box of pastel paints, dressed for a funeral. Jocelyn reassured me, saying, "That is one of the perks of the job. We will be providing you with a wardrobe from the collection." Relief set in.

Thankfully, without me having to ask, she told me about the compensation. It was an acceptable base salary plus six percent commission on accessories and four percent on clothing. That was double the commission I received at Valerie's. Things were looking up. *More money and designer duds? How bad could this job be?*

"My two highest-earning associates come from New York and Los Angeles, and they each earn six figures a year. I'm certain you will too." Jocelyn sounded so convincing it was hard not to believe her. "When can you start?"

"Right away," I replied. This is how my career path always played out. Just when I was enjoying a break from the frenetic pace of one job, a new one materialized. As I left the shop, I glanced at the racks of merchandise. If you counted just the selling space, the store was only three times the square footage of Valerie's. There, I had factories ready to whip up whatever clients requested. How would I ever earn the income Jocelyn alluded to selling such a limited supply of goods? I would find out soon enough. My first day was Monday!

Before I could kindle the flames that Alan and I had ignited, I needed to bring in some business. Liv explained to me how designer boutiques operate: They have a steady client base that accounts for most of the shop's revenues. The goal known as "upselling" is to sell as much merchandise as they can to these clients, in addition to attracting new customers from walk-in traffic.

Cedric was a sales associate who was hired last season. He'd seen who the heavy hitters were and claimed them as his clients. The way we decided who was given the chance to serve a person new to the store was "the up system." Cedric and I took turns approaching a walk-in customer with the intention of establishing a rapport and making a sale. I was excited to work with Cedric. Experience taught me that certain women prefer a male salesperson over a female. They like being doted on by someone of the opposite sex. We could divide and conquer, I assumed, but I was wrong. The minute Liv mentioned I resided on the Island, Cedric felt threatened. The way he pursed his lips each time I interacted with a shopper was proof he was protecting what he considered his territory. He'd been spoiled working with Dolly, the previous manager. She'd worked at Valentino forever before she was put out to pasture due to her age. Dolly had given Cedric her book of clients before she left. Although it was smaller, I was grateful to have Liv's client book. I was willing to follow the protocol of "taking turns" with Cedric to greet the walk-ins and establish new customers; Cedric was not.

It seemed each time a well-dressed person walked into the store, he rushed to greet them, completely ignoring the up system. He had worked at every store on Worth Avenue before landing at Valentino. I could see why. The first rule of retail is not to judge a client by their appearance. No one knew this better than a girl who had been selling knitwear to an old-moneyed group of women. Let him think his bullying his way toward new business would work. I

STEPPING UP TO THE PLATE OR STEPPING DOWN IN STATUS

had too much class to declare war on the selling floor. I would find my own way to attract customers.

I couldn't call my friends; they were occupied with kids. They didn't need clothing from a designer known for dressing celebrities. The people I could reach out to had to have two qualities: an appreciation for fine things and the money to purchase them. My former clients had both. At first, I was ashamed to call them and tell them about what I viewed as a step down in status, but I shouldn't have been.

The first few I contacted were excited to hear from me. When they came to town to prepare their homes for hurricane season, they stopped in to visit. Some already loved the luxe designer brand I represented and dished out money to own it. They didn't care that I was not the one manufacturing the product. Many thought I had moved up, since Valentino's prices were higher than the cost of a three-ply cashmere car coat, one of Valerie's priciest pieces. Others thought I was the manager since selling was part of my previous job and Liv was often out at charity luncheons.

However, the type of person buying Valentino was different from the type who craved cashmere. The spring/summer line was over-the-top and expensive. I couldn't expect to build a clientele from walk-ins strolling down Worth Avenue during summer. Some became shoppers, but most remained browsers. I needed a plan. I never intended to be in sales. I find it distasteful to ask people to buy things. Selling was an art form to me; it was the way I connected to people. I could tell right away who would buy a black cashmere sweater and who would pick a hot pink one, and then persuade each person why they needed both. I offered luxury goods to those who desired them. The fact that they paid for them was merely a formality. It felt more like giving than selling. The only thing missing was a few more people who couldn't live without the gift of Valentino.

The Little Prince

In Palm Beach County, Wednesday was the standard night for visitation for children with their noncustodial parent. That's why I told all my single friends hunting for husbands to go out on Wednesdays. They would get a preview of the men on the market and the offspring they would inherit if they were lucky enough to marry one of them. Despite this being my only night *sans* child, Alan wasn't free. His son, Noah, dined with his mom, but he didn't sleep over. The nonprofit she worked for was far from her home and she couldn't risk being late. She was still finding her footing in the business world after spending 15 years as a stay-at-home mom. It didn't make sense for Alan to drive for an hour and a half just to take me to dinner. The rush hour traffic in Miami, even in June, made it difficult to meet halfway. This meant our dates were limited to weekends.

Alan had recently bought a house but had not moved in yet. After seeing my house, he hinted that he was embarrassed to show me his current place. However, his desire to see me must have outweighed his pride. He invited me to lunch the Sunday before Noah's bar mitzvah. He was excited to take me to a French café where he was a regular. I asked if his son would be with him that weekend. "Yes, of course," he said. I thought it seemed a little early for me to be meeting Noah, but my hormones let it slide. I was drawn to this man. I disregarded my mom's advice about keeping kids out of the dating ritual until it became a more permanent relationship.

THE LITTLE PRINCE

My heart raced as I exceeded the speed limit on Interstate 95 while listening to Will Smith's "Miami." As I approached the address Alan gave me, I saw a tiny house with a one-car garage. I looked down at the piece of paper where I had scribbled the address to be sure I was in the right place. This house did not seem like one where a lawyer would live, even if he was renting it. I confirmed the address was correct, walked to the front door and rang the bell. Alan opened the door and kissed me on the cheek. From my perch on the front stoop, I could see every room of the house. He showed me around, which took no more than five minutes.

His eyes focused on the beige cargo pants that hugged my body in all the right places and the white James Perse T-shirt I purposely left unbuttoned in the front.

"Wow, you look great, Kari." Years in fashion had taught me how to get a guy's attention, even in the afternoon. We went to the café, where he impressed me by greeting the hostess in French. After a lunch of quiche and onion soup, he took me on a tour of South Miami. It was a mix of chic eateries and small stores that carried stylish women's apparel, tabletop items and linens, like the boutiques on the Island. Noah was home from baseball practice when we returned to the postage-stamp-sized house.

I was nervous. I was comfortable around boys this age—my daughter was a year younger—but I had never dated a man with a son. My mind raced. *How many women had this boy seen walk in and out that front door in the last three years? What if Noah didn't like me? Isn't it hard enough to get along with one guy, let alone two? What was I thinking showing up and intruding on them like this?*

Noah came out of his bedroom and greeted me with "Hi! Are you here for a sleepover?" If any of the sofas in the living room had been big enough, I would have dived under one. They were not. I glanced toward the brown cardboard boxes stacked up against a wall and said the first thing that came to mind that might explain what I was doing there on what was now Saturday afternoon.

"Nope. I'm here to help you and Dad pack."

"Wow, that's great. I wasn't looking forward to that."

This boy was adorable. He was tall and lanky with a head of hair the color of black licorice. Thinking I better back up my story, I turned to Alan and said, "Let's get to work." To the outside world, the fashion business is glamorous. Anyone on the inside knows how much manual labor it requires. I sprang into action and carried the boxes Alan had assembled into each room. Using a black Sharpie, I printed the name of each room on the top of every box. Alan and Noah wrapped items in bubble wrap and newspaper and placed them in boxes, room by room. I made a list of each item going in each box, tore the page from the legal pad and taped it on the lid.

"What's that?" Noah asked.

"It's a packing slip. Before you unpack the box, you'll know what is inside."

"Wow," he said, "what a great idea, Kari."

Suddenly, I felt grateful to Valerie for making this task part of my job description. If being a skillful packer could make me look good to this boy, all the drudgery would have paid off. I knew eventually I'd be rewarded for my years of hard work; I thought it would be in the form of equity or a title, not admiration from a 12-year-old. When Alan sealed the last box, he smiled at me and said, "You made this fun for Noah, Kari. He never pitches in to help with these things; I think he likes you."

My heart felt warm, like a tray of chocolate chip cookies fresh out of the oven. Then I reminded myself of the pain I endured after allowing myself to get close to men too soon. I wasn't ready to be vulnerable again. I started to plan my exit, but before I could say I was leaving, Alan said, "Let's go for smoothies."

"I'm in," said Noah. I guessed I was too.

THE LITTLE PRINCE

The three of us trudged across the unkempt lawn to Alan's midnight blue Lincoln Navigator. Noah climbed in the back, leaving the passenger seat for me. Alan opened the car door, and I got in like it was the most natural thing in the world to be sitting next to this 53-year-old man with his son in the back seat. It all seemed too easy. Whenever things are too good, I worry something bad will happen—essentially, I wait for the other shoe to drop. There was a big step down from the running board of the vehicle to the ground. Luckily, I was wearing Nikes, not Louboutins. I wouldn't want the little prince seated behind me to have to rescue me if I fell.

Dating or Mating

Liv empathized with me when I told her I had never expected to earn a living by selling merchandise in the summer because previously I'd spent mine on the road doing trunk shows.

"Clients will come back in when the pre-fall line arrives at the end of July. Until then, you can only sell what's left of the spring/summer collection. Don't be discouraged, Kari."

It wasn't necessary to confide in her that after a long hiatus, there was a man in my life, and that he was much more interesting than clothing. At night, when our kids went to sleep, Alan and I had slipped into a routine of speaking on the phone for hours.

"I want our next date to be at night," Alan said, sounding like he was treating the courtship ritual more like a business deal than an enjoyable evening out. "With the move and all, I can't come to Palm Beach for a while. And I wouldn't feel right about having you drive home in the dark after a date in Miami."

What a gentleman. Before I could suggest that I could stay over and sleep in the guest room, he suggested I stay at Beth's, and he could pick me up there. The timing was right. My mom was in town for Emmy's dance recital; she could babysit. When I told Beth about his chivalry, she was all for it. One of the best things about having like-minded friends is you share the same values.

However, our date was on a Friday. Beth would be busy preparing Shabbat dinner for her husband Doug and their two kids. Luckily, her nanny had picked up some of Beth's cooking skills and was able to help. Beth was always eager to aid a friend in the romance department. She helped me dress for my date like she did when we were students. In college, her curvy figure and blond hair always made me feel like Skipper to her Malibu Barbie. But her bohemian touches, a suede shoulder bag and beaded bracelets, gave my outfit a softer edge.

Doug greeted Alan at the door. I watched Alan's eyes look toward me as I made my entrance in a leopard print pencil skirt, flesh-colored sleeveless shell and nude slingback pumps with a pointed toe. The first few dates I had kept my clothing casual on purpose. I wanted this man to want me for what was on the inside, not be taken in by the packaging. However, in the dating game I played, the man must be the pursuer. And the best way to get one to chase you is to dress the part. Years of outfitting fashionistas gave me an advantage in this arena.

Over entrees of eggplant parmigiana, Alan and I bared our souls. He confessed he hoped to marry again. I filed that remark in a folder that would be easy to access in the future. I sensed that I could spend the rest of my life with this man, and we would both be incredibly happy. But was he husband material? I would need to find out.

He held my hand across the small bistro style table and listened intently when I spoke. As his face brushed up against mine, I thought my leopard print skirt might be stirring up his animal instincts. But instead of moving in for the kill, he tamed the thoughts that were tingling more than my senses.

"Kari," he said softly, "there's something I need to discuss with you." *Maybe we're about to do more than discussing.* But out loud I innocently asked, "Yes?"

"I feel this is going somewhere, and I want you to know we can't have sex until we've gone on eight dates." *Okay, that was unexpected.* My face must have communicated my confusion. He continued speaking.

"In the five years I've been divorced, I haven't felt a connection with any of the women I dated. I spoke to my rabbi, and he gave me this book called *Kosher Sex*. After reading it, I came up with an 'eight date rule' for dating."

"Okay..." I said slowly, not knowing where this was going. "What's the eight-date rule?"

"It is based on the principle that sex should be the icing on the cake in a relationship, not the glue that holds the cake together. Before getting to the physical part, a couple should be committed to the relationship for the long term. Every woman I've dated jumped in bed with me on the first or second date. When I realized she wasn't for me, I stayed for the sex. Then I got stuck and didn't know how to get out of the relationship. This time I want to do things differently."

I didn't know what to say. I could tell he was serious. Somehow, he thought I would be the same as those girls.

"Kari, why are you so quiet? Is this okay with you?"

I laughed. I didn't think I needed to go into a long explanation about how I was not some desperate girl who couldn't wait to sleep with him. Or that I wouldn't entertain such an encounter unless *he* was marriage material. I could tell he was waiting for me to say something.

"It won't be a problem...I can wait. We both have a lot going on. You have a new house and a son who has just come to live with you. I have a new job." Then I couldn't help but give him a taste of his own medicine. "By the way, the icing is my favorite part of a cake."

"I'm so glad," he said, appearing relieved. Then he grinned. "Believe me, by that eighth date you'll be dying to sleep with me."

Now I was the one laughing. I had never been the first in any relationship to want it to get physical.

"I doubt it. I've had two boyfriends and more dates in the last three years than I had in my entire single life. Not one of them has led to a lasting relationship. My guard is up."

We both dipped our spoons into the crackly top of the crème brûlée. At the end of the evening, he came around to my side of the car and opened the door for me. He walked me to Beth's front door and gave me a long, passionate kiss. It was the best kiss of my life. Hmm...If this kiss was any indication of his lovemaking, perhaps *I would be* the one who came begging.

My mind agreed we should take things slowly; my body refused to listen. I lay awake in Beth's guest room longing to be next to Alan in that little house, which only made our proximity closer. Would we make it to date eight?

I woke up early and shared the details of our date with Beth: how polite Alan was to the waiter, the way he draped his sports jacket over my shoulders when I said I was cold and how he opened the car door for me both times, getting in and getting out. It's funny how married people enjoy the escapades singles encounter as we try to navigate our way to coupledom. Beth insisted on hearing everything about our date, including if he was a good kisser.

"That would be a deal-breaker for me," she said.

I assured her he was, but the only deal I was thinking about now was the one I made with my mother to fill in for me as a chaperone at the dress rehearsal for Emmy's dance recital. Like Cinderella, I had a curfew. I'd promised Mom I would be back by noon to resume my parental responsibilities. I blamed Beth's challah French toast for making me late. As I pulled up to the parking lot of Suncoast High School, I could see my mom at the concession stand, clutching her purse, engaged in what looked like a debate with Summer's girls, Alex and Jax. I hurried over to see what the problem was. Mom turned to me and said, "These girls are asking me for money to buy lunch." Lunch and dinner during these rehearsals consisted of a hot dog or a slice of pizza and a drink from the concession stand.

"So what?" I didn't understand what the issue was. It wasn't like she didn't know them. They went to school with her granddaughter. They had been to every one of Emmy's parties. She'd been a guest at their home.

"Am I supposed to give them money?" Alex and Jax were 11 and 12. They didn't have any cash. The code between us dance moms was, whoever was chaperoning paid for everyone's food.

"But their father is a multimillionaire; they live in a huge house on the ocean."

"Mom, that is irrelevant," I explained. "We're all part of the same community. This is what we do for each other's kids."

By this point, Emmy and the girls were cranky and hungry. I asked them what they wanted, placed the order and paid. I explained that it had been a long time since my mom had done the dance recital thing. They laughed as they carried their trays of food back to the cafeteria, the place that served as a waiting area, until it was time for their next number to go on.

Emmy was taking ballet, tap, jazz and hip-hop, which meant she was in four routines. I loved watching her dance. Her passion came alive through the movements of each number. She had talent, but the lessons helped. Summer had found this jewel of a dance company—Palm Beach Ballet. When I had been hesitant to leave the Island and drive through a rough neighborhood to get the girls to dance class, Summer convinced me the dancers produced by Palm Beach Ballet were far superior to those of our local company.

And Summer was more than a mom I shared carpool duties with. Ever since that first ball at The Breakers, our families stayed close. She and her husband, Ray, sponsored our membership to The Beach Club. Despite my fear that I'd asked a silly question at the interview, she assured me we'd be accepted. I couldn't help it. I respected the club's "no cell phone" policy," but I had to know if Scott could talk to a client if necessary. The committee politely told me they would page him so he could take the call in private.

Summer hoped her girls would be ballerinas. I had no expectations Emmy would dance professionally, but I felt the discipline and the experience of being on stage would help her in whatever career she chose. That day at dance practice, I saw Miss Joan, the head of the company, and told her how impressed I was with the quality of the choreography this year. I especially loved the originality of Emmy's hip-hop routine set to "Work It" by Missy Elliott. This surprised her as this style of dance was new to the studio.

But hip-hop was anything but new to me. I learned about it back in my college days from the roommate of my then-boyfriend. He worked at his father's label, which was one of the first to feature Black artists. This opened a new world for me, including visits to Queens, the Bronx and Brooklyn as he sought out emerging talent.

"And I love that color on you," I said to Miss Joan, referring to the ballet-slipper pink cashmere tunic I'd given her for Christmas. I already missed giving sweaters as gifts. Valerie let me buy whatever I wanted at exactly what it cost the factory to produce it. *Maybe I should have thought about that perk when I asked for more money.*

That was in the past. I needed to think about the future. This job at Valentino was different from any position I'd held before. Did they give employees a discount? I was so focused on the company's savings plan, I forgot to ask. It would be nice to buy Alan a gift for Father's Day. The Worth Avenue store didn't carry the full menswear line, but I'd noticed a display case of red silk ties that would be perfect for a powerful defense lawyer.

Prince Charming #2

On Father's Day weekend, Scott vacationed with Bri and Drew and all three kids. I was glad Bri and Drew were able to remain friends with both me and Scott without having to choose sides. Emmy thought of their kids, Chloe and Jordan, as her younger sister and brother. I contemplated a weekend of reading, swimming in the ocean and watching my favorite show—*Sex and the City*—on Sunday night. Now that I had agreed to this eight-date rule, the show might be the best sex I would be getting for a long time. Then Alan surprised me and asked if he could come up for the weekend.

"Noah is going to be with his mom. I'd love to spend some quality time with you," he said on one of our nightly phone calls.

I was excited and nervous at the same time. It had been a long time since I spent a weekend alone with a man.

"What would you like to do?" I asked.

"I'd like to meet your friends, attend services, go to a French restaurant for some fine dining Saturday night and do brunch on Sunday." I remembered that he played tennis every Sunday morning.

"What about your tennis game? Do you want me to see if the pro from my club can hit with you? The courts are walking distance from my house."

"That would be amazing! I can't believe you remembered."

PRINCE CHARMING #2

I thought about mentioning that I remembered everything but decided not to. It wasn't something he needed to know yet. *Or maybe ever.*

"See you on Friday after work. Bring your tennis whites; that's the dress code at the club."

I smiled as I hung up the phone and thought about what a treat it would be to spend an entire weekend with him. Right away, I called my friends Ben and Elys who I'd met at the temple. They hosted a dinner every Friday night, the beginning of the Jewish Sabbath. After my divorce, they promised that Emmy and I would never spend a Friday evening alone; we had a permanent place at their table. I told Elys I'd be coming this week, but instead of my daughter, I was bringing a date.

I had been afraid to tell my Island friends about Alan. I didn't want to be the girl that cried wolf, saying I was serious with someone only to have to admit that I had been wrong again. I called my favorite restaurant, Chez Jean-Pierre, and booked a reservation for Saturday. Luckily, the owner, Nicole, recognized my voice. She was able to give me a table by the bar, which was where the action was and the section people my age dined. The pro at The Beach Club laughed when I called to reserve a court and his services.

"So, we've finally convinced you to play, Kari?"

Tennis was a popular pastime for Palm Beach ladies. It was a sport my dad had been obsessed with. Because of him, I had insisted Emmy take lessons beginning at age five. I wanted her to have a sport she could take with her into adulthood. Competitive cheerleading, mine, had lost its cachet after high school.

"It's not for me—it's for a man I'm dating."

"I'm booked for Sunday. Can he play Saturday afternoon?"

"Yes," I said as I gave him Alan's name.

I remembered that my junior membership would expire on my birthday. The Beach Club was the only club in town to offer a junior membership to people under the age of 40. Scott and I joined when we moved to the Island. We planned to upgrade to a regular membership when the time came. Now that I was single, I couldn't afford to. We had so much history here: holidays, family nights, Emmy's day camp and cotillion where she learned the art of table manners, ballroom dancing and social etiquette. Years from now, Emmy would credit those days for giving her confidence to deal with celebrities in her entertainment career. But even then, I knew it was a special place and I couldn't imagine our lives without it.

I loved calling Lucy at the front desk to leave the names of my houseguests. A short walk to the end of the street and they had the beach, a pool, tennis, croquet and fine dining at their disposal. Where would I swim laps and work out? Did they open the camp to kids who weren't members? It was too much to think about. Instead, I was grateful to my mom for giving birth to me in the latter part of the year. We would have the pleasure of using the club for one last summer.

Work was slow that Friday, and since Alan was coming, I left a little early. I stopped at my florist, The Gazebo, to buy a hostess gift for Elys and some flowers for my house. The owner led me to the refrigerators in the back room where the best blooms were kept. The scent of the lilies I picked would make the house smell like an English garden.

"When are you going to let me do your entire house, Kari?" At one time, I intended to fill my home with potted plants and trees. Scott's departure put it on hold, along with the art collection I'd hoped to display on the walls.

"One day. It's just not in my budget right now."

"It's okay, Kari. We're thankful for the customers you send our way."

"And vice versa," I said.

Their shop and Valerie's shared the same street address; it was easy for us to refer business to each other. And of course, I sent friends in.

"Please put everything on my house account," I said as he held the door open for me. I stepped outside as he placed the flowers in the front seat of my car. Service, loyalty and street-level parking... there was so much to love about this town. I'd canceled my bikini wax. Despite our scheduled sleepover, I knew the extent of our physical intimacy wouldn't move beyond kissing. Instead, I took a walk on the trail with my neighbor Erin. She laughed when I told her about Alan and his eight-date rule and asked if she thought he would stick to it.

"You're hopeless, Kari. Stop obsessing about everything. Look where that got you with Seth and Sam. Let the relationship evolve." Erin had yet to get Todd to propose, but her job as a teacher taught her a lot about men. "Men are like children; they'll do whatever they can get away with," she said when I cried on her shoulder about mine and their shenanigans.

When I opened the door to greet Alan, he was holding a bouquet of daisies. I led him into the kitchen where I cut the stems at a 45-degree angle and arranged them in a crystal vase. I placed them on a coffee table in the living room.

"Gorgeous," he said. "I love flowers."

"You do?" I asked, surprised.

"Yes, gardening is a hobby of mine. Wait 'til you see what I do with the landscaping at my new house."

I smiled and thought of my grandfather, Michel, the perfume maker. He loved gardening and passed that down to his daughter. Scott always criticized me for spending money on fresh flowers. To him they were frivolous. No matter how often I told him they connected me to a place and time I was happy, I could never get him to see things from my perspective.

I served Alan a Coke and walked him through the house. As we made our way back to the foyer, I noticed the small overnight bag he must have put down when he came in. Awkwardness overtook me as I realized I had not thought out the sleeping arrangements.

I picked up the bag and placed it in my bedroom. I wanted him to feel relaxed, and my room was the most luxurious room in the house. The walls were painted a soothing sage green. The carpet was plush. To ensure a good night's sleep I had blackout shades sewn onto the floral printed drapes. French doors looked out to lemon trees planted in the side yard of the house. I had planned to put a pool in that spot before Scott left.

"I'll sleep in Emmy's room or the guest room," I said, trying to hide my embarrassment.

"No security system?" he asked as I locked the front door.

"Nope, never felt I needed it here." Palm Beach was patrolled by the local police who did a thorough job of keeping those who didn't belong off the Island. Alan opened the car door for me, and we headed south on County Road toward Costa Bella, Ben's rambling three-story estate that resembled a Spanish castle.

Ben and Elys were the envy of many families on the Island. When the Preservation Society voted to tear down a 1925 oceanfront house built by society architect Addison Mizner, Ben went to the town and offered to buy it. At his own expense, he moved it one lot to the west. In doing so he saved Costa Bella from the wrecking ball. Now he used it to house his growing family. It was a luxury to be invited to the lavish Shabbat dinners they hosted. The rooms in the house were grand in scale and filled with antiques. Sitting at their long dining table, sipping wine from crystal goblets made you feel you were living in the Gilded Age. Ben and Alan discovered they shared a love for construction. Alan hung on every word as Ben told him how he gave up practicing law to manage his family's malls and joined the house-flipping craze that swept the Island in the early 2000s.

We were enjoying ourselves so much we lost track of time. It was close to midnight when Alan and I left. When we got back to my house, I headed to Emmy's room. Alan gave me a long kiss goodnight in the hallway that separated her room from mine. I

PRINCE CHARMING #2

felt my heart race. The Torah says a man should please his wife on Shabbat. Could he please me? Would he try? We were dating, I wasn't a wife; did the same rules still apply? I wondered if Christian girls knew about this rule. Maybe *this* was the reason, not the myth that they make good husbands, that made these women want to marry Jewish guys? But there was no need to worry; that kiss was all I was getting.

I'd guessed wrongly that because it was June, the crowd at morning services would be light. There was a bar mitzvah, which meant more people were present than usual. I knew everyone would be curious when I walked in with Alan. The temple was Modern Orthodox, which required men and women to sit separately so the men would not be distracted by the beauty of the women while praying. Ben waved Alan over to his pew. I found a seat near Elys.

I made sure I had a view of Alan from my seat. He was reading in Hebrew and had brought his own *tallit*, which is the Hebrew word for a prayer shawl. I never understood women who had fantasies about police officers or firefighters. To me, a man in a fine tailored suit with a tallit over his shoulders was the ultimate in sex appeal. Harriet, my colleague at Valerie's, thought so too. She was Scottish, Catholic and pushing 70, not the type who'd find a young rabbi sexy, but she smiled like a schoolgirl when she told me about the handsome bearded man who walked by our shop wearing a black suit and an ivory pashmina. I explained to her that the "pashmina" was not a men's version of the garment women used to keep warm, but a prayer shawl, worn by men of the Jewish faith while praying.

The other men gave Alan such a warm welcome we stayed for the second half of the service, the kiddush luncheon. Alan couldn't believe how good the food was. He laughed when Ben told him he joined this temple for two reasons: the food and the women. Ben was right about both. The temple had a great caterer. Because many members were young families, the mothers were pretty. But no one compared to Dinie, the rabbi's wife, my close friend since the day we met shopping at Pastel. With her heart-shaped face and bee-stung lips, she looked like she stepped off the cover of *Vogue* magazine instead of the streets of Crown Heights where she came from.

As we walked across the street to the Paramount Building, I pointed out Valerie's boutique, my second home for the past five years. Of course the shop was closed; this was the time of year Valerie traveled to Scotland. As we made our way toward Worth Avenue, I pointed out Valentino. It was too soon to introduce Alan to my co-workers, so we hit my favorite shop, Eye of the Needle, where a 75-percent-off sale was taking place. Only locals know that summer is the best time to shop in Palm Beach. Since so few people were in town, the only way stores could make money was by marking everything down.

I grabbed some dresses from a rack. When I came out of the fitting room to model them for Alan, he told me he loved the floral one with the empire waist and pointed out the bias cut on another. I couldn't believe how much he knew about women's clothing. He explained that he took classes at the Fashion Institute of Technology, a school in New York, to better understand the garment industry as that's where he made his living then. *That was exactly the kind of thing I would do.*

I placed the items I was buying on the counter. I added two pairs of Havaiana flip-flops, which had emerged as trendy footwear instead of something you wore to the beach. Green and white canvas beach bags with the initials G and H completed my purchase. Susan, the manager, wrapped them for Alan's girls. Alan spoke of Goldie and Hannah so often, it felt like I already knew them. Surely, they would like a souvenir from Dad's weekend. As I stepped away to add an item for Noah, Alan placed his credit card down on the counter.

"You're not paying," I said firmly. "Please put them on my house account," I instructed Susan.

"I got it, Kari. Really, it's fine," he said, smiling.

I was not about to let this man, who was not yet a boyfriend, buy me three dresses, especially when he had just bought a house. Susan didn't know what to do. "Charge them to my house account, please," I said again as I picked up the credit card and handed it back to Alan. "You can buy me a coffee before your tennis match."

We walked to Bice, a restaurant nearby, before heading back to my house. Francésco, the maître d', smiled at me and gave me a wink of approval as he sized up Alan. Francésco and I had a history going back years. It started when I threw a baby shower for my friend Nina, who was pregnant with a baby girl. I preferred to host parties like this at home, but I had just moved into mine and it was short on furniture. I trusted Francésco and his staff to create the atmosphere I desired.

What I didn't account for was the amount of alcohol the native Palm Beach girls could drink. There were nine of us. Nina and I were not drinking, she because she was pregnant and I because I was hosting. Amid the conversation and opening of gifts, I lost track of the wine being consumed. I had sticker shock when the bill came and I saw that seven girls had gone through *12* bottles of wine. I had purposefully chosen a price-fix menu and a house wine to keep the cost of the party down. "Francésco, you know my husband, Scott. He'll be furious if he sees a bill like this. Can you please adjust it?" He removed the cost of all the bottles but two from the bill. By doing so, he gained a loyal customer. Whenever Scott asked where we should take a potential client, I chose Bice, not only for the delicious food but as payback for what Francésco did for me when we were newcomers to town.

As Alan and I drove back to my house, I pointed out the tennis courts. I told him I would take a bike ride while he played with the pro.

"I want to go with you," he said.

"Are you sure? You won't be tired after tennis?"

"Not a chance."

"Okay, I'll wait for you. I have things I need to catch up on." I thought about the pile of bills I had put off opening. I knew I would need to pay them from my savings until I got my first commission check, which wouldn't show up in my account until the middle of next month.

After Alan's match, we biked to the tip of the Island. There, we sat at the edge of the pier and let our feet dangle as we inhaled the smell of saltwater. I pointed out my favorite homes and told him who owned them. When we returned to my house, I showered in Emmy's bathroom. When Alan saw me pull out a hair dryer and round brush he asked if he could dry my hair. "I'm good at it; I do it for my girls." Surprisingly, he did a salon-quality blowout. I pulled out the printed dress I'd bought earlier and slipped it on along with a pair of high-heeled sandals.

"You look beautiful, Kari," he said as we met in the entranceway and walked to his car.

As we approached Chez Jean-Pierre, I began to get nervous. Even though it was the off season, I worried about who would see me. I hoped they wouldn't ask too many questions. Dating in New York in my 20s was easy. The city was big; girls knew how to avoid the places where they may run into an ex-boyfriend or a boss. In a small town it's challenging to be discreet about your personal life. Palm Beach is like Pandora's box. If you keep it locked, your secrets are safe. But if curiosity got the best of you and you lifted the lid, then beware: Its contents would scatter in the air for everyone to see.

I started to feel I was overthinking this whole situation and scolded myself. *Really, Kari? Scott left the Island when he remarried; no one cares if you're dating.* The Season was over. The society photographer, Lucien Capehart, was more likely to be on vacation than taking pictures at Chez Jean-Pierre. Upon arrival, Alan gave his name to the hostess and started speaking to her in French. Not only was I impressed, but this warmed my heart, as Grandpa Michel spoke French. We sat next to each other at a small table for two. Our conversation was delicate, just like the Pouilly Fuisse white wine he ordered. The Dover sole *meunière* was deboned tableside and tasted so much better when shared with a man who appreciated this service. I don't know if it was the wine, Alan's voice or the gentle way he held my hand, but all I could think about was getting home and letting this seduction continue.

I saw Lori and John, friends of Drew and Bri, seated a few tables away. They were dressed in their usual head-to-toe attire of black and bling, fitting for a couple who owned Fantasma Productions, South Florida's largest independent concert promoter. I thought about pretending not to see them but decided against it. Like me, Lori didn't have family in town. We shared many holidays together at Bri's.

"Hi, guys," I said quietly as they walked by my table. Lori was model-tall with giraffe-like legs that went on forever. I had to tilt my head all the way back to see her face. Before I got that far, I spotted her bare midriff. Every outfit she wore, whether it was for athleisure or a formal affair, exposed this section of skin. How she kept it so toned after 40 was the best-kept secret in town. It struck me that she could be the perfect client for Valentino. Before I got a chance to mention my new job, the waiter brought dessert. There wasn't enough room for him to serve us with Lori and John standing there. I was glad they said goodnight and left; my neck hurt from straining to look up.

As we waited for the valet, I returned my attention to Alan. Despite being dressed like the male inhabitants of the Island, he looked so regal in his navy blazer, button-down shirt and khakis. Although he was wearing the Island uniform, something about his attitude made the clothes look different on him, as if each piece had been tailored with attitude. Unlike most men in Palm Beach, he wore socks with his loafers. I couldn't help but think about him slipping those off. What would happen when we got back to my house? It was date six. His rules prohibited us from doing anything physical, but I wanted to sleep next to him, not in the room next door. Would he be okay with that? Should I even suggest it? Thankfully, I didn't have to. He kissed me as I unlocked the front door. He continued doing so as he led me to my bedroom. As we slowly undressed he whispered, "No sex yet, Kari."

"I know," I whispered back, glad he had been the one to say it. We fell asleep in each other's arms as if it were the most natural thing in the world. Our bodies stayed entwined until morning, like a delicate spool of thread tightly, neatly wound. What wasn't natural was waking up with mascara on. Removing my makeup was a ritual I rarely deviated from. I wandered into the bathroom to wash up, then slipped on a robe and went to the kitchen to brew a fresh pot of coffee. I walked outside to pick up my copy of *The Shiny Sheet*. Sunday was the only day I had the paper delivered. The other days it came to the boutique. Alan walked into the kitchen dressed in long black nylon shorts and a white T-shirt.

"Do you have a newspaper?" he asked casually.

"Yes, right there," I said, pointing to *The Shiny Sheet*. He looked at it and laughed.

"I mean a paper with real news like *The Palm Beach Post* or *The New York Times*," he said, smiling at me. *Oops.* This guy was a lawyer; of course he needed real news. I hadn't read *The Times* in years. In my 20s, I had spent many a cold snowy Sunday lounging around my apartment with only the "Styles" section to keep me company. But I didn't feel like Alan was judging me.

"It's just part of my morning routine. I need to read a paper with my coffee," he said.

"I have the perfect place to take you. Let's go!"

PRINCE CHARMING #2

I took him to Green's Pharmacy, a drugstore where one side looked like a kitschy five-and-dime that sold overpriced beach pails and saltwater taffy. The section to the south resembled a 1950s luncheonette: Red vinyl round stools faced a counter where short-order cooks tossed up a skillet breakfast as customers looked on. If you were lucky enough to grab any of the small creaky tables, you'd be so impressed your server remembered your name that you'd forgive her for throwing your food at you. After all, she'd been there as long as the restaurant itself. Green's sold *The Palm Beach Post*, *The New York Times* and *The New York Daily News*. I couldn't decide if Alan was more pleased with the newspapers or the pancakes with homemade maple syrup. Back at my house, he packed his things. He planned to spend the rest of the day with his family.

"Don't forget the gifts for the girls and Noah," I said, bringing the pink-and-white striped shopping bags from the family room. The store carried mainly women's apparel but stocked a few menswear items, for the ones who accompanied these women and most often footed the bill for their purchases. I'd bought Noah a belt for his summer-school uniform. Outside, I stood by the window of Alan's car, kissed him goodbye, and thanked him for coming. I'd forgotten it was Father's Day. Having lost my father at a young age, it was a day I chose not to remember. The image of my dad driving off to his job in the city as I waved goodbye, never to return, was one that still haunted me.

But today I felt happy. The fact that this man was a father of three appealed to me. His son living with him was an added bonus. Despite Alan's boyish appeal, he was responsible and decisive. With Scott and other men from my past, I had always felt like the wiser, more mature one in a relationship. With Alan it was the reverse. Like a new dress, I was trying it on, and I liked the way it fit. I hoped it wasn't cheating to count these last three days as dates five, six and seven.

Date 8: Would You Care for Dessert?

June was coming to an end, and Alan was in the middle of an important trial. At the same time he was preparing to move. That didn't stop him from calling me every night. We spoke about his case and our kids going to sleepaway camp for the first time. I'd found a camp for Emmy in North Carolina that was much closer than Maine and popular among Palm Beachers. Since I'd just started a new job, I couldn't fly up for visiting day. Scott complained when I asked him to go instead. He'd never gone to camp and didn't understand why parents needed to visit. He said he'd go, then sent his wife, Candace, in his place. Apparently, she understood why a parent should be present, and I appreciated her for going.

Alan's parents were joining him on the drive to Bradenton where Noah went to baseball camp, and before the trip, he had one final round of packing to do before the movers came. It could be weeks before we'd see each other again. I missed him already.

Alan must have been feeling the same way because he called and asked me to spend Monday night with him. Wednesday was my usual day off, but Cedric was eager to trade with me. Monday is to shoppers what it is to businesspeople: a day to get back to work. In this town, that meant the business of shopping. In Palm Beach, Monday followed the retail sabbatical that was Sunday. This town still abided by the rules established long ago that insisted businesses stay closed on the day of prayer. It wasn't unusual for one of our clients to have been photographed wearing Valentino in Sunday's *Shiny Sheet*. Smart salespeople knew this meant their

DATE 8: WOULD YOU CARE FOR DESSERT?

client would be back for a second helping. By Wednesday, they'd have forgotten about shopping and moved on to a lecture at The Preservation Society or a class at The Four Arts.

Before driving south, I took a bike ride. The beauty of the Island always made me feel like a mother seeing her child for the first time—awe-inspired. The ocean sparkled like sapphires scattered with diamonds; the dunes of the sandy beaches resembled untouched heaps of flour in a mixing bowl. The fragrant blooming jasmine, the smell of saltwater and the palm trees hugging the coastline gave this place an aura unlike anywhere else in the world. And now my little family was part of it.

At the end of each block were beach cabanas shared by the residents of the street. Emmy, Scott and I had biked to these cabanas for countless children's birthday parties over the years. Unlike the parties of my youth where pizza was served and the cake came straight from Mom's oven, these affairs were catered. Except for one, where an oceanfront pool was covered so a mini golf course could be installed, there was a simplicity to them: catching waves and making sand art activities instead of musical chairs and Simon Says, the games of my youth.

I glanced back at the to-do list that I planned to tackle on my day off, but I remembered Alan wasn't working today. Maybe it was getting caught up in the emotions of the beautiful Palm Beach vista, but I felt anxious to get to Miami to be with Alan. My to-do list could wait.

The smooth leather seats of my Mercedes stuck to my bare legs as "Hot in Herre" by Nelly blasted from my car radio. It was a humid day; I imagined my car cutting through the thick air to get me to Alan. I arrived to find him and Noah playing catch on the front lawn. In my eagerness to see Alan, I'd completely forgotten that school was out and Noah would be with him.

Once Upon a Time in Palm Beach

"Kari," Noah said, smiling as he ran over to my car. I cringed as his eyes moved toward the small overnight bag that sat on the passenger seat. "Are you here for a sleepover?" This time I had no excuse; there was no getting around it—I was. Thankfully, before I could muster a response, Alan walked over and kissed me on the cheek.

"Hi, Kari," he said as he picked up the bag and walked to the front door as if there was nothing at all embarrassing about this scenario.

"I need some things for the new house. Do you want to go to T.J. Maxx with me? Noah has a friend coming over."

"Sure," I said, thinking this was the perfect way to avoid answering more questions.

When we walked into the store I tried to stay with Alan, but the small kitchen gadgets he tossed into his cart were of no interest to me. However, the selection of candles, vases and table linens made me feel as if I'd stumbled upon Aladdin's treasure trove. This store did for home goods what Loehmann's did for designer clothes. I didn't even know stores that sold off-price home décor existed! It was a status symbol for Palm Beachers to claim they never left the Island, and except for a date or the dance carpool, I rarely did either. This discovery was proof I should borrow a dinghy and go boating every so often.

At one point, I drifted so far from Alan that I lost him. I started calling out his name in two syllables: "Al-an...Al-an." As he and I turned a corner, we bumped into each other. Standing beside him was a petite brunette in a pink tank top and Juicy Couture velour sweatpants that flared at the bottom. He introduced her as Kim, his former paralegal. She smiled at me. "The way you were saying that name, I knew exactly which Alan you were looking for," she said.

"Really? Why?" I asked. The name "Alan" was not that unusual.

DATE 8: WOULD YOU CARE FOR DESSERT?

"It's just the perfect 'nag' name. And believe me, you will be nagging him a lot," she said. I thought this was an odd remark for a secretary to make about a former boss.

"Kim was with me for 10 years," Alan said by way of explanation. I smiled sweetly.

"Lucky for me, I'm dating him, not working for him."

Why on earth would I have to nag this man? I wondered. *What did Kim know?* But I didn't read into the exchange as much as I normally would. How could I? My mind was on one thing: This was date eight. We could finally have sex. Alan was right—it was me who wanted to get to the next step first.

Alan's new house was a one-story Bermuda style painted sky blue. The first thing I noticed was the fireplace in the family room. I loved fireplaces—there was no better place to curl up with a book. He pointed to a bedroom off the kitchen that he called Noah's room. To the right of the living area was a hallway that led to the other bedrooms: the premier bedroom and en suite bath and two smaller rooms with a bathroom for his girls. French doors led to a covered terrace and rectangular shaped pool that was long enough to swim laps in. *Perfect for when I visited.* As we'd discussed before, he'd driven around the neighborhood looking for a house. This one had a "For Sale by Owner" sign on the lawn. Alan negotiated a good price for it. I relayed my journey to home ownership. We laughed at how similar our stories were.

Back at the rental house, Noah was waiting for us to go to dinner. At their local sushi hangout, Alan introduced me to the owner, who teased Noah about all the girls who were glancing his way. Noah didn't notice; he was happy to just be with us. I had never been out with a man and his child before; it felt warm and fuzzy, like the first time I slipped on a pair of cashmere socks. When we got back to the house, I pretended to be interested in what was on TV, but all I could think about was what would happen when Noah went to sleep.

This was Alan's last night in this house. It was the only house he had been able to afford next to the larger one where his kids and ex-wife lived. It was the one where his oldest daughter, Goldie, came to live during her last year of high school. Noah had been here three months. Alan never thought his kids would even sleep here, other than on weekends. They wanted more time with him. He said it made him feel whole again.

The fact that he shared this with me was the best foreplay I could have asked for. Suddenly, I was nervous. I had so much invested in this man. What if there was no chemistry between us? We hadn't done more than kiss until now. I wish I knew what that rabbi's book said about what to do if everything else was right except the physical part. I thought of each first time with a man, like the Christmas list teachers had us write to Santa. I knew exactly what I wanted but was too afraid to ask for it. Then, when I didn't get it, I was disappointed.

Alan grabbed my hand and led me to his bedroom. The king-sized bed looked like an oversized raft in a kiddie pool. He tore off my clothes like a present he was anxious to unwrap. He sensed my hesitation. "Relax, Kari, we'll take it slow." I took a deep breath. It was time to blow out the candles and see if the icing tasted as good as the cake.

It seemed like all he wanted to do was please me. I wondered if this was because he was older. If that were the case, I'd seriously been remiss by not adding this demographic to my dating pool sooner. I drifted off to sleep dreaming this was my best Christmas yet. But this was no dream; he'd given me everything on my list.

My head was spinning when his alarm sounded. I tried to get up, but Alan's arm was tucked over my waist. I savored this moment before I squirmed out from under his arm and leapfrogged into the bathroom so as not to make any noise. I showered off the scent of sweat and sex. I dressed in the outfit I'd packed for work: black linen pants and a white blouse with a black satin ribbon that tied

DATE 8: WOULD YOU CARE FOR DESSERT?

at the waist. "Bye, Allie," I whispered as I brushed my lips on his forehead as he slept. "Alan" seemed too formal a name to call this man who'd treated me like a goddess just hours ago. That name could be saved for the courtroom or everyday conversation.

I tiptoed out the front door, peep-toe pumps in hand, and slid into my car. There were 75 miles between me and the Island. Beyoncé's "Crazy in Love" played on the radio. Certain songs always brought me back to the time when I first heard them. From this day forward, this one would remind me of last night. The sparks between Alan and me were more than I'd hoped for. Next weekend was the Fourth of July. I had a feeling mine was going to sizzle.

Training & Gaming

In September, Jocelyn arrived from New York with a list of strategies lined up to entice clients to buy the fall/winter collection. *The Shiny Sheet* was delivered every day. While Cedric flipped through the pages, fantasizing about being a guest at the galas, I studied the society section to memorize the names and faces of people who attended them. This way, when they walked through the door, I would recognize them right away. That's how Hilary and I became acquainted. She wrote for *New York Social Diary* and *Quest* magazine, and her upcoming wedding to billionaire Wilbur Ross was sure to be splashed across the pages of every society column.

Hilary had shoulder-length blond hair that turned up at the bottom. Her trim figure was the ideal canvas for our clothes. Plus, I had a soft spot for second wives. These gals weren't ashamed to admit the frog they kissed was a toad, not a prince, before throwing themselves right back into the dating pond.

These women, along with some first wives and girls desperate to join either group, trusted me as their go-to stylist to make them look elegant. Soon, I had a client list that read like a who's who of Palm Beach. These ladies wanted everything that was Valentino: gowns, cocktail dresses, daywear, shoes, handbags, scarves and jewelry.

I had been selling solely cashmere for so long, I was unaware that in 2004 the stock market was soaring, the economy was booming and women couldn't spend this newfound money fast enough. The atmosphere of the time consisted of two things that made it easy for me to earn my keep: excessive wealth and insatiable longing. Fashion is a business of instant gratification. When my clients wanted something it was like a drug: They had to have it. I became their supplier.

It helped that the 2004 collection was youthful and that our brand was exclusive. The best way to get a customer to want more of something was to have less of it. Valentino only had five freestanding boutiques in the United States: New York, Los Angeles, Las Vegas, Bal Harbour and Palm Beach. All five boutiques were connected to a computer system that allowed us to view the inventory in the other stores in addition to ours. We could request anything from our fellow sales associates on one condition: that we send them an item from our store in return.

It was as if I was in a Middle Eastern bazaar. I had to bargain with an associate from another store to give up an item so I could sell it in ours. Although this seemed futile in theory, if you were fair, as I was, it worked. And I was grateful for this system as it gave me access to the inventory of five stores instead of one. More sales equals more money. My alimony was about to end. By February, I would be a single mother paying for a house in Palm Beach.

The only people who lived on the Island had generational money or were CEOs, corporate business owners or the "hedgehogs," as Emmy had named them. Families with children on the Island had a male breadwinner supporting them. That's just how it was, given the entry-level price of a home. Store managers, salespeople and all other employees crossed over one of the three bridges that connected the Island to the mainland to serve its residents. Single women my age did not own houses, unless they had been gifted them by family or ex-husbands.

This gave me the distinction of being part of two very different communities: the one that lived here and the one that worked here. This was a plus in dealing with the Island's residents; they felt I was one of them. The person it didn't work for was Cedric.

The way he looked me up and down with disdain was proof he felt I had an advantage due to my zip code. But it was the client that should have been his that let this cat out of the bag.

When a woman strolled in with a bag with your store's name on it, it meant one thing: a return. Unless you sold the merchandise, a return didn't affect our commission. However, we earned a living making numbers add up; subtracting them doesn't add to the weight of our piggy banks. Cedric would make a beeline for the stockroom when he saw someone walk in with a bag. Instead of arguing or calling out his behavior, I saw an opportunity to turn the return into a sale and turn the customer into a repeat one.

When a soft-spoken girl named Beatrice came in with a navy crepe dress her husband bought in New York, I assured her it would be no problem to return it. This husband, who the receipt listed as Ned, owned a venture capital firm. Beatrice needed a dress for the company's Christmas party. She was drawn to the collection that just arrived and ended up buying three.

Cedric must have smelled a sale taking place. When Stella, our seamstress, came to the floor to fit the dresses, he resurfaced from his hiding place in the stockroom. I asked him to translate the conversation going on between Beatrice and Stella in Spanish to make sure I understood what Beatrice requested. I could see his anger boiling as I rang up her purchase. Beatrice not only became a regular customer but a regular fixture on the social circuit. These types were ideal clients to cultivate. They required lots of dresses so as not to be photographed twice in the same one in *The Shiny Sheet*. Beatrice sent in the wives of the other executives, all eager to emulate her by wearing the designer preferred by the boss's wife.

Beatrice lived on North Lake Way, like I did. When she needed something in a hurry, I would drop it off at her house on my way home. If it was cocktail hour, which Palm Beachers treated as ritual, she invited me in for a drink. At the end of the day, I would have preferred a cup of coffee over a glass of Cabernet—Emmy needed me at home to start my second shift as a mother—but Beatrice and my other clients enjoyed my company as much as they liked having their clothing hand-delivered.

One day it came up in conversation that Beatrice and Ned were traveling to New York at the same time I was. They insisted that Emmy and I fly with them "PJ"—Island talk for "private jet." Liv had given me the weekend off to attend my sister Leslie's bridal shower. I was elated; Emmy had never flown private. She'd only heard about how I had for business; it would be fun for her. There was one person who did not find this fun at all: Cedric.

"This has gone way too far," he snarled.

After Beatrice extended her offer, Cedric requested a meeting with Liv. They disappeared into her office behind closed doors. I planted myself near the cash/wrap area, opened my client book and pretended to be absorbed with it. When they emerged, Liv initiated the conversation. "Cedric seems to think that you are laying claim to clients because you know them from living on the Island. Frankly, I am too busy dealing with the pressure from New York to increase our sales figures so the store can be renovated. The last thing I need is to be in the middle of a catfight between the two people I need most to help me accomplish this."

I trembled as Cedric crossed his arms over the black cashmere and silk T-shirt that clung to his perfectly toned chest. His silicone-injected lips looked more pronounced than ever, and his smugness declared victory. My instincts were to defend myself and say that Cedric was the one with the advantage, as he was hired during the Season and claimed the biggest spenders for himself. Or to point out that because he was Latin, he had a connection with the Spanish-speaking customers, who were some of our best. Or that he could have had Beatrice if he hadn't assumed she was there only to make a return. Instead, I chose to see the big picture and offered a solution.

"I'm sorry you feel that way, Cedric. I am here every day for the same reason you are, to earn a living, not climb the social ladder. Yes, my customers invite me in when I drop something off at their homes, which I happen to pass on the way to mine. Your clients would be happy to meet you outside of work if you let them know you were open to it. Customers don't care where you live. You're the one putting up that wall."

To say Cedric and Liv were shocked was an understatement. Emboldened, I went one step further and said: "If you would like help taking your relationships to the next level, I'd be happy to show you how it's done." I could tell Liv was relieved. New to management, she didn't know what to do in this situation. The stress of running a store was getting to her. Playing referee between Cedric and me, the pressure to make our numbers and the task of opening and closing a store did not lend itself to her around-the-clock social life. Often, Cedric opened the shop when she couldn't show up on time after late nights out. I was the one left to answer to Jocelyn and fend for myself against Cedric when she disappeared for hours at midday to mingle with friends from high places.

Shortly after our impromptu staff meeting, one of Cedric's clients, Tess, began taking him out to lunch. After a bitter divorce, she had sworn off men but craved attention from the male population. The fact that he was good-looking and gay made Cedric the ideal companion. The more he swooned over her, the more cash made its way to Valentino's coffers. Tess was just a start—it seemed there were lots of lonely ladies willing to trade money for time and attention.

I gave Cedric a way to cash in, but my strategy helped me too. Surprisingly, most of my clients were not former ones, but just like Beatrice, came purely from my pursuit of making a connection and offering exceptional service. That was how I bewitched Wendy.

TRAINING & GAMING

Because we were the smallest store in terms of square footage, we had the least staff compared to other Valentino boutiques. Our team consisted of Liv, me, Cedric, Stella and Bob, the bookkeeper, who divided his time between our shop and the one in Bal Harbour. Unlike the other boutiques, ours had no shipping clerk. Each salesperson was required to ship the merchandise they sold from the back of the store, an area away from the view of clients. We also needed to ship the pieces being sent out to other stores, often up to 20 items per day.

When I was shipping, Cedric took advantage. He didn't follow the protocol of coming to get me when a customer asked for me or stepping back if it was my turn with a walk-in. I quickly learned I couldn't resign myself to the space allotted for shipping and let Cedric steal my clients. Instead, I took the necessary tools and wrapped outgoing shipments on the selling floor. I was glad there wasn't a security camera filming the day-to-day activity of our store. I'm sure Jocelyn would have thought it less than chic to see me holding an oversized tape gun like a weapon, sealing brown boxes on top of a display case of jeweled evening bags, but it served me well.

Once, while I was wrapping a crystal-beaded suede jacket for a client, Wendy, a hedge fund wife, saw it and had to have it. It turned out I had discovered an amazing selling strategy. Our store didn't stock her size, but the Vegas one did. Stores didn't like to give away big-ticket items without good reason, but standing in front of me was a client willing to plunk down $16,000 for a jacket. Wendy was happy to learn that if I shipped it to her, there would be no sales tax since we had no store in Connecticut. While I was wrapping Wendy's purchase, it happened again; another client saw the jacket and ordered it. I managed to sell the company's entire stock of this piece. Jocelyn was amazed at how our tiny shop was able to do this. I couldn't reveal my secret, but when I needed to make my numbers, shipping from the selling floor worked every time.

Once Upon a Time in Palm Beach

Wendy referred friends who were happy to let me handpick their wardrobes. When I asked why they didn't shop at the New York store, they said the staff there had no time for them. They were too busy helping the hedge fund wives of the Upper East Side. Word traveled quickly that a girl in Palm Beach was good at getting the Greenwich gals the best pieces before they sold out. If only they didn't all take a size two and dress the same way—I would have had a lot more things to sell to them! It turned out competing for customers with Cedric was the least of my worries. I was driving home from the dance studio when Summer called to warn me about a diva who was a bigger threat: a hurricane named Jeanne.

When It Rains It Pours

I rushed home after my carpool duties. It seemed like more than bad luck that my first fall at a new job, the weather report predicted a severe hurricane aimed straight for Palm Beach. The last hurricane to hit South Florida was Hurricane Andrew, 12 years ago. Back then, I lived in New York and I'd never experienced one. As a single mother, I felt vulnerable enough, and now my home—our sanctuary and my source of strength—was at risk.

Barrier islands like Palm Beach are the first to be evacuated before a hurricane. It's too risky to leave people stranded in a place that requires entry by drawbridges that go up and down to allow boats to pass. If a bridge was in the up position when the power went out, it would be disastrous. No rescue workers could access the Island in case of an emergency. Twenty-four hours before the storm, Island residents were ordered to leave. When I told Alan this he said, "Pack some stuff and bring Emmy. It'll be fun; we'll have a party."

Early on, Alan had let me be a part of Noah's life. I loved taking him shopping and helping him with homework. When Noah learned I was redecorating my daughter's room, he asked if I could do his too. But when it came to Emmy, I was protective. She had yet to meet Alan or Noah. All she knew about them was what I told her. Being trapped in a house with no electricity while a storm raged didn't seem like the best time for the four of us to become better acquainted. Scott took her to Disney World instead. I was thankful for my ex in times like this. No matter how scared I felt, Emmy had a father she could count on.

I wish I could say there was a calm before the storm, but it was the exact opposite. I spent my workday wrapping clothing in plastic, then came home to do the same with my artwork and antiques. I panicked when I looked at the floor-to-ceiling glass doors and windows throughout my house. They had no shutters. Scott left before we got around to ordering them. Island residents had staff on call to help them hurricane-proof their homes. As a newcomer to the task of storm preparation, I had no one, so I called Ben. He had enough extra plywood to protect my windows. Together, we rolled up my two Persian rugs, lifted them onto the sofas and wrapped them in plastic. If the roof leaked or a storm surge came, they would stay dry.

The town was more desolate than a ski resort in summer. Homes were vacated, shops were boarded up and no people or pets were in sight. The only cars visible were the lengthy line of ones filling up at Testa's gas station. Before the storm struck, I hunkered down with my friend Deb who owned the salon across from Valerie's shop. I spent so much time there she joked she should charge me rent. I could never master the art of doing my nails and a good blowout. Painting my nails made me feel like a kid who couldn't color within the lines. As for my hair, the dryer was heavy in my hand and I could never reach the back of my head, so that part of my hair remained wet. It was so much easier to leave these tasks to a professional. Deb loved fashion and understood the protocol required to deal with high-profile clients. We figured if the electricity went out, we could trade war stories about work. Her townhouse in West Palm seemed safe.

After the storm hit the power was down for 10 days. Schools were closed. Emmy stayed with Scott at his new house in Boca Raton. When residents were finally allowed back on the Island, I was required to show proof that I lived there. Law enforcement worried about looters. I flashed my driver's license at the officer on duty at the north bridge and drove down my street at a snail's pace, observing the trees and shrubs that Mother Nature had toppled.

A musty smell filled my nostrils before I even opened my front door. As I paced the room, I realized the smell was the least of my problems. My house looked like it had been watered with a hose. Erin relayed what had happened: The rain came fast and hard. The power went out and the drainage pumps malfunctioned. The excess water flowed into my house and the ones on the low-lying interior streets. Todd's Porsche was submerged in water. The carpeting in my bedroom and Emmy's was drenched and the baseboards had warped. When I opened the bottom drawer in my walk-in closet, I found my sweaters were soaked and the colors had run together. I should have known better than to accept cashmere, instead of cash, as overtime pay.

My neighbor, Dean, a custom home builder, was glad to help a damsel in designer clothes who had once done him a favor. Dean bought the house next to mine—Brenda Straus'. At the closing, Brenda produced the note I left in her mailbox when Bella, Dean's wife, confided we might be neighbors. It read, "All offers being equal, please consider the one from my friends, Dean and Bella, as their daughter is a friend of Emmy's. Since Emmy is an only child, and this neighborhood is short on kids, it would be nice for her to have a playmate next door." Dean wrote up an estimate of the damage for me to give to my insurance company. His crew ripped out the closet and wet carpets in the bedrooms. My wrought iron bed frame sat on the concrete floor for months while I waited for the insurance check to arrive.

I never used four-letter words, but all around me, everyone was saying one in particular: mold. My fellow homeowners told me it was paramount to prevent it from invading my house. Apparently, it could poison a person. Worse yet, a house associated with this word became unsellable. Great, our health *and* our home. What else was left to lose? I hired a company to test for mold. I replaced the carpet in Emmy's bedroom with leftover tiles from the hallway. The test came back negative. The adjuster told me I was lucky—my policy didn't cover mold.

To get reimbursed for damages, my insurance company required me to list every object that was ruined. The most important things to me—family pictures and Emmy's school projects—I couldn't replace. I called Valerie to ask for a receipt for the ruined sweaters. Secretly, I wondered if this was serendipity. Was this a chance to ask for my job back? When I called, Valerie didn't say a word about my job, and I was too proud to bring it up. I prayed the insurance company would reimburse me before I needed to write the final check to Scott that gave me the deed to our house.

I spent my last paycheck on stuff for Emmy's room; Noah's was next. Decorating his room was a fun distraction from everything going on at my house. Plus, I'd never done a boy's room before. Each time I visited, I brought swatches of rugs and bed linens. Noah was bogged down from the stress of school and sports. I thought a room designed to his taste might help him flourish in the life Alan and I were slowly beginning to create together. Alan's mom, Sondra, was glad I volunteered to do this. Before me, she'd done these things for her newly single son. Alan's parents would do anything for their kids and grandkids. A few days after I had laid down the area rug I'd bought for Noah, Alan pulled a bigger rug from underneath me.

"I can't see you anymore, Kari," he said at the end of our nightly phone call. "I'm overwhelmed. I feel like I do my law job in the day only to come home to cook, clean and study with Noah. Noah is getting Ds in two classes. I can't convince him about the importance of doing well in school. All we do is yell at each other. I have no time to work out or play tennis, let alone have a girlfriend."

My first reaction was to think it was my fault. Had I burdened him by talking about the damage to my house? Why would he want to hear about water in my house when he was knee-deep in hot water with his son? Other than being exclusive, he had never led me on. Even in the height of passion, neither of us had said the "L" word. But I was devastated. Was it only me who felt a connection? I was already imagining our life—I could *see* it. In one week, I'd lost not only my most cherished belongings, but the boyfriend I had hoped for a future with. I knew it was hard to raise a child on your own. I'd been doing it with Emmy for years. *Welcome to the world of single parenthood.* Emmy was studying the same subjects as Noah; I knew how to quiz him for tests. Didn't Alan see this? How would he be better off without me? I'd never trusted any man enough to let them become part of Emmy's life. Alan let me drive Noah to school dances and tutoring. We bonded over the music of Lil Wayne. His lyrics had a southern feel and a party vibe that was different from the other rap music we liked. But once again, someone up above had a different plan for my future.

I told myself the soaking wet sweaters were a sign I needed to move on from both Alan and Valerie. Valentino's cruise collection was due in the store soon. Liv told me this was where I could make my numbers for the month. Inhabitants of our Island flew to the ones in the Caribbean in December. These jetsetters had finished buying winter clothes. They would be looking ahead toward vacation. I needed to not think about Alan and how he had stomped on my heart or the rainwater that had invaded my house like a burglar and stolen my possessions. If I could make these ladies look good, they could make it rain money for me. I spooned Alan's words into a Tupperware container and moved it to the back of my fridge. I was four months away from owning my home outright, and I needed to gather every bit of energy I had and put it toward two things: my sales goal at the store and repairing my house.

I thought about running in the arms of the sweet guy with the shy smile who moved in down the road. He had asked me out when we bumped into each other on the trail. He was walking his Cavalier King Charles Spaniel. We volunteered together at Ballet Florida. I decided to run the other way. He was newly divorced. We were both on the rebound. I was determined to stay focused on repairing my house and healing my heart. Romance was the last thing I needed. Or was it?

Prince Charming #3

What was going on? County Road had more traffic than the Long Island Expressway in the summer when the entire city headed east toward the Hamptons. As I passed Bethesda-By-The-Sea, I noticed crowds of elegantly dressed people walking across the manicured lawn to get to the Gothic Revival church. Then I remembered it was the wedding day of Donald Trump, the real estate mogul who transformed New York into an "Emerald City" of excessive wealth in my day. His bride was a European model named Melania. Mr. Trump owned Mar-A-Lago, the estate referred to as "The Queen of Palm Beach" by its former owner, Marjorie Merriweather Post. I thought about pulling over and trying to get a glimpse of Melania's gown, but it was a new year and Jocelyn had set my sales goal at a number that was more frightening than confessing my sins on Yom Kippur.

To do my part, I was browsing through an old client list, hoping to find some former customers to introduce to the Valentino brand. The February deadline for claiming ownership of my house was a month away. I needed steady sales to cushion my commission check, the last one I'd receive before I signed on the dotted line. Three years ago, when I made this deal, I thought it would be easy to come up with the money. My career trajectory had changed but the deal didn't. If I couldn't hand over the funds, I would be forced to sell the house and split the proceeds with Scott. The stakes were high and the clock was ticking.

Just then, a distinguished man with a full head of gray hair walked into the store. When he turned to face me, his strong jawline was visible. It was Larry, an old cashmere client of mine. He gave me a big bear hug. He had just arrived from Maine. He smiled when he saw the gold Bulgari necklace around my neck. Last year, at Christmas, he watched as I wrapped the sweaters he was giving to his family members. He decided I deserved a gift too and demanded to know what I wanted. I'm shy about receiving gifts, but his offer seemed genuine, and the holiday spirit was in full bloom on the Island. Since I started dating again, flowers were the most any guy had delivered. My request for an everyday necklace led to this piece. "I told you I loved it, Larry," I said flirtatiously.

This man was 30 years my senior. He'd had a crush on me since we first met at Valerie's shop. He wore a canary-yellow cable-knit sweater with the confidence that only a self-made man could pull off. Maybe it was because he was in the oil business, but each time I was in his presence I felt like we were about to step out to The Wildcatters' Ball, a gala for people employed in the oil and gas industry. Once, when I was in Houston for a trunk show, clients took me as their guest, and the extravagance of it surpassed the galas in Palm Beach.

"What else can you tell me, Kari?" Larry asked. "I'm hoping you'll say you're single and you'll have dinner with me."

"Well, you happen to be in luck, Larry," I teased. "That 'man in Miami,'" (which was what Larry called Alan) "broke it off, so I am."

"What a fool to let a girl like you go. How about Friday? Is Club Colette okay?"

Club Colette was a private supper club. Most people my age found it stuffy, but I liked the British atmosphere. For another reason, it held a special place in my heart. Their sister location in Southampton was where I held my first solo trunk show. I remembered how hard it was to convince Valerie that a show without her or a socialite could be successful. She refused to believe anyone would come if I was hosting. I'd begged her to give me a chance. The percentage of sales we usually donated to a socialite's charity went to a much needier cause—mine. Instead of the usual three days, I scheduled the show for two days. Valerie was shocked when she wrote me my commission check. After expenses, we netted more than we had the previous year: no pedigree or design degree required.

"Kari, did you hear me?" Larry asked. I focused my attention back on him and nodded. "I'll pick you up at 7:00," he said.

This is how our courtship began. Larry lived on Breakers Row. If you weren't given precise directions, you might never find the entrance sandwiched behind the post office and Root Trail. This was low-rise living at its finest. Some of the residences had their own yoga studios and massage rooms. Larry's apartment was decorated in cool blue tones and boasted views of the golf course. From the balcony off his bedroom, the ocean seemed close enough to greet you in the morning and drag you out of bed with the tide. Residents were given use of the amenities at the five-star Breakers Resort that was walking distance away. I was familiar with this place from my days with Valerie and Lana. Back then, I was here as a delivery girl. It felt different being here as a guest.

It was nice to date someone who lived nearby. I skipped my midweek book club to dine with Larry at the best places in town. Everyone knew him. It was a luxury to be treated like a princess after standing in high heels on a marble floor catering to clients all day.

Marzotto, the company that bought Valentino, got wind that Palm Beach now allowed stores to open on Sunday and Jocelyn thought we should give it a try. As a local, I knew this would never work. The business of Islanders was shopping. This took place Monday through Saturday. Sundays were spent at the private country clubs. Rather than complain, I made the most of it. This was the bar and bat bitzvah year for Emmy's age group. These affairs took place on Saturdays. Larry saw one of the invites on my dining table and noticed it said black tie, and he asked if I needed an escort. I told him I didn't.

These celebrations honored the children and families Emmy grew up with. It would not have been proper etiquette for me to bring a date, let alone one that resembled the kids' grandfathers. Larry understood the first part completely. I would never intentionally hurt anyone's feelings, so I didn't mention the "grandfather" part. To take off the Saturdays I needed, I worked Sundays instead. The hours were shorter and there were rarely any customers, but Emmy and I never missed a Bar or Bat Mitzvah.

On my days off, Larry and I read books at the private pool reserved for residents of Breakers Row. We both favored biographies and historical fiction. When I saw he was absorbed in one about a pope, I asked him to explain to me who the Holy Ghost was. Emmy was scared to go to bed after learning about him in elementary school at Rosarian. Larry explained that it was not a physical being like the ones on Halloween, but God's presence in the form of a spirit, more akin to an angel. I couldn't wait to tell Emmy.

However, another ghost still haunted me—the ghost of Alan. He may have ghosted me, but I couldn't rid myself of his presence. When I heard the voices of guys with a Long Island accent talking sports, I felt his spirit. And unlike Casper, his ghost wasn't friendly; it spooked me. Instead, I chose to focus on Larry, who praised my keen intellect. He was impressed with how I'd grown Valerie's company. Larry's compliments helped me push memories of Alan to the side, at least part of the time.

"I can't believe she brought that silly girl Elinor back," Larry said, referring to Valerie as we strolled down Worth Avenue and looked at the fashions, one of our favorite pastimes. "She is not equipped to handle the business at the level you took it to. I refuse to step foot in there. Let me know if you have an idea for a business, Kari; I'll back you."

It was nice to know that an accomplished entrepreneur had this level of respect for me. If only I had known this while I was with Valerie, perhaps he could have helped me. As we passed Saks, he saw I was drawn to something in the window and suggested we go in. I hadn't set foot on the designer floor since I was a guest at a fashion show. The price tags on the gowns were bigger than my paycheck. Thankfully, the staff was new and didn't recognize me. For fun, I tried on formal dresses for him.

"Please let me buy one for you, Kari. The American Ireland Fund's Gala is next week, and nothing would make me prouder than having you on my arm in one of those gowns."

I said no, to the annoyance of the shop girls, who right away thought a man accompanied by a much younger woman was a guaranteed commission. Larry persisted as he tried to get closer to me. "When can I meet your daughter? My plane's available. It's 'wheels up', anytime you two want to get away. She'll have fun, Kari. My grandkids are her age; they can come along too."

I confessed why I couldn't take time off to travel. I relayed the details of my agreement with Scott. I had to earn the money I needed to buy out Scott's share of our house, my daughter's home. "Geez, Kari. How much do you need? Heck, I'll *give* it to you. Let me pay off the mortgage, so you never have to think about it again."

I laughed. If all this seemed perfectly normal to him, it wasn't to me. In my 20s, guys measured their level of commitment to a relationship by the gifts they bought a girl. I never merited more than a designer dress or a sterling silver trinket from Tiffanys. This man wasn't asking for anything more than my affection. In return, he offered not just the glass slipper, but the castle to go with it.

In his gentlemanly way, he hinted about our relationship moving to the next level. I wish I could say I didn't need his help, that I was certain I'd make the money I needed on my own or that I felt no chemistry with him. All three would be a lie. I had one month left to earn the necessary funds; there was no guarantee I could come up with enough. As far as physical attraction? I had never been with a big burly guy like this. I wondered how it would feel.

When I mentioned Larry to my friend Matt, he said I must have daddy issues to consider a man this age a prospect. Matt was wrong. I lost my dad when he was 33 and I was eight. My dad was my hero. He remained in my memory as youthful and strong, the man that taught me how to steer my sled away from the ice in a snowstorm. My attraction to Larry was not fatherly in any way. When I relayed this to Matt, it didn't change his opinion. "This guy has one foot in the grave. He could kick the bucket any day and you'll be back to being alone again." I refrained from asking Matt if that was why he chose to marry a girl 14 years his junior.

I told Larry I found him wildly attractive. If I didn't, I wouldn't waste his time or mine. I explained my hesitation. It was too soon for me to get close to someone and risk being hurt again. As I reflected on our conversation, I realized what was holding me back. My heart was still with Alan. I'd fallen for him, and I remembered exactly when it happened: We were seated directly across from each other at a table for two at The Palm restaurant. A couple were seated at the table adjacent to ours. The woman wore a Gucci scarf tied around her neck. The emerald-cut diamond on her left hand was so big I thought it was an ice cube that had fallen from the cocktail she was drinking. She had been staring at Alan all evening. Suddenly, she blurted out his first and last name as if she had been searching for a missing earring and was surprised to have found it. Alan moved his gaze from me to her and said, "Yes, that's me."

"You saved our son's life," she announced.

It took Alan some time before he remembered her son. The details they rattled off about the case jogged his memory. The woman showed us pictures of her son and said he was working and the father of two boys. She asked Alan if her son could contact him. Alan agreed and handed her his card. That's when my heart climbed over the fence it had erected to keep me from getting hurt. If my heart is with a man, there is not even a piece of it I can break off to give to another one. I was honest about this with Larry.

"Well, I'm extremely patient, Kari, and I plan to stick around until you're ready." Larry reserved a little table at Café L'Europe for Valentine's Day, but there was no room in my heart for Valentine's Day this year—my entire future would be determined by the events of one week!

London Bridges Falling Down

The store was bustling with excitement. Mr. Valentino was flying in for a runway fashion show at the Mar-A-Lago Club. Everyone was excited to sit at the tables reserved for the boutique's best customers. Everyone except for me; I had a different agenda. While Cedric was cozying up to the models on the catwalk, I could work the store alone and not have to divvy up the commissions. I relished the glamour of a runway show as much as anyone, but I was about to turn over all my savings to my ex-husband.

The show was scheduled for the weekend before The Palm Beach International Art and Antique Show. Each year, this event brought a host of bigwigs to town. I loved the museum-quality paintings, art deco furniture and jewelry. I was a browser, not a buyer, but I knew the revenue from this show was important to the town of Palm Beach. Ladies who shopped at Valentino were the type of women who would spend on collectables. I called a contact I had at the show and explained why this crowd was the kind the show needed and asked for a stack of free passes. Meanwhile, back at the shop, I was in my element running my own show again.

Just before closing, a Hugh Grant lookalike and his model-perfect wife walked in looking for a tie. I began to show some ties to Jonathan as he introduced himself, while Claudia, his wife, began browsing. Having dressed the wealthiest men in the world, choosing a tie was easy for me. I noted the suit and shirt he had on and selected a navy one with "just a pop of pink in it, perfect for Palm Beach," as I told him. As I placed the tie around his neck and adjusted it, I told them how they had picked the ideal weekend to come to town, due to the timing of The International Art and Antique Show. "Mr. Valentino flew in for a fashion show that's taking place at Mar-A-Lago. I made sure passes to the show were placed in the goodie bags." Jonathan beamed as I said this.

"You just said the perfect thing, Kari," Claudia remarked. "Really, what was that?"

Claudia looked at me with the easy elegance associated with royalty. "Because my husband owns the show, the tie is for tonight's opening party. Jonathan forgot to pack one. We're on our way there now, but we'll be back." When I got home, I glanced at my invite and learned my new clients were Viscount Jonathan Rothermere and Viscountess Claudia Rothermere, of London.

Fortunately, Valerie and I were still on speaking terms. I'd made sure to never burn any bridges, especially on the Island, where one wrong move could land you in Lake Worth or "Lake Worthless," as the locals referred to the blue-collar town just south of Palm Beach. I phoned Valerie and got the scoop. Not only was Jonathan English aristocracy, but he owned *The Daily Mail*, part of a British media empire founded by his great-grandfather. As promised, Jonathan and Claudia returned to the store on Saturday. Lady Rothermere, which Valerie told me was the proper way to address Claudia, bought so much I made my goal for the week!

Cedric, who had been sulking in a corner, suddenly got excited when Claudia said she needed everything delivered to her hotel by Sunday morning before they boarded a plane to England. Certain items had to be brought in from California. I was not going to lose this sale or disappoint my new clients. Surely this situation had come up before. I called James, the top producer at the Rodeo Drive store, and explained my predicament. He'd used Federal Express to make Sunday deliveries in an emergency. It was possible but it depended on where the merchandise was going. I held my breath until I got someone on the phone at Federal Express who assured me they could get a package from Beverly Hills to the Four Seasons Hotel in Palm Beach before noon on Sunday. I tracked the package to make sure it arrived. My resourcefulness benefited not just me, but the store. Liv was so delighted she let me have Monday off to attend the show.

A year later, that same weekend, Jonathan and Claudia strolled through the doors of the boutique and asked for me by name. I walked to the sales floor, greeted them both and said how delighted I was to see them again. After a day of shopping, I asked if they had ever visited the Valentino store in London.

"Oh no, we never go there; we only shop here, Kari, so we can see *you*," Claudia said.

It never ceased to amaze me how far courtesy, respect and curiosity could take a small-town girl. When I called Valerie to tell her the Rothermeres came back, she wasn't surprised. "It's because you saw them as people, not a paycheck, Kari, and they picked up on that."

A Happier Valentine's Day

Larry refused to let me skip Valentine's Day. Since I couldn't join him at the table he reserved by the piano at Café L' Europe. He did the next best thing for a girl who wasn't ready for romance: he sent flowers. When I got home, a huge vase filled with three dozen roses in pink, white and yellow sat at my doorstep. The card was signed: "Worth Waiting For, Love, Larry."

    I'd just finished placing them on the round glass table in the entranceway when the doorbell rang. It was a delivery boy from The Gazebo, bringing a modest bouquet of red roses surrounded by baby's breath. He set them on the console table as he glanced at the larger arrangement. I could only imagine what he was thinking. Then, to my surprise, I saw Alan's name on the card! I hadn't heard from him in three months. My heart jumped just seeing his name. Before I could decide who to thank first, Alan's number flashed on my phone. I took a deep breath before I answered.

    "Happy Valentine's Day, Kari. I know you love this day," Alan said softly.

    "Wow, I can't believe you remembered."

    "Me either. I've been thinking, Kari, it was a bit reckless of me to just end things; you did so much for me and for my kids when we were together."

    "It was my pleasure. All of it. How are you and Noah and the girls?"

"We're doing okay, actually. I'm getting the hang of this single parenthood thing. I'm feeling less overwhelmed by the day-to-day stuff."

"I'm happy for you," I said. Before we could ask each other any other questions, another call came in. It was my divorce attorney. Tomorrow was D-day; there was a lot to do. I warmly, but hurriedly, said my goodbyes to Alan. I wasn't sure when we'd speak again, but I had a feeling it would be soon.

The next morning, my commission check showed up in my bank account. I calculated the amount correctly and made my goal! I was able to write the check to Scott. Now I was the sole owner of a house in Palm Beach. With that title came the bills that went with it. How would I pay them on a retail girl's salary? There must be a way; I just had to find it. Season was in full swing. Valentino's cruise collection was selling faster than the ships leaving the Port of Miami. The spring/summer collection was expected to arrive in our store in March. The advance buzz of the runway fashion show and a personal appearance by Mr. Valentino had our clients crossing the days off their calendars in anticipation of its arrival.

When Alan called and asked to see me I was tempted to say yes, but I had no time. The frantic pace of work required at least one weekend day. Bar and bat mitzvahs took up a good portion of every weekend, too. Plus, Emmy was co-captain of the cheerleading squad. Along with a group of parents, I attended every basketball game to root for the team. Did I have any desire to rush back to playing house with Alan? *No, thanks.*

On the few days I had off, Larry was free to see me. Without the commitment of work or kids, he could put me first. Importantly, Emmy thought he was nice, and like me, she was blind to his age. I was certain I wasn't the only girl he was seeing. I assumed he desired sex, and I just wasn't there yet. I didn't give it too much thought. My work and Emmy were my focus now. Our big discussion of the moment was whether or not Emmy would have a bat mitzvah.

A HAPPIER VALENTINE'S DAY

She was up for the party but wasn't sure she could commit to the learning part. She spent three days a week at the dance studio, had a lead role in the school's spring musical and played soccer on Saturdays. She struggled to fit Sunday school in on her one day off. I left the decision to her. After all, I was a latecomer to religion.

"Don't worry, baby, we can do a dessert party at The Beach Club or something simple that doesn't require much planning if you decide to do it at the last minute."

The last weekend of April I found myself alone on a Saturday night, a rare occurence. Larry was hosting Easter with his sons and grandchildren. He'd invited me to join the festivities, but I declined. I didn't know his family; I wouldn't feel comfortable. As fate would have it, Alan called and asked me to visit that very evening. "Or I'll come to you," he volunteered. The choice was easy. "I'm coming," I said. Bees, not butterflies, churned in my stomach. Alan seemed pleased. He preferred to be with me at his house where he was in charge.

We went to his neighborhood hangout for dinner. When the owner greeted me by name, I was surprised, considering the length of time since I'd been there. Words flowed easily between us. It was as if we had never been apart. Back at his house, we watched a movie—*Finding Neverland*. We both cried at the end. I had a soft spot for men who were able to cry in front of a woman. It was late, and when Alan asked me to sleep over, I hesitated. He sensed my uncertainty.

"You could stay in the girls' room if you feel more comfortable," he said softly.

"How do you feel?" I asked, looking into his eyes, hoping they would tell me what my heart wanted to hear.

"I feel exactly as I did before. Nothing's changed, Kari. You're the only one for me."

I longed to be close to him, to feel his arms around me and share intimacy with him in the way I hadn't been able to do with

Larry. I let my intuition guide me, praying it was right this time. But in the game of love, as anyone who's played it knows, there is no return policy.

It turned out that make-up sex was better than first-time sex. There was a hunger between us after time spent apart and an intense energy in not knowing where we would go from here. I stayed until Monday. As the weeks passed, we slowly returned to our routine. On my days off, I drove to Miami. When he came to me, I set up tennis games for him with guys I knew to be skilled players. He planted purple hibiscus flowers in my yard and tended to my lawn. Months passed before the check for the damages from the hurricane came. My clothes hung from rolling racks until the closet company rebuilt the one that was ruined. Finally, I was able to replace the carpeting in my bedroom.

I told Larry I was back with Alan. He said he was sorry to hear it but was grateful for our time together. Emmy left for sleepaway camp. Noah played baseball for a travel team. I spent every weekend with my two guys. When camp let out, Emmy spent time with us in Miami. I thought decorating my house would make it feel cozy, but something was missing. Alan had more hand-me-down furniture than I did, but to me his house felt like home. When we were with him, and especially him and Noah, the four of us were a family.

Family is what I yearned for. My mother lost her husband at 33, nine years and four children after she was married. With her wavy black hair, green eyes and willowy figure, she looked more like a Greek goddess than a grieving widow. Her fairy tale life turned into a nightmare when my father drove to his job in the city and never returned. The roads were icy, and his car was hit by a truck. He died instantly.

The dads in our small town tried to help. They pitched in to rake leaves in our yard in the fall and shoveled snow from our driveway in winter. Nonetheless, my enchanted childhood was never the same. I promised myself when I grew up, I would never live far from my work or allow my husband to either.

If only Mom had chosen one of the many suitors who proposed marriage, my sisters and I could have grown up with a father. She said she didn't remarry because no man had the same qualities as my dad. Perhaps they didn't, but maybe they had other ones. Eventually, I came to understand it was her life and her decision to make. But I was determined not to make the same one.

Despite my desire for a husband, I could never trade my heart for the kind of security a man like Larry could provide. My love for Scott and Seth had been real. Scott walked away and Seth refused to commit. That didn't mean I'd be alone forever. Alan was a dreamer, like me. He was passionate, emotional and brave. I was certain he was my destiny. He said he wanted to marry again. I prayed that time would come...*soon*. That's when a suitor from my past turned up and caused me to question my decision.

Prince Charming #1 Returns

In January, I was standing on the selling floor questioning how I could survive another season in Valentino's cutthroat environment. Corporate had raised our monthly sales goals to numbers that seemed impossible to achieve. It was beneath me to fight over clients with Cedric. Jocelyn decided that Deirdre, the intern she sent to help out, would now be a commissioned salesperson. Our store didn't have enough square footage, clients or merchandise to support three salespeople. Carol, Liv's replacement, had been useful in keeping my clients away from Cedric, but now Deirdre needed her as an ally; she had no time to concentrate on my customers. If ever I needed a Prince Charming to rescue me, it was now.

Suddenly, as if a fairy godmother waved her magic wand, in walked Harry Kent. I hadn't seen him in three years, when we went on a series of dates that turned from bad to worse—the prenuptial agreement he brought up way too early and the drastic steps he took to make sure he wouldn't have kids. My mind reviewed these reasons I ended it with him as if I were studying for a pop quiz I had just been given the chance to take over. As I thought back, my eyes landed on his tan work boots. I guess it hadn't registered when I told him that work boots were not proper footwear for Palm Beach unless you were employed in the construction industry, which he was not.

He looked the same, but there was a sadness lurking underneath his cheery demeanor. He relayed the news of his father's death. He was in town trying to collect pictures of his dad to display at the funeral.

"Do you have any connections at *Palm Beach Society Magazine*, Kari? I just came from their offices. They sent me away." I told him I was sorry for his loss and that yes, I did. James Jennings Sheeran, the publisher, was a good friend of mine. During my time at Valerie's, his magazine was the best place to advertise our products, after *The Shiny Sheet,* of course. Year after year, I gave their staff writers fresh material and print-ready photos to make sure our editorial made its way to a prime spot in the magazine. Scott and I had graced its pages many times. Harry asked if I'd call James on his behalf. I said yes, thinking it was unlike James not to honor the request of Sidney Kent's son.

"By the way, did you tell them who you are?" I asked. Now my eyes were drawn to his crumpled ivory fisherman's sweater. Maybe his attire was the reason they shunned him. He hadn't lasted long enough to receive a cashmere sweater from me.

"No. Why would that make a difference? Where I come from it doesn't matter who you are when you're trying to get some help."

"That's nice, Harry," I said sarcastically. "But this is Palm Beach. Here, who you are is the only thing that matters. Go back to their office, ask for Mr. Sheeran, mention my name and tell them you are Sidney Kent's son. I guarantee, they will help you."

He did as I suggested, and the magazine gave him the pictures. Despite his grief, I could tell Harry was happy to see me. Alan and I had been dating for almost two years and I still had no idea where we stood. He still had not said those three words that begin with "I" and end with "you" every woman waits for.

Should I give Harry a second chance? Alan and I had vacationed in Aspen last July. People from Palm Beach called it a winter wonderland, but it was magical in the summer. It had so many things I loved: mountains, clement weather, shopping and a small-town feeling like that of the Island. How bad could it be to have homes in Palm Beach and Aspen, like many of my clients did? Could it be more than a coincidence that Harry showed up now, just as I was plotting my way out of this job and its toxic atmosphere?

My dream of having more kids ended when I fell in love with a man who had three. The prenuptial agreement Harry insisted on didn't matter now—the equity in my house would take care of Emmy and me if the relationship didn't last. The reasons that I'd crossed Harry off my list, at least on paper, were no longer the dealbreakers they once were. But as I mulled it over, I concluded that my instincts had been right the first time. He didn't have the fire in his belly to make a big mark on the world like I hoped to. His ancestors had made sure he didn't need to.

My friend Lynn, from my city days, had smarts that were way more valuable than the CPA degree she held. I trusted her insight when it came to both finance and love. As I caught her up on my "will we, won't we" with Harry during one of our weekly phone calls, she told me in no uncertain terms that Harry was not the one for me. She didn't say why, only that I'd figure it out myself.

I knew what it was. I was searching for a soul mate, someone whose dreams aligned with mine. I hoped that the love between us would allow us to create something bigger than either of us could on our own. I wanted my own legacy, not to live off one started by someone's grandfather that I could play no part in building.

My heart told me Alan was the prince that held the missing glass slipper, the mate to one I had in my closet. He just had to get down on one knee and slide it on my foot. He may not have said he loved me, but I was committed to loving him. I wasn't ready to give up, not yet. What was two years when I was looking for a love to last a lifetime?

As I pondered these thoughts my phone rang and beckoned me back to real life. My babysitter was sick, and Emmy was stranded at school. It was too late to call another mom to pick her up. I asked Carol to show my client, Hilary, the pieces I had on hold for her. Hilary needed to buy these items before they mysteriously ended up walking out the door with one of Cedric's clients and I lost out on a big commission.

Spring Fling with Faith

There were so many days I wanted to quit this job, give my keys to Carol and never look back. It was all too much for me: the pettiness, Cedric trying to sabotage every sale I closed and a corporate office in New York, 1,500 miles away, telling us what to do to make a store in this idiosyncratic town succeed.

Each time I wanted to hit "send" on the resignation letter I'd saved on my laptop, someone or something happened to make me stay. This time, it was Faith from Philadelphia. She and her husband left The Colony Hotel, crossed County Road and entered Valentino. Faith had a huge heart-shaped pink diamond on her ring finger and a wedding band underneath. Any good salesperson knows an older man shopping with his wife means a sale. And this time it was me who made it happen in a big way. They left a few hours later after spending $100,000. I enjoyed sharing Faith's excitement as she discovered the Valentino brand and our spring/summer collection. I was unaware how much she'd spent until Carol rang it up.

Unbeknownst to me, no other salesperson at the company had ever sold this dollar amount to one person in one day. It was nice to have Jocelyn congratulate me and gift me a red cashmere and lace Valentino shawl. But the niceness soured when she took my accomplishment and used it to question the associates at the other stores as to why they never had a sale this big. Now, when I spoke to the sales associates from the other boutiques, they were cool and distant. The income gained from this sale wouldn't be worth it if colleagues I considered friends become foes.

Nonetheless, Faith and I formed a bond that day that led to a lasting relationship. I was flattered when she asked me to meet her at our New York boutique to be her personal stylist. As nice as the commission may have been, the aggravation that followed wouldn't be. The New York store had a staff that could assist her. I referred her to a colleague whose sense of style surpassed mine.

I disagreed with Valentino's philosophy that competition between salespeople drove sales higher. I'd built my client base to a level where I earned a good living. My nest egg was replenished. After two years, I was earning more from just selling than I had as a store manager, supply chain coordinator, marketing director and salesperson at Valerie's. The sales report released each month was proof that Cedric and I reached our goals, as did the store. So why did work feel like a war zone?

I hadn't smoked since my single days. Now, before I went to sleep, I found myself outside on my loggia, slipping back into the nasty habit of puffing on a cigarette to ease my stress. Each time I thought I couldn't stand this job another minute, a customer would make me feel so valued I couldn't go. The next one to do so was Daphne.

Ring-a-Ding Daphne

Daphne represented the kind of wife I would have been if I'd married a guy with money. She had wispy bangs that she wore with shoulder-length brown hair. She carried herself more like a Girl Scout than a wife getting a wing of a museum named for her. I could picture bumping into her midday at Forty Carrots in Bloomingdale's. The oversized cups of frozen yogurt they served were the go-to food for girls like us with an appetite for shopping. Apart from being one of my best clients, I adored Daphne. She and I were close in age, as were Emmy and her daughter.

Our bond was cemented when I gave Daphne's daughter a gift. I'd hoped to get her something at Aristokids, Emmy's favorite shop, but Cedric called in sick, and I couldn't step out. In a pinch, I had our seamstress, Stella, sew together two Valentino silk scarves. Spaghetti straps at the shoulders secured it. Daphne's daughter would never forget the day she became a teen and got her first bespoke designer dress. Daphne valued my taste so much she was determined to never let me leave Valentino. I had become so good at choosing her clothing, she promoted me to fine jewelry.

"Kari, I need you to go look at a ring I saw at the estate jewelers next door. My husband has agreed to replace my engagement ring with a bigger one for my 40th birthday."

I told Carol I needed to get some fresh air. I stepped outside and turned left. The gleaming jewels in the adjacent shop's window would cause any passerby to stop in their tracks, even if they were too shy to go in. I entered the store and asked the owner to show me the ring Daphne had her eye on. He and I knew each other. Emmy and his daughter were in the same Sunday school class. He seemed a bit surprised at my request, as if he was trying to figure out how someone like me knew the caliber of person who might become a customer of *his*.

When I mentioned Daphne was a client of Valentino, his pace quickened as he walked over to a display case and pulled the ring out. It wasn't big by Palm Beach standards, about six carats, but the cut and color were perfection. He told me it was an antique piece by JAR, a jeweler from Paris. I saw a price tag dangling from it that read $200,000. That didn't seem like so much, considering Daphne spent half that amount at Valentino last year. Daphne called the following day. She didn't care that I was with a client. She insisted that Carol get me on the phone.

"Did you have a chance to see the ring, Kari?" I could tell she was desperate to hear my opinion.

"I did."

"Well, what do you think?" I could hear her holding her breath on the other end of the line as she waited for my reply.

"It is the most stunning ring I've ever seen, and you must have it," I replied. She asked me about the family that owned the business. I assured her of their reputation and my personal relationship with not just the owner but his wife, who supported the same charities I did.

"Kari, I completely trust your taste and if Craig gets it for me, it's all because of you, so you better tell the owner I'm only buying the ring if you get a piece of the sale." It seemed vulgar to me that clients knew about the commission structure that existed in the luxury goods industry. Not once in five years did a customer mention compensation at Valerie's.

I figured if the commission for jewelry was the same as it was at Valentino, my share would be $12,000. I was never comfortable negotiating about money. Instead, I asked the owner to give Craig a fair price for the ring. Despite Craig's hesitation, Daphne got the ring. Like most "Old Testament" types, as Valerie called people of the Jewish faith, Craig hoped to get one wholesale, not a piece from an estate jeweler and not one sitting in a showcase on Worth Avenue. His wife, like me, had exquisite taste. However, I had read the price tag wrong. I was off by one zero. The price of the ring was $2 million, not $200,000! That meant my cut might have been $120,000. That was more than I earned in a year! That kind of cash could have come in handy. I didn't dwell on it. After all, I had gained a regular client. I was overwhelmed by her loyalty. Daphne insisted on taking me to lunch to celebrate the ring acquisition. Once we were seated at Ta-boo, she presented me with a jewel-encrusted gold picture frame.

"It's a small token of my appreciation. I can never thank you enough, Kari." She told me I was "too good a girl" to remain single. She insisted on fixing me up with one of Craig's friends, a guy who worked at his hedge fund. "The Robin Hood Gala is next month—we can all go together," she said. This affair was the biggest charity event in the country. It would be a dream to go, especially after Daphne told me Beyoncé was performing. But I declined. After Seth and Scott, I decided I was finished with guys in the finance field. Their inability to share emotional intimacy in a relationship seemed directly related to the cash they were always counting.

"Thanks, but no thanks," I said.

Daphne looked at me as if I were a kid who had just turned down an extra piece of candy on Halloween. It wasn't every day that a client offered to introduce you to a well-heeled friend of her husband.

"I think I need a guy who's smart, but also creative and sensitive, maybe more of an artist type," I said. Daphne shook her head.

"I don't think so," she said, sounding like a physics professor teaching an advanced-level class. "Don't you know why that type is called starving?" Before I could respond, she answered her own question. "Because they are known for eating from everyone else's table. Really, Kari, I want the best for you, but you're never going to find a guy who is a money earner who's an artist."

"I think I already have," I said, smiling. "The guy I'm dating used to make women's clothing. Now he is a powerful trial lawyer who defends people for free if they can't afford his fees. He loves the theater and ballet, and he plays the clarinet," I went on, hoping to change her mind. Daphne laughed sarcastically.

"The guy you're describing sounds like one that could only exist in a fairy tale. Keep me in the loop, Kari, if it doesn't work out. Craig has lots of single friends that would die to meet a girl like you."

"Okay," I said to be polite.

As I walked across Worth Avenue to the shop, I tucked the frame inside my tote bag. I was tipsy from the mimosa Daphne ordered for me. I had no desire to deal with the devil in the shop named Cedric, whose horns would sprout if he learned Daphne had given me a gift. I reflected on what she had said. I knew I wouldn't find my prince among Craig's friends. I'd almost given up hope he was even out there. Would Alan ever be ready to audition for the part? Even the beast from *Beauty and the Beast* displayed his affection for Belle by presenting her with his library because he knew she loved books. Alan hadn't done anything yet to show me he was anything more than a boyfriend. Then, someone resurfaced and gave me the clarity I needed.

No More Knights in Shining Armor

As my two-year anniversary at Valentino approached, I'd fallen further into Dante's hell and Virgil was nowhere in sight. Now that the Season was over, I was about to embark on a third summer where business basically shut down as clients left for cooler parts of the country. I complained more and more to Matt that I needed a Prince Charming to rescue me. I was half joking, but Matt and the other men in my life felt my only way out of this madness was, well…a man. "How about that trust-funder from Colorado?" Matt asked. "Or the oilman from Maine?" I explained my recent run-in with Harry and why he was no longer a prospect. As for Larry? Well, poor Larry—he was so respectful and patient. As I reflected on our relationship, I remembered I still had a home to run and a child to feed, and that meant going grocery shopping.

Grocery shopping was a gruesome chore for me. Unlike fashion, which thrived on novelty, food stores could get away with selling the same items year after year and still make a profit. In luxury retail, a season could completely flop if, God forbid, the designer didn't produce a collection that captivated buyers. I was deep in the throes of analyzing this concept when my cart crashed into another customer. When I looked up, I realized it was Harriet, my former co-worker from Valerie's.

"I'm so sorry," I said to her as I gave her a hug. "How are you, Harriet? Happy Mother's Day."

"I'm well, Kari. Happy Mother's Day to you too."

NO MORE KNIGHTS IN SHINING ARMOR

"Have you spoken to Larry?" I asked. Harriet's daughter was married to Larry's son, so if anyone knew what was going on with him it would be her. It was odd for Larry to let a season pass without calling me. Even though we were no longer dating, he had stayed in touch.

"I called to wish him a happy New Year. A woman answered and said she would give him the message. When he didn't call back, I assumed she was a girlfriend who wasn't too eager to let another contestant enter the competition to snag a sugar daddy," I said.

"You didn't hear, Kari?" Harriet asked, giving me a strange look.

"Hear about what?" I asked.

"He died of a stroke in February."

"I didn't. I'm so sorry, Harriet." The first thought to cross my mind was a selfish one.

I'd always thought of Larry as a backup plan—like when you splurge on a new outfit for a party but know if you change your mind, you have another one in your closet that will work just as well. This was not something I wanted to share with Harriet.

"He was quite a guy, wasn't he?" I said instead. How could I forget his generosity during our courtship, especially when he offered to pay off my mortgage?

"He always carried a torch for you, Kari," Harriet said. I hated to think of him dying alone.

"Was he with anyone?"

"Apparently, several young women; let's just say there were a lot of little black dresses at the funeral."

I briefly relayed the story to Matt, who said, "I told you dating a guy that much older was a bad idea. With Harry and Larry out of the picture, I guess the only prince left is Alan."

"No...I don't think he's ready to ascend the throne. He can barely take care of himself," I said without hesitation. "He's still supporting his first wife, his college-age daughters and his son. The last thing he needs is another person to take care of."

"Well, if he can't take care of you, why are you with him?" Matt asked in his ever-practical way. In the world of 2006 Palm Beach, a grown woman like myself would be a fool to settle down with a man that couldn't provide for her. Matt was just saying out loud what everyone else was thinking.

My customers felt the same way. Mr. Curtis, a trims supplier from New York, was convinced Alan was in it for the sex. I don't know why it's always assumed that the man is the one in a relationship for sex. In this case, because of the distance between us geographically and age-wise, it was me who was left wanting more in that department. Didn't Mr. Curtis realize how hard it was to find sex in a town where most of the men were either married, senior citizens or both? It seemed like a curse that now, when I wanted sex more than ever, I was single and living in a house with an adolescent daughter who refused to be left with a sitter. It was as if God made the early 40s the sexual prime for women to give them one last chance to procreate.

Even Les, our visual merchandiser, was no fan of Alan's. Once a month, Les and I worked together when he came to change the display windows. It takes two pairs of hands to dress and undress mannequins. While Cedric often vanished into a closet of Valentino couture when Les arrived, I always helped. I'd learned from doing the window displays at Valerie's how valuable they are to attract clients. Les thought it was ridiculous that I was driving through three counties to pick up the son of a man who wouldn't commit from baseball practice.

"Kari, this guy needs to sign on the dotted line. You are doing way more than what the job of a girlfriend entails."

"Les, are you my fairy godmother?" I would ask him teasingly.

"Kari, this is no fairy tale, so stop pretending you are Cinderella. If this Alan or Allie or whatever the hell you call him can only be a part-time prince, seeing you on weekends, you need to find another knight in shining armor. Stop worrying about this boy and baseball. You live in Palm Beach. Balls take place every night of the week. Borrow a gown and go to one."

I laughed. I had never bought into the Cinderella story my mom told me. My prince wasn't spending his evenings at any ball. I imagined my fairytale ending would be more like that of Princess Jasmine's from the Disney version of *Aladdin*. The kind of guy I would fall for would be a diamond in the rough, who by some act of magic, or perhaps faith, would become a prince. A casting agent would be hard-pressed to find a better actor for the role of Aladdin than Alan. If I pronounced it differently, "Allie," the nickname I gave him that first night we were intimate was the same as the prince's in the movie—Prince Ali. Alan's empire might be smaller than those of the other suitors, but together we could make it grow. With Harry and Larry out of the picture, I knew in my heart Alan was destined to be my prince. He just needed to rub the magic lamp.

Until then, I had my own kingdom to rule.

One Door Closes, Another Opens

December, just before season, was an inopportune time to leave my job at Valentino. But after 12 collections I knew that luxury retail was not for me. I missed overseeing a product from the design phase to the finished one, whether it was a cashmere sweater, an exotic skin handbag or a men's suit. I longed for the calls from Dee, my columnist friend at *The Shiny Sheet*, that bordered on harassment, to deliver advertising copy to her before the paper's deadline. I craved the collaboration with a designer I'd had in my last three jobs. I despised competing for customers. I liked seeing my efforts turn into profits for a company but hated that my contribution was only measured by the dollar amount in a commission check.

Starting in September, Carol agreed to let me work three days a week until our core clients returned. After Thanksgiving, I'd be required to work a five-day week, including two Saturdays a month. If Alan couldn't come to Palm Beach, that meant two weekends without seeing him, and I wasn't willing to give up that time. Our relationship had advanced from algebra to calculus. He finally confessed he loved me. He told me while we were on vacation in Aspen. How could I forget the suite with the spacious outdoor terrace he booked? When I suggested we switch rooms because it was so grand, he laughed. "I love you, Kari! I wanted to impress you." That wasn't the setting I'd imagined when I'd dreamed about how he'd deliver those words. It didn't matter. *He said them!* I wanted to enjoy this moment. I didn't want to turn the dialogue to me by saying it back. He knew how I felt; I'd told him months ago.

"I'm happy you finally said it. I was beginning to think you didn't have a heart."

"Even the Tin Man had a heart. Mine just stopped beating for a while. Don't worry about the room. I'll let you in on a secret. You know my friend Lenny, who travels a lot? He gave me a tip. He told me to reserve a regular room and when I get to the hotel, slip a hundred-dollar bill into the clerk's hand and ask for an upgrade. The suite cost the same as a regular room."

Alan and I were enjoying one last weekend in Miami before we settled into our separate routines of packing lunches, dropping off and picking up our kids from school, working, preparing supper and helping with homework—all without the companionship of the other's presence at the end of the day.

We were sipping smoothies on a park bench when Alan's casual demeanor turned serious. In his soft voice, with just the right bit of roughness that let everyone know he was a New Yorker, he turned to me and said, "Noah thinks it would be good for you and Emmy to come live with us so we can be together all the time, not just in the summer and on weekends." I smiled, thinking it was so typical Alan to embark on a subject as weighty as this one from his son's viewpoint.

"What about you, Allie? Is this what you want?" I was almost afraid to hear his answer.

"I know we've talked about this, Kari, and I would never bring it up if I wasn't ready to make a commitment. I don't have a lot of money, but I have a big heart, and I'm willing to give it to you if you will take it. I want you to marry me, stop working at that stupid job and be a real mother to both kids."

My first thought was to debate what working had to do with me being a "real" mother, but my mind clung to the word I had been longing to hear for the last year. It was the one that began with "m" and ended with "y." (And it wasn't money!) It had taken Alan two years to tell me he loved me. I had figured it may take two more before he even thought about marriage. Each time I doubted we had a future, I reminded myself that he spoke of marriage. I prayed in time he'd commit. I had completely missed the signs that the time was *now*. If missing those signs wasn't enough, his next statement left me breathless.

"And if everything goes well, you can have a baby."

Not only was I short of oxygen, but I was also speechless. Since his divorce, Alan struggled to support the kids he had on his own. Even for a lawyer, a mortgage, two girls in college and Noah's private school and sports expenses along with day-to-day living in Miami added up. Why would he think of having another baby? As I tried to process all this, I thought about what I loved the most about him. The first thing that came to mind was that he was a family man. Life was best for him when he had his kids and me and Emmy around. If he was asking me to marry him, having another child was just a piece of that puzzle.

I, being the practical one, had imagined a future that consisted of the two of us and the four children. The girls would be away at university, coming home on holidays. I'd be taking care of Emmy and Noah—watching their games, volunteering at school and making party favors—without the pressure of full-time work. A baby had never been part of the plan. Did I really want to start all over again? At my age, was it even possible? Alan was waiting for an answer. I chose my next sentence carefully.

"I've been waiting to hear those words since our eighth date," I said. He laughed. "You know there is nothing I want more than to be your wife and bring our lives together, but I have to see how Emmy feels first." Every decision I made since I gave birth to Emmy had been about what was best for her. She just started eighth grade. I couldn't imagine deciding her fate for the next four years without her input.

"If Emmy agrees, it's a yes."

"Kari, Emmy wants you to be happy. She's going to say yes. And she likes me, I can tell." Alan was right; Emmy was on board. That meant we would be heading to Miami in May when school ended.

I needed to make my house shine like the star it was and get it sold before the luxury buyers left town. Could I work one more Season and do repairs on my house at the same time? I'd prioritized Emmy, my clients and Alan over caring for it. The neglect showed on the torn screens, chipped floor tiles and outdated appliances. Despite Alan's efforts, the landscaping was never restored to its pre-hurricane glory. I pulled out my property tax bill. Column one told me how much I owed for the year. Column two listed the value of my house. Based on column two, each year for the past five years, I'd saved more than I earned. The money just happened to be deposited into my "house account" instead of my bank account. In school, I'd gotten A's in every subject except math. Calculus was as foreign to me as the language spoken by my Greek relatives. Grandma Margaret told me to put aside 10 percent of my income each year for the future. How could I go wrong if I had saved 100 percent of it? The lakefront home across the street sold to private equity titan Henry Kravis for a record price. It was time to make a withdrawal.

Builders were grabbing up lots the size of mine to tear down the existing homes and construct new ones. My realtor told me buyers who couldn't wait needed homes that were move-in ready. She said if I did some minor repairs, mine could fetch $2.5 million. This amount was five times what I paid for it nine years ago!

I recalled my last home improvement project. It was stressful ordering materials, coordinating deliveries, scheduling tradesmen and making sure the job was done properly, all within the time limit allowed by a permit. At that time, I worked a mile down the road and had Valerie to cover for me if I was needed at the house. Valentino was farther away. Carol's strength was in operations; she couldn't close my sales like Liv could. Cedric refused to help, even if it meant money for the company, because it meant no commission for him. That was my dilemma. I couldn't be in two places at the same time and earn income from both. I had six months of expenses stashed away and a home equity line of credit in place to pay for house repairs. Did I stay at a job I despised to earn a paycheck, or did I use that time to do work on my house and gain access to the seven-figure profit I would have when I sold it?

I wish I could say I left Valentino because I no longer needed to earn a living by selling a designer label along with my soul. I wish I could say it was because I had the foresight to see that the housing market was about to come crashing down just as quickly as it had gone up and the time to get out was now. I wish I could say it was because I loved renovation projects and couldn't wait to tackle this one. It was none of these things that made me resign.

In fact, it wasn't things at all, but people: Emmy and Noah. I'd held a full-time job for most of Emmy's life. For the last few months of middle school, I wanted to be the first one to see her when school let out, instead of my babysitter. I planned to relish every minute in the pickup line. I promised not to be annoyed by the distracted moms chatting on their phones while trying to merge into one lane. For years, I told myself I wasn't missing much time with Emmy. Four out of five days she had activities, I reasoned. But soon that time would be gone. In the same way a child squeezes a mother's hand in a crowd, I wanted to hold onto these months and not let go until graduation.

"It's good Emmy sees me and Scott working during spring break," I told myself as all the other families departed for the Keys or Colorado. "Our clients are in town then," I told Emmy, without guilt, when she asked why we couldn't go away like everyone else did.

ONE DOOR CLOSES, ANOTHER OPENS

"My clients need to be dressed for the remaining parties of the season, and tax time is an important time for Dad," I said, wondering who I was really trying to convince. Suddenly, it hit me. Despite what Alan hinted at, I might never have another child. This was her last spring vacation before high school. I wanted to travel somewhere neither of us had ever been. I was tired of the reasons why we couldn't.

Then there was Noah. Alan's office was 45 minutes from their house, and Alan was often stuck in court in the afternoon. Noah was left stranded at school. Noah was a poor student. Alan was convinced his only path to college was a baseball scholarship. The public high school had a much better team, so Noah transferred from his private school to the public one. Neither Alan nor Noah knew the kids or parents at his new school; it was difficult to find a carpool.

After spring break, Scott asked if he could have Emmy two nights a week instead of one. I was happy to grant his request. I knew from not having a father how much a girl needs one. This schedule gave me time to pick up Noah midweek, make supper and help him with homework. It broke my heart to think of him stranded on the baseball field after the other boys had been picked up. The four of us would soon be family. I wanted to show Noah I was just as committed to him as I was to Emmy.

As every working person revved up for the Season, I switched gears and looked forward to being a mother to two teenagers. Before I ever bought my first business suit, I longed to be a mother. My childhood friends talked about being fashion designers or teachers. When the conversation came around to me, it was always the same. I dreamed of being a mother. I wanted to have a boy first, then a girl, so the girl would have a big brother to look after her.

In the home I grew up in, it had been my mom and four girls. Instead of feeling like she was the head of our household, I felt like we were dolls she was playing house with. I worried what would become of us if we didn't meet husbands and marry in our 20s like she had. Mom said she supported us with money from her father's fragrance company. What would happen if those funds ran out?

I yearned for a family like the ones behind the white picket fences in the town I grew up in. That meant one headed by a hardworking husband who valued his wife, the kind who came home for dinner and had time to coach his kids' sports teams on the weekends. Beginning in college, with one boyfriend after the next, I pictured my future family with this man at the helm. My dream was about to come true. I couldn't be happier. Nothing could make me change my mind about resigning. That's not to say people didn't try. Carol asked, "Are you sure you want to leave just before Season? This is the last collection to be designed by Mr. Valentino before he steps down."

"Why don't you take a leave of absence instead of resigning, Kari?" Jocelyn suggested. "You've built up such a nice clientele; they won't forget you after one Season." I pictured Cedric and Deirdre fighting over my clients. Once they sank their claws into them and began taking care of them "Kari style," it would be difficult for me to reclaim them. Cedric and Deirdre had learned from a very good teacher. The methods I used to attract clients were what kept them coming back. Once I left the company, I couldn't expect these customers to remain loyal to me.

In the past, every decision I had ever made—both personal and professional—I had been uncertain about. This time, I had no doubt I was making the right choice. My tenure as a salesperson at Valentino lasted a little less than three years. In that time, I'd established a loyal clientele and only twice missed my sales goal. There were some wins to be proud of, but my mental health was at risk. On my last day at Valentino, I handed over my keys and the clicker that opened the gate to the private parking lot behind the store. My days as a shopgirl were done. I was never coming back.

There Goes Someone Pulling the Rug Again

It was December. Hurricane season scooted out the door behind November and the holiday season was upon us. This was the first time in years I was able to enjoy the festivities with my family and friends instead of helping clients choose gifts for theirs. My life was on track, or it was until disaster struck.

The storm hit while I was out holiday shopping with Bri. I made it home despite unusually heavy rain and hail. When I entered the house, I saw that water had gushed over the threshold of my front door, past the foyer all the way into the living room. The Persian rug that survived three hurricanes was soaked! I walked into the house, my arms loaded with gifts, and cried. The pinks, blues and greens had run onto the ivory wool background. Had I been home, I could have rolled it up and saved it. To make matters worse, I was alone. Emmy was skiing with Scott and Alan was behaving oddly. Ever since his dad's birthday dinner, he took longer to return my calls. When he did, he seemed distant. I had accepted his proposal and promised him that Emmy and I would move to Miami in the spring. Why wasn't he making plans to get together?

Before Christmas he called to say he was going to Washington, D.C. for a federal case. Did he think I was naïve enough to believe this? Unless you worked in retail, which up until two weeks ago I had, most businesses shut down right before the holidays. Alan said he'd call when he arrived. He never did. My calls to him went unanswered. My emotions vacillated from anger to grief at the same time.

I did the only thing I could do and made a date with the insurance adjuster to document the rug, damaged dining table and other items. He asked why a pretty girl like me was alone during the holidays. *A series of poor choices in men.* As he examined the rug, I told him how my boyfriend of two and a half years had just pulled an even bigger rug from underneath me. I explained about quitting my job to begin a life with this boyfriend who recently proposed. I wasn't looking for sympathy or special treatment; I was simply venting. I could tell this guy felt sorry for me. He said that most insurance policies don't cover antique rugs; however, he would try to get the company to reimburse me for mine.

"How much did you pay for it?" he asked.

"I have no idea…it was a gift from my mother."

"Can you ask her if she has the receipt?"

"I can, but it was a gift, so I doubt she does."

"Well, for now, let's roll it up so the restoration company can pick it up." We each took a side and started rolling, and he pointed to a price tag sewn on the back. I was shocked to see it said $46000. The adjuster took a picture of it.

The Island was abuzz with holiday spirit. I attempted to join the festivities, but my heart wasn't in celebration mode. Alan returned before New Year's and acted like nothing was wrong. I told him I wasn't buying his fictional account of his last-minute business trip. He tried to present every piece of evidence possible in his defense. I should have known better than to go up against a guy who argued for a living.

He didn't even ask what I was doing for New Year's, which was nothing. I thought we'd be spending it together, like we did the previous year. I had imagined a fire roaring at his house and the two of us and Noah would sip champagne, dine on stone crabs, creamed spinach and key lime pie and watch *Dick Clark's New*

THERE GOES SOMEONE PULLING THE RUG AGAIN

Year's Rockin' Eve. Alan knew I looked forward to watching the emerging hip-hop artists showcased each year. It had become our tradition. Or at least, I thought it had.

When Lynn heard I was alone, she invited me to fly to New York to see the show from a private box in Times Square. I declined her offer. I was in no mood to celebrate with anyone. It would just be me and Dick this year, rocking around my living room. *How could I have read this situation so wrong?* When Alan didn't call all week, I called him and left a message. When he returned my call, it was as if he was doing so out of duty, not because he wanted to talk to me. I couldn't believe this was happening.

"Alan, I don't know what's going on, but whatever it is, I deserve an explanation."

"I'm so sorry, Kari. You're right, I owe you at least that, but I'm not ready to talk yet. I think it's best I text you." *Coward.*

"That is not acceptable. Call me when you feel you can talk."

I tossed Emmy's applications to the private high schools in Miami in the trash. I reminded myself of the real reason I quit my job: to spend my daughter's last semester of eighth grade with her. I flung myself into that role, along with getting my house in saleable condition and creating favors for charity events and friends' parties. I had come up with the idea to use cellophane to wrap gifts when Emmy was in preschool. For a new mom saving for a house, wrapping paper was expensive; using cellophane and tissue paper was an affordable alternative. Pulling the sides of the cellophane and tissue around the gift and tying a velvet or satin ribbon at the top looked festive. Crafting these gifts was an outlet for my creativity. Ben was starting a Jewish day school on the Island, and the fundraiser was next week. Mountains of notebooks and pencils were stacked on my dining table waiting to be turned into favors. Without a job, I had no money to give, so donating these gifts was my way to support my friends and give back to the community.

Breaking Free From the Valentine's Curse

Valentine's Day comes each year, whether you're in love or not. That year, not being in love was trumped by a fiancé who took away the love I had waited for so patiently. My heart was in pieces, like the individually wrapped chocolates Emmy gave me from Hoffman's. Even my favorite, milk chocolate with a peach crème filling, tasted bitter this year. I didn't expect to hear from Alan. When he called to say he was thinking of me, the warmth of my favorite holiday was hanging in the back of my closet next to my summer wardrobe. Alan wasn't ready to talk so I made up an excuse to end our conversation. A week later, he called again, and said he was ready to talk, if I was ready to listen.

"Go ahead."

He proceeded to tell me he got cold feet at the thought of me moving in. He didn't realize the seriousness of it all when he asked me to marry him. He panicked. At the same time, a woman he dated in college called him. She'd seen him with me in Aspen and wanted a do-over at a chance for a relationship with him. *Nothing like seeing an ex with a much younger woman to make an old flame want you back.* I listened quietly as he spoke. Alan said he needed to see if there was anything between them before I moved in. He thought he could do it without me finding out.

"You must not have loved me enough to commit. Thanks for being honest. I'm glad I found out before we moved to Miami." There was silence on both ends of the phone before he spoke again.

"Are you okay, Kari?"

"I have been through much worse than this. I'll be fine." That's what I told him, but truthfully, I was worried. Ever since he brought up the idea of me having a baby, we'd stopped using protection. The red-cloaked friend that visited like clockwork hadn't come in two months. My doctor was on vacation. I drove to a Planned Parenthood in a strip mall in West Palm to find out why. As I exited the clinic, I spotted Rabbi Moshe dining outside with another rabbi. I'm sure my face was redder than the Valentine's Day decorations in the store windows. How would I explain what I was doing here to a man whose religion didn't condone sex before marriage?

"Dropping off an auction item, Kari?" *What a perfect cover up,* I thought.

Season was in full throttle. The smartest charities asked for donations early in the year before businesses could say they had exceeded their budget.

"Yes, I was," I said. "Can I bring the one I have for the temple's auction to you tomorrow?"

"Of course."

The next day, I found myself sobbing in Rabbi Moshe's office as I rehashed the story of Alan and our breakup. He smiled as he slid a box of tissues across his large walnut desk so I could take one.

"Everything will work out the way it's supposed to. Look how long Rachel waited for Jacob," he said, referencing a woman in the Bible who waited seven years before she married the man she loved. I told Rabbi Moshe that Scott and Candace were expecting a child, the sibling I'd hoped to give Emmy. Candace had been trying to get pregnant since their wedding. Four years and numerous rounds of IVF later, she'd succeeded.

"Man plans, God laughs. Everything will turn out how it's supposed to. You've heard my sermons enough times to know this, Kari. You can still have children. If that's what's meant for you, it will happen. Sarah gave birth to Isaac when she was 90."

In the Hebrew Bible, Sarah was the mother of the Jewish people. I had always thought this story was metaphorical, but Rabbi Moshe wasn't one you questioned about these things. He had a way of spinning a story that could turn anyone into a believer.

"Do you know why divorce is permitted in the Jewish religion?" he asked. Before I could come up with an answer, he told me. "It's because by staying with someone you're unhappy with, you're depriving someone else of their 'bashert.'" *Bashert* is the Hebrew word for destiny. Used this way, it refers to the person you are meant to be with. I reflected on his words. If Scott had stayed with me, he wouldn't have met Candace.

Emmy might never have had a sister or brother. Candace understood Scott in a way I never could. She was sensible. If we were shoes, she would be ballet flats and I would be stilettos. Unlike me, Candace wouldn't venture out at night in search of a maroon Sharpie to match the ink on a trunk show invitation; not if her husband found it a waste of time to write a note on each one, as I did, to entice people to come.

I'd heard Rabbi Moshe had a career selling life-saving medical supplies before he decided to lead a congregation and save souls instead. At this moment, I was grateful he gave it up. I wanted to jump out of my seat and throw my arms around him. However, in the Orthodox version of Judaism he practiced, a man is not allowed to touch a woman unless she is his wife. I would never do anything to disrespect him. Instead, I used those arms, which suddenly felt much lighter, to pull out the Valentino clutch for the auction from my canvas tote bag. I was rushing to get Emmy to a high school interview, but Rabbi Moshe's words soothed me as much as those of the nurse who assured me I wasn't pregnant.

It felt like forever, not three months, that I'd driven Emmy to and from school, play practice, tutoring and dance classes. In addition, I'd emailed every builder in town to partner with me to build a spec house on my lot in case my realtor couldn't find a buyer. I did all this while mending my heart, which hadn't just broken but shattered like a crystal vase when Alan changed his mind about marriage. I felt like an actress in a Hallmark Channel movie—like the feeling of abandonment snowballing me was happening to her and not me. It would have been one thing for Alan to break it off with me, to say he wasn't ready. However, before he did, he'd asked me to quit my job, uproot my daughter and move in with him—not to mention to become what mattered most to me—his wife. An engagement accompanied by a ring never mattered to me, but maybe the ancient Romans who came up with this tradition were onto something. Perhaps the purpose of the ring was to show that a man was investing in marriage.

Alan knew the money I earned at Valentino was my livelihood, how I supported myself and Emmy. He was 13 years older, a professional and a business owner. How could he do this to me? If he wanted out of our relationship, he should have thought about that before he asked me to marry him. Emmy was at a turning point in her life; she was leaving the Island to attend high school. Without relatives nearby, this community was her family. Didn't Alan realize what a huge decision it was for us to relocate to Miami?

Emmy's transcripts and letters of recommendation had been sent to the three best private high schools in the area. Today, we were off to Saint Andrew's High School, the only one in South Florida that had both day students and boarders. We left early, not knowing what type of traffic we would encounter.

"Are you excited, honey?"

"Not really. I wish Palm Beach had a high school so I could just stay on the Island."

"The Island doesn't have enough kids to fill a high school. Now that you're older, you need to see that the world is a much bigger place than Palm Beach. Kids from all over the world go to this school. There's so much you can learn from them."

We arrived ahead of schedule and decided to walk around the campus. We trekked across the carefully mown athletic field and peeked over the fence to the aquatic center. A group of boys were in the water. When I suggested they were playing Marco Polo, a game I knew from my pool club growing up, Emmy laughed. She explained it was water polo, a popular sport at prep schools. The cafeteria looked more like a trendy café than a dining hall. Pale yellow buildings that resembled pieces in a monopoly game held the classrooms. All these structures were strewn over 200 grassy green acres.

More than these things, what mattered most was the school's mission statement. They prided themselves on educating the whole student, mind, body and spirit. We made our way over to the correct building and waited for Jayne, the admissions officer, to call us. When it was our turn, she said it was customary to interview the child first and then the parent. She escorted Emmy to her private office and closed the door behind them.

There was no one else in the waiting room. I snuck over and put my ear up to the door and listened to the answers Emmy gave to her questions. She aced it. When I heard the scuffle of their chairs, I jumped up and scurried back to my seat, so they wouldn't know I had listened in. Emmy smiled at me as she took her seat. It was my turn.

"How did you learn about our school, being that you live in Palm Beach?" Jayne asked. This question surprised me. Children from Palm Beach had attended since the school's inception. Emmy listed the names of the kids from the Island in her application: the Fanjul kids, whose grandfather founded a sugar company, and the Merck siblings, descendants of the pharmaceutical company of the same name. New to the Saint Andrew's community, maybe Jayne didn't know these families and how valuable their contributions were to the school. But she might know Candace.

Candace, Scott's wife, was an alumni and a member of the Board of Trustees. Although they shared the same last name and it may have helped Emmy, I told her not to list Candace as a reference. There was a reason for this—Candace didn't want Emmy to go to Saint Andrew's. She cited reasons like "Kari and Emmy live too far" or "there are other good schools for Emmy." Scott told me the real reason: Candace considered Saint Andrew's "her" school. She didn't want to share it with a stepdaughter.

I learned about the school when I worked for Lana. Lana's son thrived at Saint Andrew's. He attended a well-respected university upon graduating. Since then, I planned for Emmy to go there. Jayne asked how I learned of the school beyond the Palm Beach families, and something pulled at me to mention Candace's name. I didn't want Jayne to think I was hiding anything.

"Well, my daughter's stepmother is on the board. I didn't say something sooner because it's kind of a tricky situation."

"Really? Why is that?" Jane asked.

I explained Candace's position and went on to tell her that she had made Emmy feel bad about her score on the math part of the admittance test, which was the truth. She told my daughter that she was not "Saint Andrew's material." I relayed this to the young, fresh-faced admissions woman whose blond hair was pulled off her face with a headband. I wondered if she could possibly understand the complexity of the dynamics I was describing or if this would hurt Emmy's chances. "I was upset, because I feel my daughter has so much to offer this school." We talked a little more and then Jayne escorted me to the door. As I pushed it open, I caught a glimpse of the crimson fabric of Emmy's shirt. She had been crouched outside the door listening as I had. Unlike me, she hadn't gotten back to her seat as quickly.

In mid-March, Jayne called me on my cell phone. She wanted to personally let me know Emmy had been accepted to Saint Andrew's School. She assured me that, despite what Candace thought, Emmy was worthy of a slot.

"That was not a nice thing to say to a child. Not to mention simply untrue."

"Thank you so much, Jayne."

"Look for the acceptance letter in the mail."

Hurrah! All of Emmy's hard work, and mine, had paid off. And I knew before any of the other parents. I was tempted to tell Scott but decided against it. When Emmy slid into the front seat of my car at pickup, I shared the good news. She was thrilled.

"Let's celebrate tonight! Where do you want to go?"

"The Grill," she said, referring to our go-to spot for family celebrations. It had been a favorite of Emmy's since she was a kid. Once, when we had a party of all adults, a waiter placed crayons and white paper on the table so she could draw during dinner. Emmy never forgot that. It may have been a coincidence, but the next time we dined there we noticed the white paper had become the standard tablecloth. Crayons lay on the table along with the usual utensils.

"You got it, baby."

Scott called later in the week to tell me he was happy Emmy got in.

"How did you hear?" I knew the letters hadn't been mailed yet.

"Candace told me. She found out at the school's board meeting. She had no idea why the other board members rushed over to congratulate her until they told her about Emmy's acceptance." I pictured this scenario and couldn't help but laugh. Candace may see herself as some fancy financial analyst, but she had no idea what lengths a mother would go to to do what's best for her child. Just wait until hers was born.

Buyer's Remorse

Emmy's acceptance to Saint Andrew's School made me realize how much I missed Alan. I couldn't help myself—he was the first person I wanted to share the news with. When I called to tell him, he insisted we celebrate. "I have a case in Palm Beach. Have dinner with me Thursday? I'll be done with court by 5:30."

I agreed to dinner but refused his offer to pick me up; he didn't deserve that benefit yet. "Meet me at Echo at 6:00," I said, referring to an Asian fusion restaurant in my part of town. Over dinner he told me how sorry he was. There had been no chemistry between him and his former girlfriend. He was a fool to think there would be. I wondered if it had been necessary to sleep with this woman to find this out, but I decided not to ask. I didn't want to know.

"Do you want to go to Los Angeles and Newport Beach with me this summer? Noah has baseball tournaments in both places." I stayed quiet. Alan tried to persuade me. "Come on! You deserve a trip, Kari. It wouldn't be the same without you. Emmy can come too, like last year." I wondered how men knew that asking women to vacation with them was a sure way to weaken us and forget any transgression on their part.

"I'll think about it. It will depend on what's happening with my house. There's an offer pending. If it goes through, I may take Emmy to Europe after we get settled in Boca."

"I'm happy for you, and happier for me—you'll be closer to Miami. I want you back, Kari. I miss you. What do you say?"

Part of me wanted to forget what happened, to reshuffle the deck, deal the cards again and pray for a winning hand. But this was the second time he had broken up with me. His commitment issues were more serious than I thought.

"Let me think about it, okay?" When the valet pulled our cars up, he wrapped his arms around my waist, pulled me into his chest and kissed me.

"I love you, Kari." I didn't say it back. He continued to call me to share news about his cases and Noah. I listened to him because both topics still interested me. However, the igloo I built to protect my heart wasn't melting so fast. When Alan asked to see me again, I said no. The wound he'd inflicted was still raw. Seeing him would only make it worse. Nonetheless, when he invited me to sit courtside in his box at the Sony Ericsson tennis tournament, I gave in. Last year when he asked me, I couldn't take time off from work to accompany him. I grew to love tennis from watching my dad play. "I'll go with you, but only because I want to see the tennis. Don't read anything into it," I warned.

"Meet me at my office and we'll drive to Key Biscayne together." I gave extra thought to my outfit that day. Being unsure of my feelings was no excuse not to look my best. I chose a white linen maxi dress with a wide-brimmed hat and silver and white Navajo Palm Beach sandals. Despite the heat, I couldn't warm up to Alan. He tried to joke about what happened in December, comparing it to buyer's remorse. I didn't find it amusing.

A week or so later, Alan returned to Palm Beach for his case. We were having dinner at McCarty's when my realtor called me to say the offer on my house fell through. The buyer couldn't get financing.

"You guys can come live with us so you can save on household expenses," Alan suggested. "Emmy can commute to school from Miami during the week. She can be with her dad on weekends when the fun stuff goes on."

"That doesn't make any sense. Your house is farther away from the school than mine. The house will sell. This is only the first offer. My plan is to move to Boca Raton and stay put until Emmy finishes high school. You had your chance to have us live together as a family and you ran from it. I cannot place my future in your hands again. I understand the distance thing is hard, but I need to do what's best for me and my daughter."

"Of course, Kari. I get it," he said, looking like a kid who had been sent to "time out" and was begging for a shorter sentence.

"Alan, do you want to continue this relationship knowing we will be living apart?"

"I do." I searched his eyes, looking for a sign he meant it. He seemed so sincere. Maybe that was why juries always believed his clients were innocent. I remained silent while I collected my thoughts.

"I will give you one more chance, Allie. If you screw up, that will be three strikes and I promise you, we're through. And another thing: I feel no desire to be intimate with you right now. You are going to have to earn my trust all over again before there is anything physical between us."

"I'll wait as long as it takes, Kari, whether it is eight dates, eight months or eight years." I burst out laughing. Laughter is what this man gave me that no other man could. Shortly after, I began to pick Noah up from baseball practice, not because we would soon be family, but because I wanted to and he wanted me to. I smiled each time I arrived at school or the baseball field and spotted him with the other boys. He no longer seemed anxious; he knew I'd be there.

Often, Noah's travel ball games were in my area. He slept at my house and brought boys from the team to stay too. Alan drove up on weekends and we watched Noah's games as a family. Alan cooked for the four of us. Emmy seemed happy to have them around. The sheet of ice that shielded my heart like a coat of armor slowly melted. I was able to be intimate with Alan again. In a way I never expected I would, I got to mother a teenage girl and a boy. We didn't all live in the same house all the time, but we made it work. I didn't need the title of stepmother to make a difference in Noah's life. Finally, I was a full-time mom instead of a full-time employee. I enjoyed every minute of it.

Season ended, leaving my house behind like merchandise a store returns to a vendor. Before I could worry about my diminishing bank account, the insurance company sent a check for my damaged belongings. Surprisingly, it included the amount on the price tag of the Persian rug. This was a better gift than the denim blue Celine bag Alan gave me to celebrate the May anniversary of our first date. These extra funds bought me time to come up with a plan. But what exactly would that plan be?

Baseball took us all over Florida and back to California. When it came time to vacation with our kids in the summer of 2008, Alan's dad, the firm's bookkeeper, told me that business was slow. He asked me to keep our travel budget in the realm of Holiday Inn, not Hilton. Even with "The Lenny," three rooms at the hotels Alan liked were too expensive. Luckily, a friend from my private equity days let us stay at his guest house in Mulholland Estates in Beverly Hills.

But as Emmy began her second year of high school, a storm was brewing that was about to make landfall on the Island. Like the tornado that swept Dorothy's house from Kansas, the damage it would inflict was worse than any hurricane to ever strike Palm Beach.

Beware of the Black Swan

The power on North Lake Way was down again. This happened often during thunderstorms. Desperate to see Emmy's grades, I was headed to the office of Christian Angle Real Estate. When my house didn't sell after two seasons, my friend Ben suggested I switch realtors and hire Christian. "He's young and just starting out, but he hustles. He sold my last listing in a month." I trusted Ben's industry knowledge, and luckily, one of the benefits of working with a family firm included the use of their office. As I logged into my email, my friend Lori walked in.

"Hi, Kari. I didn't know you worked here."

"I don't." I smiled, knowing that everyone on the Island knew I was always working in one way or another. "I'm here to pick up the Valentino dress and wrap I lent Christian's wife for The Ultimate Dinner Party." The Ultimate Dinner Party was an invitation-only charity event that took place every November. It was a favorite among Islanders due to the venue: cocktails for guests at a grand Palm Beach estate, followed by intimate dinner parties at private homes hosted by Palm Beach's most celebrated chefs and residents. Scott's firm was the corporate benefactor. As a favor, I'd asked him to add Christian to the list. When Christian's wife, Ann, confided she had nothing to wear, I stepped in to play fairy godmother.

"How funny, I let Ann borrow my jewelry for that same event," Lori said. Leave it to the ladies of this town to welcome a newcomer this way. It was good to know there were a slew of fairy godmothers on call to prepare women for the charity circuit. Ann's scrubbed

Ivory Girl looks hinted at her age, late 20s at most—equivalent to a toddler in this town.

"Are you still making party favors, Kari?" Lori asked. "I could really use something with a music theme for my son's bar mitzvah. If you have anything, I'll be glad to pay for them." Before I could get excited about earning money for something I did for fun, the "D" in math on Emmy's report card jumped out from the screen and practically assaulted me.

Just as I was thinking how bad this would look on Emmy's transcripts, Christian walked in with news that sent everyone into a panic. It was all over the media that a money manager named Bernie Madoff had been arrested for carrying out a $60 billion Ponzi scheme. *Why did it matter to us?* Because most of his crimes took place in our own backyard-—Palm Beach.

I could never have imagined the impact this man named Madoff who, true to his name, *made off* with his clients' money, would affect my life and those of many other Island residents. Palm Beach had seemed out of sorts since Bank of America bought Countrywide Home Loans last year. Bear Stearns was sold to JPMorgan Chase in a fire sale in March. Lehman Brothers went bankrupt in September. This was yet another event leading up to the global financial crisis of 2008. I had never heard of this man, but many of my former clients invested with him and unbeknownst to me, he lived in one of the waterfront homes on North Lake Way.

The Palm Beach Country Club was the setting where this scoundrel carried out this scheme. This club was two blocks north of my house and highly respected. Members had to prove themselves worthy of belonging by making substantial donations to charity. Living around the corner from this club was a positive when I bought my house; now it was a negative. The real estate market went from piping hot to lukewarm to ice cold since I listed my house in March of 2007. Because of this, Emmy and I were still living on the Island, 50 miles north of her school. We left the house at 6 am so Emmy could board the train that dropped the Palm Beach students in Boca Raton. A van took kids from the train station to the school. At 4:00, I headed south to pick up Emmy. She had cheerleading practice in fall and dance team practice in winter. The school offered no bus to take kids home; they all had different after-school activities.

I used the hours in between to fix up my house, hoping the market would turn. With Emmy's school so far away, I couldn't look for work. When Emmy visited Scott, I played house with Alan and Noah. Everyone predicted things would get better, but I wasn't betting on it. It seemed like a permanent black cloud had settled over always sunny Palm Beach. When Season began, instead of the usual flurry of activity, Palm Beach was deserted. My house sat between Mr. Madoff's and the now newsworthy Country Club where he lured clients for his phony fund.

My neighbor Lionel replaced Erin as my walking buddy when she decided to give New York a whirl. Erin was lucky she left town after ending it with Todd. Lionel and I bonded over the textile industry, which was where his inheritance came from. Lionel was sophisticated, aloof and spoke with an accent. He wore sports jackets cut from the finest fabrics. I only learned he moved to the street when his dog ended up in my front yard. Rumor had it his summer home in Ireland was a castle. When he traveled, his copy of *The Financial Times* landed on my doorstep.

When he was home, we'd have tea at my place or walk his Yorkshire terrier, Gigi. She was the love of his life. It was real love, the unconditional type, not the kind offered by a bevy of beauties coming and going—but never staying—at his two-story Georgian-style house. Lionel couldn't get close to anyone. Bri attended high school with him. She remembered how his parents left him to fend for himself when they sold their business and moved back to Europe. He never got over the loneliness that followed. I wasn't a threat to him. I was looking to get rid of a house, not attain one, like most of the single girls hoping his would become theirs.

On one cool Sunday morning we set off to walk the trail. As we made our way toward the water, Lionel pointed to the window in the coral reef where a witch supposedly lived.

"You know us local guys tell girls that story to scare them into sleeping over?"

"You know, in all the years I've lived here, I've yet to see her," I replied, laughing. As we walked farther south, we saw Madoff's boat, Bull, docked behind his house. I'm sure the name came from him selling his clients the belief that, by investing with him, it would always be a bull market for them. Instead, he sold them a bunch of bull *you know what*.

What would happen now? I wondered. I had bet my future on the equity in our house and now there were no buyers. How could Emmy and I begin a new chapter during this storm? The Palm Beach parents who sent kids to Saint Andrew's gave large sums of money to the school but kept within the realm of society life on the Island. Since I was no longer a regular on the charity circuit, I didn't see them much. Nina, Summer and Kate were still friends, but Nina and Kate's kids were at boarding school and Summer's girls attended a Catholic high school. It was important for me to meet the moms of Emmy's classmates, many of whom had known each other since kindergarten. Living closer would help. Who knew how long this crisis would last? Where was the life raft to get off this Island?

The atmosphere in Palm Beach changed overnight. Excess was out, caution was in. Reckless spending was viewed with suspicion. Everyone was guarded. Just as one should exercise caution when investing, it was now fashionable to be prudent when shopping. This behavior carried over to the housing market.

With my savings sinking, I considered finding work. I swallowed a piece of humble pie and called Carol at Valentino. There were no openings. Deirdre's clients were the first to stop spending. She resigned and moved back to the Midwest. Cedric struggled to keep his customers coming in.

Since my departure, I'd heard from former clients that Valerie found a capable person to replace me. I'd missed my chance there too. When I saw my former boss Lana at a fashion show, she confessed she was selling her products abroad. Except for her flagship store and one in New York, she had closed all her shops in the States. The department stores hadn't carried her collection in a decade. So, there was no way for me to sell my house or my skill set.

And Emmy was suffering. She was never an early riser. I am sure that "D" in math had something to do with not getting proper rest. She didn't complain, but I felt guilty for putting us in this predicament. Scott paid Emmy's tuition. It was my responsibility to drive her to and from school. I needed to hold up my end of the bargain, even if it meant the only job available was that of chauffeur.

Alan felt badly he couldn't help, but his finances were hurting too. His daughter Hannah was getting her professional degree at Harvard—her tuition wasn't cheap. Our days of fine dining were done. Little did I know the family trip we took to California last summer would be our last. With my savings dwindling, I had to tap into my home equity line just to put food on the table. When Emmy wasn't home, sometimes that food was nothing more than rice, just like back when I first moved to New York. The only difference was that now the rice was brown instead of white.

Apparently, the only people not affected by the financial crisis were the ones with inherited money. And when a multi-generational business decides to cash out, their descendants cash in. In July of 2008, Anheuser Busch, known as "The King of Beers," was taken over by a Belgian-based holding company for $52 billion. It was the largest cash deal in American business history. Six months later, the heirs to this brewing fortune moved into the brand-new two-story Mediterranean revival house across the street from me. *Who were they? How come I didn't know them?* This clan must have splurged on gowns or cashmere at some point.

My new neighbors were a couple a bit younger than me. Their children were babies. The husband, a big teddy bear type, introduced himself as Chip and his wife as Bitsy. There were many women named Muffy and Bunny in Palm Beach. Island dwellers like to adapt to their habitats. In this town, that meant having a "society" nickname. Margarets or Marys morphed into Muffys. Barbaras and Bernices became Bunny's. A Nettie was formerly a Jeanette. The name "Bitsy" was unfamiliar to me, though. The only Bitsy I knew of was the spider who climbed up the waterspout in the nursery rhyme "The Itsy-Bitsy Spider."

I recalled the countless hours I spent coming up with a name for my daughter that sounded pretty and had meaning. Emmy means sweet and cute. She was named after my maternal grandmother, Edie. I couldn't imagine why a mother would choose to name her child after a spider. This girl was blond and willowy, the exact opposite of a tiny black spider. I tried to come up with a way to approach the topic of her name; I couldn't find one.

One morning, Bitsy and I chatted by the mailboxes that stood at the foot of our driveways. She was certain we'd met before and was trying to place me. I asked if she ever shopped at Valentino or Valerie Louthan and mentioned that I'd worked at both places.

"I don't, but maybe you know my mother. She's been a customer of Valerie's for as long as I can remember," Bitsy said.

"What's her name?" I asked. When she said it, I recognized it at once.

"Yes, of course! She's lovely." And she really was. Bitsy's mother came from the family that had once owned a chain of women's clothing stores. They had shops all over Philadelphia, New Jersey and Delaware. It struck me that I now had the heirs of not one, but two scions of American business dynasties living across the street from me.

On my side of the street, I picked up the palm fronds scattered over my yard and placed them in a neat pile for public works, who picked up the yard trash every Wednesday. Thankfully, it was February and I suspected, like most monied residents, my new neighbors would be leaving by the end of the Season to summer somewhere other than Palm Beach. I was outside retrieving my mail when Chip asked if I would like his gardener to mow my lawn.

"My guy is right across the street doing mine; he may as well do yours too, Kari."

"Sure," I said, "that would be great," thinking it was one less cost I would have to incur.

Then a second thought struck me: Is he just being nice or is my yard not up to his standards? His home sat high on the coral reef looking east at mine. My excitement turned to embarrassment. Bitsy and Chip had laborers at their house around the clock, making it more perfect than it was. Across the street, my house seemed to be held together with Krazy Glue.

Word spread fast about the brand-new house on the north end and its high-end interiors. Bitsy was hosting charity soirees on a weekly basis. Perhaps she needed favors. The ones I did for Lori with a hip-hop theme were as popular as the entertainment she hired a hot new DJ named Khaled. After the party, many women placed orders. I decided against mentioning it. This was not the right way to welcome her. We were neighbors, not friends. Lori and the other moms had asked me to make the favors. Palm Beach had an unwritten protocol about soliciting residents. Instead, I offered Bitsy use of my driveway. It had more space to park cars than hers. She thanked me and accepted.

Later that month, spring break arrived, and it was special that year. Since I was no longer employed, as in the nine-to-five,

I was free to spend time with my mom, unlike past visits when I required her babysitting services. We'd just returned from Disney World with Bri and her kids, and guest passes at The Beach Club were waiting for us. I explained we would go there after I finished giving instructions to the crew doing repairs on my house. When I glanced toward the front doors, I noticed a multicolored lawn chair and a beach towel propped up against the glass.

"Mom, you know the club provides chairs and towels, right?"

"Yes, I know," she said. "I thought I'd get a head start on sunbathing and take my chair and sit in the front yard for a while." If you're thinking that my front yard is large, then this may not sound unusual. But my front yard stretched a mere 15 feet from the front door to the road, and a large part of it was a half-circle driveway.

"No, Mom, this isn't Astoria," I said, remembering how our Greek relatives parked themselves outside their homes on tiny plots of grass when we visited. I explained who the new neighbors were. I told her I didn't think they would appreciate the view of her sunning herself in a lounge chair. Nor would the people rollerblading, jogging or driving by on the way to their homes: my friends, fellow parents and former clients. Thankfully, she understood.

Then May came, and the beer prince and princess packed up and left for St. Louis, where they hailed from. They left me a white double orchid with a note saying they couldn't have wished for a better neighbor. Relief set in. I could relax about my inferior home-maintenance abilities. Bitsy and Chip weren't grading them; only I had been.

Gin and Toxic

A third Season swept by, and my house still hadn't sold. I couldn't understand why. The repairs I made got it in tip-top condition. Every surface glistened, even the garage floor that was freshly painted in a pale gray shade. What I came to understand, along with the rest of the country, was that the collapse of the financial markets was the result of a catastrophe in the mortgage sector. Housing was to blame for the worst monetary crisis since the Great Depression. When I asked Christian for advice, he said, "Your price is in the boom numbers in a market that has gone bust. The house will only sell if you lower it by a lot." This was not what I wanted to hear. Instead, I changed course and asked Christian to list the house for rent. Many people who weren't ready to take the plunge into Palm Beach real estate eagerly put down money to rent.

"Are you sure you want to do that, Kari? What if a tenant ruins the house?" My instincts told me the kind of people renting a house in Palm Beach would not be the type to trash it. But now was not the time to think about this. Time and money were running out. We needed to move so Emmy could have a normal high school experience. That meant living near her school, not commuting to it. Older kids from the Island had started driving. I wouldn't let Emmy ride along as a passenger. I lost my dad in a car accident; I refused to lose a daughter.

Prospective tenants came to look at the house. No agent could entice a taker, despite it being offered furnished, unfurnished, monthly or yearly. Lionel rode in like a white knight. His girlfriend wanted to move in with him. He found female companionship confining, so renting my house could be the perfect compromise. Lionel had never seen the walk-in closet with its felt-lined jewelry drawers, alcoves for handbags and long hanging space for gowns. One look later and he offered to pay a year's rent and utilities up front. Before Christian could draw up the lease, the girlfriend nixed it. Her goal was to live with *him*, not pay for her *not* to.

I canceled my listing and decided to strike out on my own and market the house myself. Palm Beach had strict rules regarding the size of a sign that could be displayed to advertise homes for sale or rent. Signs could be no bigger than a brick and must hang from a thin post so as not to obstruct the beauty of the houses. The sign I had made stated my intentions in simple terms: "By Owner: Sale or Rent" and listed my number underneath. Hopefully, someone hunting for a bargain would take the bait. The sign had been up barely a week when a fish was on the hook. I needed to reel this one in. My bank account was nearing zero.

My "fish" was a woman named Mona. Her fiancé, Arthur, a tall pasty-skinned man in his late 60s, saw my sign and sent her to scout out the house as a place where they could nest. Mona stepped out of her jeep sporting the look Palm Beach women wear as a uniform: Lilly shift dress, Jack Rogers sandals, a straw hat with a ribbon around the brim and a Hermès Birkin bag—hers in turquoise blue. The sunspots on her face gave away her age—early 50s. Her blond hair resembled hay, but her body was toned, a prerequisite for any girl on the Island looking for love.

When I opened the front door, her eyes let on that she was impressed. She asked how much it was to buy the house, which surprised me. When Arthur knocked on my door, he said they were renting. I threw out the last listing price to gauge her expectations, and she seemed unfazed. When she revealed her last name, I knew why. She was part of the Canadian family who were heirs to Seagram's liquor and had a presence in Palm Beach going back decades. They gave more money to Jewish charities than any other family in the country. Between Lionel, Chip and Bitsy, and now Mona, my street, North Lake Way, could have been called "Trust Fund Way" to reflect the new demographic of people moving in.

I led Mona through the wide-open spaces of the house—the dining room with the bay window that invited the flora and palm trees inside, the family room with French doors that led to a private garden, the sun-drenched kitchen and separate all-white laundry room. When she saw my snow-colored marble bathroom and custom closet she was sold.

"I'll make sure Arthur signs a one-year lease with an option to either buy the house or renew the lease for a second year," she said. A week later, she did a second walk-through and handed me a punch list to be completed before they moved in. This gal knew about houses. I was eager to oblige since it meant money in my pocket. But the more I gave in to her whims, the more demanding she became. She wanted to change the color of the walls. She asked if I would pay the painter if she supplied the paint. I agreed. She requested a new dishwasher, to which I said yes, and a new washer and dryer, to which I said no. The ones I owned functioned perfectly. She said she'd buy a new set and have them delivered. This woman was accustomed to getting her way.

She asked if the ceiling fans in the bedrooms and loggia could be removed so she could bring her own. Anxious to close the deal, I said yes. Mona couldn't be doing this for a one-year stay. The house was owned by two women before me. Mona was a shoo-in to be the fourth. Despite her family name, did she have the funds to buy it or was she counting on Arthur's? His business card said he was in finance; surely, he had them. It didn't matter. Theirs was the only offer on the table.

It was easy to get references for both of them. Another plus of living here was the one degree of separation between Island dwellers. Christian rented Arthur a place after he left his first wife.

He said he drove a tough bargain but paid on time and left the place as he found it. Liv, my manager from Valentino, vouched for Mona. They resided on the same floor in a building near Worth Avenue. She said Mona treated the apartment as if she owned it. She made several upgrades, which she paid for herself.

Arthur was relentless in asking me to lower the rent. I gave him a discount on one condition: during Season, he and Mona would let my realtor show the house to buyers. He and Mona would be allowed to stay until their lease was up, even if the house was sold. The sum we agreed to was enough to cover the costs of the house and the rent on a small apartment farther south for Emmy and me. Arthur gave me two checks: one to be used as a security deposit and one for the last month's rent. He promised to provide the first month's rent once the punch list was completed. He and Mona first saw the house in June. It was late October when they moved in. Mona confessed she was waiting until the month was up so she could get every dollar's worth from the company storing her furniture.

I wish she had told me that sooner. I'd called in favors from every tradesman I knew to repair my house. In this town, it wasn't uncommon for divorced women to sell jewelry when they needed cash. Because I had a job, I never thought I'd be part of this group. But the work I was doing now, like theirs, came with no paycheck. House repairs didn't seem like a valid reason to sell off family heirlooms. Luckily, the gowns I bought in the off season fetched a hefty sum at the consignment stores. This money paid for materials and labor. When I was down to my last dollar, the workers told me to pay when I could. In a small town, one's word is everything. Thankfully, mine was good.

Mona was curious how Alba, my housekeeper, got the limestone floors to sparkle; Alba agreed to show her. Mona arrived while I was cleaning out the garage. When Alba drove up, Mona didn't remember her. She ran out the door and demanded that Alba get off her property or she'd call the police. When I came to see the cause of the commotion, Alba exclaimed: "I'll do anything for you, Mrs. Kari, but I'm not coming back while Miss Mona is here." This incident should have been a warning. Despite the wreath Mona placed on my door, she was less of an angel and more of a devil disguised as "the lady of the house."

In private, I called Mona "Miss Seagram's." Often when we spoke, she seemed to have sipped too much of the product her family sold. Mona lived in a grand house near Worth Avenue with her mother. On the eve of the Jewish New Year, a holiday we both celebrated, I rushed from my lawyer's office to meet her to finally close the deal. Beads of sweat clung to the knit dress I was wearing, which was too warm for the October weather. Mona was perched on the porch in a skirt suit that was new; I'd seen it in the window of Chanel. In Judaism, it is customary to wear new clothes on this holiday. I was in favor of any tradition that includes adding to one's wardrobe. However, I was mad that Mona was sitting pretty, her straw-like hair sleek from a salon blow out, while mine resembled a damp mop. I presented the lease, the fourth revision, and the house keys. She looked like a mouse who just stumbled upon a large wedge of cheese. She hugged me, handed over a check and invited me in for a cocktail. I thanked her and said no. Emmy was at Bri's helping her prepare for the holiday. Thirty people were expected for dinner. It would be rude to walk in after everyone was seated.

The new year couldn't have come at a better time. Christian told me I'd done what no real estate agent in town could do. He was so impressed, he asked me to join his firm. He said he'd cover the cost for me to get licensed. I laughed and told him I couldn't sell a product I knew nothing about. However, what I learned was this: Presenting a house for sale or for rent isn't much different from selling luxury goods. If you have a product that stands apart from the rest, price it right and get an ambitious person to promote it, it will sell. For now, my house was sold, at least for the next two years. And if Mona prevailed, maybe for good.

Escape from Palm Beach

In the rush to make my place perfect for Mona, I had no time to find housing for me and Emmy. Boca Raton, like Palm Beach, was seasonal. I needed to find a place before the good ones were gone. Alan said I could stay with him until I found something. Somehow men are much more willing to let women move in when no commitment is involved. In the end, I did move in with him—but only temporarily. Scott and Candace, meanwhile, were happy to have Emmy with them. Once they had a baby, Emmy was no longer just Scott's daughter; she was part of their family. I was angry when Scott left the Island and moved to Boca Raton when he remarried. Now I was glad he got there first.

Anyone who works in retail knows holiday shopping begins in October, not November. Unlike luxury goods, which people buy for themselves, Matt's desk sets, day planners, memo pads and totes made perfect gifts. Trendsetters needed to sell as many goods as possible before Christmas. To accomplish this, Matt hired people to promote his goods in the stores that sold his collection. This work, called merchandising, was my fallback when I was in between jobs. Matt gave me a list of stores to visit before the holiday shopping rush. Setting up displays, along with apartment hunting, kept me from missing Emmy. Two nights a week, we met at the library near school and grabbed dinner.

Finding a place to live took longer than I expected. Emmy said "no" to each apartment I showed her. Some weren't nice enough. Others were too small. She insisted the second bedroom be large enough to fit the furniture from our house: her queen size bed, nightstands and the antique vanity that doubled as a desk. Despite my hesitation, Scott bought Emmy a white Audi for her birthday. We needed two parking spaces. Emmy's new car wasn't going in the street.

Just as I began to think that what I wanted didn't exist, I discovered Boca West Country Club, a second home heaven for snowbirds. It had a real estate office on the premises. Their agent showed me a furnished townhouse directly across the street from the high school. The art deco mirrors and curved sofas gave it a glamorous feel. It checked the boxes on Emmy's wishlist with its spacious second bedroom and a two-car garage. There was a bonus room for me: a screened-in sun porch overlooking a lake.

Emmy agreed to meet me there after school. "It's perfect, Mom, and I like that the kitchen is near my room, so I don't have to walk so far to get a snack if I'm hungry." I agreed to the lease terms; someone was looking after me, and I didn't want to lose it. Mona taught me that even when renting, things are negotiable. The owner, a solicitous type who asked me to call her Ms. Gladys, was happy to remove the furniture from the second bedroom so Emmy could bring her own. The other furniture in the townhouse wasn't high-end, like mine, but it could stay. We'd only be there a short time.

Management requested three local references. Luckily, I had a lawyer, a realtor and a rabbi to list on my application: Alan, Christian, and Moshe. They must not have checked my bank account; the application was approved. Finally, we had a home! As a thank-you, I dropped off paper storage trunks in a red heart pattern for Ms. Gladys. I hoped they would push her to pack up and move out by Valentine's Day.

I liked waking up to Emmy, especially since I no longer needed to coax her out of bed. We discovered a Starbucks outside the gates of Boca West. She couldn't wait to get an iced caramel macchiato in the morning. One morning, while the barista brewed our drinks,

ESCAPE FROM PALM BEACH

I brainstormed with Emmy about ideas for a business. Emmy seemed more interested in the yoga gear worn by the women bringing goods to the estate jeweler next door. Their leopard print leggings and spandex tops didn't offend me. Ladies parting with precious gems could only mean one thing—this recession wasn't getting any better.

A Hobby Lends a Hand

Trendsetters' collection wasn't selling well this year, and I had no idea why. I was using the same items to craft party favors, and people scooped them up. The country was still struggling to recover from the mortgage crisis, but this product was inexpensive and sold at places like Claire's, Bealls and Michaels—surely it was still affordable.

Boca West had a guard gate to keep the rest of the world out, so Emmy wasn't afraid to be alone in the townhouse. This allowed me to leave after supper to see if there was more foot traffic in the stores at night than during the day; there wasn't. According to the media, the recession ended in August. But the recovery was recorded as the slowest since The Great Depression. This concerned me. If customers stopped spending, stores would stop buying merchandise. If stores stopped buying merchandise, there would be no product displays to set up and I'd be out of a job. The rent from Arthur and my child support paid for the basics but didn't allow me to save or for Emmy to shop, an important extracurricular activity for a teenage girl.

The job market had dried up. There were only so many friends that needed party favors. It was hard to think of ways to eke out a living. I kept coming back to Trendsetters' products. The gift items were fashion-forward, yet the textiles they were made from—paper, cloth and ceramics—were inexpensive. I continued to merchandise the stores Matt assigned me. When shoppers saw me creating displays, they asked me what I was doing. When I explained I worked for the manufacturer, it piqued their curiosity. When I described the many uses for the products—think photo albums, storage boxes in vintage prints, day planners and ceramic catch-all trays—their buying habits changed. Instead of selecting one or two items, they filled their carts. The stores had clerks to ring up sales, but no salespeople. In normal times this product sold itself. But since the Great Recession, retail was anything but normal. Linens 'N Things went bankrupt. Many big-box stores switched to online sales. These were tough times. Tough times required a new way of thinking. By now, I'd earned a PhD in this subject. This product needed someone to sell it. Who could do that better than me? *But where?*

Off-price retailers were the new trend in 2010. Entire shopping centers were devoted to this concept. I did some research and narrowed my selection to malls that were no more than an hour away. Two were ruled out instantly. The first was outside and felt like a flea market. Trendsetters' stuff was too upscale for this type of consumer. The second was in a neighborhood that didn't feel safe. I couldn't risk being mugged for some pocket money.

The final one, The Festival Marketplace, was close to Boca West. When I stepped inside, the energy of the crowd drew me in. Each aisle was named after a famous celebration, like Carnival and Mardi Gras. Each store had a different feel. Shoppers walked up and down the aisles seeking out treasures. The press kit said the mall was looking for businesses that offered unique merchandise. Many shops sold apparel, handbags, sunglasses and perfume. None sold favors and few carried gift items.

"What kind of people come here?" I asked the leasing manager.

"Mainly middle-aged moms and older women: cruise-goers, retirees and snowbirds from all the gated communities in Boca Raton." *Bingo.* This was my target customer. So, shortly after two guys from Brooklyn came up with the idea for Etsy, an e-commerce marketplace for handmade and vintage wares, a single mother living in Boca began crafting party favors and selling them in a mall. This venue was a vast contrast to Worth Avenue, but the location would allow me to establish a new market for my product—the Boca moms.

But leaving the Island was bittersweet, not just for me but for the friends I left behind. Bri was the first one to reach out.

"I miss you and Emmy, Kari. I feel like my oldest daughter left for boarding school, instead of Boca. I know you're super busy, Kari, but can you do me a favor? I need your opinion on a gown I have on hold at Couture & More. Can you come to town to see it?"

"Of course." I welcomed any excuse to go back to the Island. I didn't realize how much I would miss it until after we moved. Her request got me thinking about a name for my business: "Do Me a Favor?" Wasn't that exactly what I was doing for people's events? Bri floated out of the dressing room in a Tiffany blue organza gown. "Stunning," I said. "You put Cinderella to shame. Get it." She loved the proposed name for my business. She asked Drew to register it. He was a whiz at this stuff. As Bri signed her receipt, Drew called me.

"Sorry, Kari, that name is already taken."

"It figures. Thanks anyway, Drew. I'll come up with something else."

As we exited the shop, Bri swung the large bag that held her gown. "Couture & More," I said aloud, as I looked at the logo. I always liked that name. It described what the store carried and had a catchy ring to it. I tossed around some words in my head until I came up with ones I liked.

"What do you think of 'Gifts Galore'?" I asked Bri.

"Love it."

"Me too." Drew confirmed that this name was available.

Now that I had a name, I needed a color for my signage. I chose an apple green background for the banner that would hang above the booth. Below the business's name, in white block lettering,

A HOBBY LENDS A HAND

it listed all the occasions the gifts could be used for: favors, wedding showers, baby showers, sweet 16s, bar and bat mitzvahs, quinceañeras and hostess gifts. Green represents money and prosperity, two things important to me now. Also, this was a "green" business. The merchandise I was selling was excess inventory or goods that stores sent back to the manufacturer. Hopefully, this might resonate with customers.

In retail, like real estate, location is key. I walked the entire length of the mall and scouted every available space. The one I chose was across from a shop that sold high-end home decor. The owners said their business was lucrative; their space took up three booths. Better yet, their products complemented mine. Alan volunteered to help with my new venture. He accompanied me to get the materials I needed to turn my 12 by 12 booth into a store. At Lowe's, we bought white backboards, shelves and shiny silver waterfall hooks to hang the canvas tote bags and backpacks, which I hoped would sell like hotcakes. When I said I'd get my handyman to help set up, he told me not to bother.

"I can do it, Kari. It's easy."

"Really? You know how?"

"Are you forgetting I was in the garment industry? And I renovated two houses and my office building."

Alan was right; he knew his stuff. His handyman skills were more valuable than the money he gave me for my cash drawer. It took three trips from my garage to the mall to bring the merchandise Matt sent on consignment. Bri helped me cart a desk and two chairs to the shop, courtesy of the townhouse.

Fear stalked me like a friend I'd promised to set up on a blind date. *What was I thinking? Who was I to think I could sell this product when chain stores couldn't? Would anyone really care about catch-all trays or memo pads and storage boxes in vintage patterns? Or how wrapping items in cellophane and tying them with a silk or velvet ribbon instantly created a gift?* My creativity, ability to forecast trends and merchandising strategies were lined up and ready to earn me a living.

While I navigated my new business venture, Scott decided Emmy should have a part-time job of her own like he did when he was in high school. My store had an opening. How fun would it be to teach my girl the art of sales and merchandising? Emmy refused to even come see the shop. She was embarrassed by it. Scott, it turned out, told her my business was low-class and not something a woman with my background and education should be doing. *Really? How was creating a business and showing up to it every day not a positive attribute?* Emmy found a position at a trendy clothing boutique instead.

I was disappointed but was too proud to show that I cared. Emmy took these products for granted. After all, she'd received gifts and party favors from Trendsetters since she was two. But girls her age loved the stuff—some of my best customers were her classmates. So as not to embarrass her, I didn't let on that my daughter attended their school.

Secretly, I was hurt. Emmy would have had fun at The Festival. There was a sweets shop that sold fudge, her favorite candy. Since preschool, each Christmas, she and I made batches of fudge and packed them into holiday-themed boxes from Trendsetters. Emmy gave the goodies to her teachers as gifts. This year, she insisted we give gift cards instead. She was afraid the teachers would trace the boxes back to The Festival and to me. I chalked up this behavior to typical teenage drama. I didn't intend to make a career out of this; it was a pop-up shop, something to do until Emmy finished high school.

I don't know whether it was luck or a case of being in the right place at the right time, or if my passion rubbed off, but people related to my concept. From opening until closing, I didn't stop selling, writing orders and wrapping gifts. At night, I sent Trendsetters a tally of my sales along with a list of items that needed to be replaced. Matt was shocked my little shop had higher numbers than the individual stores within a big-box chain.

"How is it possible that your sales are higher than a name brand store, Kari?"

"Because this is a discount mall. It has foot traffic. And I'm actively selling the stuff. It's not sitting on a shelf hoping someone finds it like it does in the chain stores." And selling was what I did—eight hours, seven days a week. Rarely did anyone leave my booth without buying. Girls like me land in fashion for a reason. We love the treasure hunt aspect of discovering unique merchandise. Despite the trend toward online shopping, to me, without a person-to-person connection, something is lost in the buying and selling process. I was a "see it, touch it, tell me about it" type of shopper. So were my customers.

In December, people rushed to my booth for last-minute gifts. I'd completely forgotten about gifts for my niece and nephews in New York. This year, there was little time and even less money to buy them. My credit card was maxed out from business expenses. I wished I hadn't closed my house accounts in Palm Beach when we moved. Suddenly, I remembered I still had a house account—the one at Saint Andrew's bookstore. It opened early; I could stop in before work.

Surprisingly, most of the merchandise was labeled with the school's logo. I grabbed sweatshirts in blue for the boys and a pink one for my niece, Michele's daughter. "Just charge it to my house account, please," I said to the cashier as I dashed out. My sisters were grateful for such practical gifts. They never asked why the name of Emmy's school was printed across the front of the sweatshirts. Better yet, I never got a bill. The store probably sent it to Scott. I'm sure he didn't see it. If he had, he would have insisted I reimburse him.

Throughout November and December, I worked every day. Three evenings a week, I merchandised chain stores and small boutiques like Franceska's. My days and nights ran together. I couldn't distinguish one from the other. If I closed my shop, even for an hour, I would be fined by the mall's management. Despite this frenetic pace, I was happy. The person who wasn't happy was Alan. The dynamic of our relationship had changed. Alan was an empty nester. Noah turned down his scholarship to play baseball in North Carolina, and instead chose a college in Florida and gave up the sport altogether. Since Alan was alone, our dates took place in Boca Raton. After fighting the rush hour traffic, he was annoyed to walk in and find me editing Emmy's college essays.

"Are we going to dinner or are you going to keep typing?" he asked.

"Dinner," I said as I polished off one last line and closed my computer. I was famished. Waiting on holiday shoppers left no time for lunch. Nonetheless, these dinners had gotten dreary. How many conversations could we have about kids and work? Yes, I was happy to send Hannah my gowns to wear to her graduate school formals. It was my pleasure to take Goldie shopping to upgrade her wardrobe from coed to professional. Didn't he see I deserved to be promoted? Noah was away at college; what was keeping him from making a commitment? I promised myself I'd bring it up over dinner.

"Kari, you look exhausted. You can't keep going at this pace. Get some help. You're too busy to see me during the week and I hate not spending weekends with you. Don't you miss me?"

"I do, and I plan to hire someone. I had to make sure the business had cash flow first."

"Based on the figures you showed me, it does. And there's expenses you can write off now that you own a business: the rent for the store, your car payment, supplies, even those favors you do for Emmy's school. All those costs can be deducted from your income. If you file your taxes early, you'll know what kind of refund

A HOBBY LENDS A HAND

you're getting. Why don't you give everything to my accountant, Garic? I'll tell him to take care of you and send me the bill."

Wow—how sweet. We sipped our decaf coffees and I dipped my spoon in the mango gelato we'd ordered for dessert; it had no flavor. Across the table, Alan looked delicious. I missed his touch. All I wanted was to get home and tumble into bed with him. The marriage talk would have to wait until morning.

Garic's office was near my work; we had an appointment for Friday at 6:00.

"Poor you," I said as I thrust a shoebox full of receipts on his desk and plopped down in the chair across from him.

"Poor me? I don't think so," he said as he looked through it. "It's more like poor you." Garic couldn't believe I had three jobs: my retail boutique, merchandising stores and the one I didn't even know was a job, property manager for the Palm Beach house. Garic claimed it was along with the money I spent to make sure it complied with Mona's standards. Every expense—the gardener, a new sprinkler system and even the induction cooktop—was a write-off.

"Kari," he said, "there must be an easier way to earn a living without working three jobs." I explained to him that I'd been on a hiatus from work when the recession hit. When our house didn't sell, I rented it, so my daughter could live closer to her school. Merchandising allowed me to make my own hours, but I worried about the stores' lackluster sales. That led to my retail venture.

"Well, from what you tell me, this company, Trendsetters, does a large part of its business before Christmas. Promise me when the holidays are over this merchandising job will be too. You should enjoy this last year with your daughter before she goes off to college. You shouldn't be hanging around strip malls at night. The good news is you didn't open your retail shop until November; you have two months of profits and a year's worth of business expenses." Alan was right; a refund was coming my way. It was in the thousands.

Whew…finally I could relax. Business was booming and in May, there would be a bonus from Uncle Sam. It was time to increase my staff. The vendor of a cosmetics booth had a niece in need of a job. It took one interview to find out Meg was a fit. It wasn't in my heart to pay my new employee minimum wage like the other shop owners did. Working on commission taught me the way to increase sales was to make it part of my employee's pay. It wasn't so long ago that these checks helped me to survive. Right now, the two people that mattered most to me, Emmy and Alan, were more important than money.

That meant I could stick to what I was best at: identifying trends and bringing in the best merchandise. I taught Meg the art of crafting favors with clear cellophane and bows. She was eager to show people how the favors gave their parties an added touch. Shoppers agreed; these whimsical items were special when wrapped. My connection to the manufacturer allowed me to get merchandise quicker than the chain stores could. The mall had more foot traffic on weekends. That meant much of my profit went to Meg. I was glad to share it with her. She used it to pay her college tuition.

Meg was thrilled to have a job, but despite the overwhelming response to the product, this was a small business. The profits from a single store, selling items priced at $30 and under, didn't generate enough income for me to see a future for this venture. My future was with Alan, and my always was Emmy. Emmy had a basketball game this Friday—she was captain of the Saint Andrew's dance team, which performed at the games—and I'd asked Alan to come. Thanks to Meg, he could stay the weekend, instead of complaining he had to leave because I was choosing work over him. Fortunately, my retail shop was quick to earn a profit, so I could give up my merchandising gig after Christmas. Nothing would have kept me

A HOBBY LENDS A HAND

from missing these games. My heart skipped a beat each time I watched Emmy dance. Her charm, combined with her poise and athleticism, made her star shine a bit brighter than the other girls.

The other parents present agreed that the activity in the school's gym beat lobster night at the private clubs that characterized the West Boca social scene. Many of these parents came to Boca Raton to raise their kids near grandparents that lived nearby. The atmosphere in the bleachers was more like a bar mitzvah than a sporting event, as parents and grandparents celebrated their sons, daughters, grandsons and granddaughters. Emmy knew how to get the crowd going. The hip-hop routine she choreographed to Hanukkah music brought them to their feet with applause.

When another mom asked who I was watching, I pointed to my girl, the one with shiny brown hair and green almond-shaped eyes, dressed in black jazz pants, a white cropped top and Puma sneakers. She said Emmy was precious. Her son, the team captain, must have thought so too. His *prom-posal* was carried out by placing balloons and a note on Emmy's car. There was one small glitch: That day, Emmy and I drove to school together in my car.

After my auction meeting, I walked to Emmy's assigned spot. Since I'd brought up marriage to Alan, our future was the only thing on my mind. When I saw the balloons, I assumed they were from him. What other reason than a proposal would explain their presence? "Josh," the name on the card, was only the first clue that this gesture wasn't meant for me.

Emmy was impressed Josh thought of such a clever way to ask her. This scene seemed like one from a reboot of a favorite show of mine, *Beverly Hills 90210*. In this episode, Emmy was asked to prom, and I was the woeful single mother, consoling herself with a pint of ice cream because her boyfriend wouldn't commit. This was not how I pictured myself. I was tired of being a girlfriend. In the hierarchy of dating, a girlfriend is an entry-level position. In business, I never stayed in these roles long. Blame it on my job in private equity, but I was after a merger. Alan and I had been dating for seven years, enough time for due diligence to take place.

This weekend, parents were hosting a cocktail party for the auction committee at their oceanfront mansion. An artist I liked was having an exhibition. Alan was coming to both. I vowed to ask him where we stood. If he didn't see marriage in our future, I would need to divest. The black cloud that hung over the Island was lifting. My friends said an influx of private equity firms had set up shop in Palm Beach; perhaps I could dig up my roots in that field. Gifts Galore had shown me the ropes of entrepreneurship. Why not start my own fashion label? My house hadn't sold; the welcome mat was still out front. Then as always, my plans were squashed. Who said a frog never turned into a prince?

Frog or Prince

It was a lazy do-nothing Sunday and Alan was sprawled on my sofa reading *The New York Times*. I walked out of the kitchen carrying a pitcher of iced tea. As I put it down, Alan appeared to bend forward to pick up his napkin. Instead, he got down on one knee, looked into my eyes and said, "Kari, will you marry me?" Then he slipped a paper ring he'd made from the napkin on my finger. I was in shock. These were the words I had been waiting to hear for years, words I thought might never come.

"Are you serious?"

"Kari, you are unlike any woman I've ever met. Nothing is too much for you. You give 100 percent to Emmy, your family and anyone else who needs your help and still manage to show up for me, Noah and the girls. I love you and can't imagine living another day without you in my life." As I looked at Alan, I imagined he was a knight in a fairy tale. Taking a knee symbolizes loyalty and respect. I was no longer doing the dance of dating. This princess had sealed the deal!

I tried to silence all the questions in my head. I wanted to enjoy this moment. A serene sensation, like the one I could never master in the *Savasana* pose during Bikram yoga, washed over my mind and body. Suddenly, everything leading up to this point was worth it. I sensed that in some reverse order, I would have the family I longed for: a husband, a son and a daughter and what I knew would come—a home shared by two parents, children and eventually grandchildren. Alan picked me up and carried me over the threshold to the porch so we could watch the sun set over the lake.

"I'm sorry it took so long for me to figure out what I wanted. I was stressed from being a single dad when Noah left home. It seemed like the right time to sell my house and move to a high-rise building downtown. I thought I'd enjoy my new freedom, but I don't. I'm miserable. With Noah gone, no more baseball and you preoccupied with work, I have no one to share my life with. We need to make a home together. One that's not mine or yours but *ours*." I was at a loss for words. I could tell he was expecting me to say something, so I said the first thing that came to my mind.

"Can I let you know?"

"Only you would give a guy an answer like that after waiting seven years to get what you wanted." I smiled, wrapped my arms around his neck and kissed him. "Of course," he said. "I deserve to wait for an answer after keeping you in limbo this long."

I was tempted to tell Emmy, but didn't know if I should. She'd been accepted at six of the eight colleges she applied to. She had yet to hear about her first and second picks. I didn't want my news to outshine hers. Nonetheless, I couldn't hold back. When she got home, I told her.

"Oh, Mommy, finally! Alan's good for you. He makes you laugh and you're so much more fun when you're with him." I laughed. The way kids see things we wise adults don't is telling.

A week later, an envelope from Vanderbilt University arrived in the mail. It was a thin one, which meant Emmy didn't get in. This would be Emmy's first experience with rejection. The minute she got home, she tore the envelope open. First, she seemed surprised, then she got angry.

"I can't believe I wasted all that time with a stupid tutor to get my SATs up," she said. The letter listed the grade point averages and test scores of the accepted students. Emmy fell below the mark in both. I didn't coddle her or try to appease her.

"You did your best. This was your reach school. Your grades and scores weren't up to par with the kids that got in. Sometimes the best fit is a school that wants you, and right now you have *six* that do!"

In April, she found out that her second choice, a school in Boston, was a yes. I was relieved my part in this process was over. It had started to feel like I was the one applying, despite having finished college decades ago. Now it was up to Emmy to decide which school was best for her and where she wanted to spend the next four years. I could concentrate on fun stuff like the senior prom, the school's fundraiser and graduation festivities. I was excited I had a fiancé to share these milestones with me. *Oh my God!* I was so caught up in Emmy's news, I forgot to give Alan an answer to his proposal. Just then, my phone rang.

"Hi, Kari, it's me. Have you had time to think about what I asked you?"

"I did. It's a yes, and thank you for being patient. And Allie…I couldn't be happier."

"I knew you couldn't say no to me. I'd love to buy you a ring ,Kari, but there is no ring I can afford that would be good enough for you. But if it means anything, I'm going to buy you a house. I can't wait for us to start looking."

He was teasing me—he knew I could care less about a ring. The one Scott gave me was jailed in a safe deposit box in Palm Beach. No one tells you that a ring given with the promise of forever loses its luster when the romance runs dry. I never understood why divorced women made necklaces with these diamonds. Hester Prynne was forced to wear a scarlet "A" to let the world know she committed adultery, but was wearing a rock around your neck to advertise you'd been married really necessary? To me the stone signified "D," for divorce, a symbol of a broken vow.

"That means everything to me, but let's wait until after Emmy's prom to start looking, okay? And don't forget, we have the school's fundraiser next weekend."

Emmy couldn't wait until Saturday, my day off, to shop for her prom dress. My business was slammed with customers leading up to Mother's Day (Trendsetters' items in floral patterns were perfect gifts), but Emmy had never been patient. Last year, we went all out; Emmy wore an emerald green taffeta gown with a fitted bodice and full skirt. This year, due to time and money constraints, I suggested we try Becca's Closet, a store near mine that sells secondhand dresses.

But Emmy wasn't having it. Unlike me, she had no budget; she had a benefactor. His name was Daddy, and he'd given her a credit card. Where else would a girl from Palm Beach go to shop for a dress? Worth Avenue, of course. The gown she bought was fit for a princess—a pale pink Badgley Mischka with capped sleeves and a drop waist. I smiled when she brought it home. The dress I'd worn to my prom was the exact same color. The difference was the neckline and the fabric: her low-cut one in chiffon registered more starlet on the red carpet, whereas mine in polyester, with its bustle and off the shoulder ruffle, resembled something worn by Little Bo Peep.

Farewell to Fundraisers

The financial crisis had humbled everyone. Even private school fundraisers were more casual affairs. Instead of a formal dinner-dance at a fancy hotel, Saint Andrew's was held in the gymnasium. Dinner was served by the bite. The cuisine, decorations and party favors were coordinated to match the theme of the affair—a boardwalk beach party. In years past, I'd attended this event alone, as it never felt right to bring a boyfriend to a school function. But Alan was no longer my bae; he was my betrothed.

The host committee decided to give out the beach bags I donated at the start of the evening, instead of at the end. This way, the bag could hold the pamphlet that listed the live auction items. The cloth fabric of the bag was printed with palm trees and hibiscus flowers. Its colors—turquoise, lime green and pink—complemented the room decor. In keeping with the theme, one guest was dressed in raspberry linen pants and a plaid sports jacket in the same lime green and raspberry sherbert color. He looked like he stepped off the croquet court of an East Coast country club.

As this guy walked away from a display of gift baskets, I realized it was Scott. It never ceased to surprise me how his wardrobe went from Wall Street conservative to WASP wannabe when he met Candace. Candace was a bit aloof and reserved around me. She either liked Alan or she was relieved he finally took me off the market, it was hard to say which, but she kissed him on the cheek and congratulated him on our engagement. Now, she would no longer have to be part of a threesome where only two of the people in the relationship had sex with one another. Of course, I would never say that part out loud.

"Hi, Kari. I'm surprised to see you here," Scott said. "Did you buy tickets, or did you come based on the donation I gave the school?"

I guess Scott hadn't noticed the signage on the easel set up as guests entered the gymnasium: *Beach Bags Courtesy of Gifts Galore.* Despite donating 300 pieces, I was eager to support the school; I bought tickets. If I hadn't been able to afford them I'd be working the event—just so I could be part of it, rather than attend as a guest.

I glanced over at the moms doing just that as they passed out the beach bags. A whole team of women wrapped those bags in clear cellophane to showcase the colors and hand-tied a ribbon at the top. Everyone has something to give: money, time, a product or service. All are equally important. I was glad not to have to police the party favor table myself like last year. I hated scolding parents for trying to take more than one item each. No matter how wealthy people are, everyone loves a freebie. That was the lesson I learned: What you don't have in cash, you can make up for with creativity. If only Scott understood this. Perhaps this was the reason our marriage didn't last. Alan *got* it. He was the guy who grasped my soul, the man who let me be my truest self. And this man was accompanying me to Emmy's graduation.

The night before the formal graduation, Saint Andrew's held a Baccalaureate Service, which was one of the Anglican traditions the school abided by despite the now more diverse demographic of the student body. This more intimate event honored the special achievements of the senior class. The attire for boys was khaki pants and navy-blue blazers, paired with a white shirt and tie. The girls donned white dresses and were given a single red rose to carry. In keeping with the school's Episcopalian heritage, graduates were part of a processional led by a Scottish marching band, complete with bagpipes and kilts. Each member of the senior class walked down the aisle and stood in front of parents and siblings as speeches were given and awards handed out.

It was hard to share these milestones with Scott and Candace. Despite being Emmy's mom, I always felt like a flat tire that was put in the trunk of Scott's car instead of being pushed off to the side of the road. My mom was so excited to marry off another daughter, she insisted I use my extra ticket to bring Alan in her place. As we entered the chapel, I looked across the room and saw Emmy standing with Scott and Candace and their three-year-old in a section reserved for Saint Andrew's alumni, which included Candace. Emmy held her little sister's hand, and I felt so proud of the mature, loving young woman she'd become.

I couldn't wait to hug Emmy and give her the long-stemmed red roses I bought for her. I'd also bought an identical bouquet of white roses, which I handed to Scott to give her. Alan walked with me to where she was standing. After Emmy left to join the other kids, Candace turned to me and said:

"During the ceremony they are going to announce the graduates of the alumni. I hope you don't mind if they announce Emmy as my daughter." I was speechless. But yes, I did mind. I'd raised Emmy for 18 years, most of that time as a single parent. Since birth, every decision of my life was made with her best interest in mind. I went to every game she cheered at, every dance recital, choir performance and parent-teacher conference. I was well known by the school's staff for my volunteer work and the favors I donated to fundraisers year after year. These parents were my friends. It would be completely disrespectful to me, as well as untrue, for this woman to claim my daughter as hers.

Suddenly I felt like Ariel in *The Little Mermaid*. The voice I used to earn a living each day was silent. Thankfully, I had an attorney present because I needed someone to defend me. Alan turned to me and said, "I will deal with this. You can leave, Kari." I turned away and walked back to take my seat.

"What did you say to Candace?" I asked when he sat down next to me.

"I told her there is no way in hell the headmaster is going to say in front of all these people that Emmy is her daughter." My first reaction was relief, and then I had an idea. I shared it with Alan.

"Are you sure about this, Kari?"

"Yes," I said, nodding my head.

Alan walked over to Emmy and whispered what I told him in her ear. Emmy approached the headmaster and said something to him. When it came time to announce the graduates of alumni, the headmaster announced Emmy as "the stepdaughter of Candace" followed by the surname they shared. *Case closed.*

"You didn't need to do that," Alan said to me.

"I know, but I wanted to. It seemed important to Candace." It was a lesson I learned in business that made me outshine the competition every time. If I could find a solution to make all parties happy with a desired outcome without compromising my integrity, I would do so every time.

Fleeing the Festival

My fellow vendors warned me that summers at The Festival meant a decrease in foot traffic in the mall. "I hope you've saved, Kari," they cautioned. I had stashed some money away; that wasn't what worried me. I had no desire to spend my last summer with my daughter at home standing in an empty shopping center, especially while paying rent. At Valentino, I was guaranteed a base salary. If a client came to town between trips, there was the potential for a large commission. My fashion career began on Fifth Avenue. Having worked for three renowned designers over two decades—Lana, Valerie and Valentino—I didn't want to end this part of my career hawking goods in a fancy flea market. Miami's luxury industry was heating up; surely there'd be a position there for someone with my experience.

May and June, when people shop for graduation gifts, was the ideal time to sell off my remaining inventory. I gave management the required notice. Soon, Gifts Galore would be "gifts no more." Matt was surprised I wanted to give up my business.

"Can't you just stay through the summer? I'm curious to see if sales really drop off as much as everyone says. Knowing you, Kari, they won't."

"Even if my sales stay consistent, the income isn't enough to justify the expense of a store in the off-season. The future of your business is to get the product online and sell it directly to customers. Even with Meg to help, I'm putting in so many hours. Without the orders for favors, I wouldn't be making a profit. When there's hundreds of pieces to wrap, I'm in such a hurry to get home, the only dinner I have time for is the drive-thru at Wendy's. Emmy needs winter clothes for college. Alan and I need to plan our wedding and find a house."

"I get it. Kari, you waited a long time for this guy. You're ready to move on." Matt had done me a favor, but I was *done*. This business had taken a toll on me. My booth didn't offer much room to move around during the day. Preparing supper and wrapping favors left no time at night to work out. I'd gained 20 pounds. I looked like a baby elephant. My small shop began to feel like a cage. And this elephant looked forward to roaming free outside the zoo of The Festival Marketplace.

PART III:
A LEGACY

A Prince, a Princess and a Castle

Alan was excited his fiancé could finally make time to look for a house. I was happy he added me to his firm's health insurance policy. Mine had been canceled when I put my profits toward product instead of paying the premium. Times like this made me appreciate Scott. I didn't fare well as a cog in the wheel of the corporate world. Thankfully, Scott made it work. Emmy was covered by his policy.

The housing market in Miami was similar to Palm Beach's. Sellers expected boom-era prices while buyers searched for a bargain. The first place we looked at was Coconut Grove, an artsy neighborhood we were familiar with from our college days. The things on our wish list—a decent-sized backyard, three bedrooms and a pool—didn't exist in our price range. We drove north, to a community called Bay Point. It was situated on the mainland and had a guard gate. Alan loved the half-acre properties. I was pleased every home had a view of the water. However, we got there too late; the last few houses in our price range had just sold.

The third area, Bay Harbor, was walking distance to the beach and the designer boutiques in Bal Harbour. This was a plus for me, but the lots were too small for Alan to nurture his love of landscaping. It didn't matter; the prices here were higher than in the first two areas. Alan was frustrated, but I refused to give up.

"Arthur's lease ends in the fall. If he and Mona buy my house, we'll have plenty of money. We can live anywhere we want. If they decide not to, I'll ask them to move out. We can live in Palm Beach."

A PRINCE, A PRINCESS AND A CASTLE

"I don't think so, Kari. I'm not commuting that far to work. And I refuse to live in a house you shared with your ex-husband. It's important to me we start fresh."

What we wanted and what we could afford didn't align. We needed a house that was "On Sale" not "For Sale." When Alan and I stumbled upon the secluded east side of Miami Shores we learned that, just like in retail, the best inventory wasn't always on the selling floor.

In Florida, there are cities, towns and villages. This one was a village. Its old-fashioned charm and varied architectural styles reminded me of the north end of Palm Beach. This neighborhood was up-and-coming—the prices were reasonable. Three streets had views of the water, but one stood apart from the rest. It had sidewalks and mature oak trees lining the block. But luck wasn't with us; most of the homes resembled the plantation style of the Old South with round columns and two floors—a no-go for Alan. "Slave owner houses," as my mother called them when I sent her a picture—but I thought the round columns that extended from the ground to the second story made these houses look grand.

"Let's compromise. Maybe climbing stairs will help me shed those extra pounds I gained working 10-hour days," I said.

"Good try, Kari, but no. I lost one house to an ex-wife and one to a recession. This will be my last and final house. I'm 60; my knees are bad from tennis. We need a ranch-style one." As we neared the end of the block Alan looked out his window and said, "Now there's a house." I turned my head and saw a house that looked like it had been sprinkled with brown sugar. That color and its pitched shingle roof reminded me of a gingerbread castle. The lawn and hedges were overgrown. Closed shutters on the windows prevented us from seeing inside, but their placement indicated the house was one story. A stack of newspapers at the front door confirmed what I suspected: This house had been abandoned.

With Alan trailing behind me, I walked around the garage to the backyard. The foliage was sharp and prickly. My arms bled as I forced my way through thorns and mangled branches. I climbed through a ripped screen that enclosed the property and found myself in a courtyard. Through a wall of sliding glass doors, I could see the kitchen and family room. I walked over to a door that was slightly ajar and nudged the handle. It slid open. Like a soft-footed cat, I crept inside. My eyes swept the room—I was awed by the architectural details of this house.

The formal living room had 24-foot ceilings with hand-carved Honduran mahogany beams that ran across the entire length of the room. The floors were the original oak. White wooden beams on the ceiling of the kitchen and family room were a throwback to the era when it was built, the 1940s. Tucked inside the small footprint of this house were four bedrooms, three bathrooms and a den. The house was in disrepair, but it was livable. The pool was narrow, but it had an interesting octagon shape at one end, and it was long enough to swim laps.

The best part was the space between the house and the courtyard. A breadcrumb trail led me to a guesthouse that ran the entire width of the main house. Alan caught up with me. We were thinking the same thing: *This is our castle.* Was it in fact for sale? At what price? Our realtor found out it had been bought at the height of the real estate boom. When the economy crashed, so did the owner's business. Unable to afford the payments, he abandoned the house and the mortgage that went with it. After three years, the bank reduced the price to less than half the amount of the loan. There was an offer pending. Alan made a higher offer and said we'd pay in cash.

"But we don't have that kind of money lying around," I said.

"We'll worry about that later. Let's figure out how to get the house first." I loved this man; he was fearless, like me.

A PRINCE, A PRINCESS AND A CASTLE

On weekends, we visited the house. The reader in me was drawn to the library in the living room. A library is the soul of a house. On the bottom shelf of the built-in bookcases, I saw a stack of note cards with an artist's rendering of the house sketched on each one. As I picked one up the scent of old paper made my nose tingle; they'd been there a long time. When I got home, I showed Emmy the card and asked if she wanted to see the house in person.

"Oh, Mom, it's beautiful, but not yet. I'll wait to see if you guys get it first." I couldn't blame her hesitation. My track record with selling houses wasn't good. When our Palm Beach house didn't sell after four years, Emmy questioned if it ever would. I did some digging through the tax records and discovered that a man named Javier owned this house. He was an architect. At first, he was reluctant to meet with us. When I mentioned we had a back-up contract, he changed his mind. As we sat in his office above Biscayne Boulevard, he explained what he called "the short sale" process to us.

"The bank can only work with one contract at a time. Only if the party under contract can't close can they move to the next contract, in this case, yours, even if you're paying with cash."

"I guess we wasted your time by coming here, then?" I asked.

"Not exactly. It was clever of you to call me, Kari. Now that I know there's another offer, there's less pressure on me to take the existing one. I'm up to date with the taxes. If the other party can't close, I'll encourage the bank to move on to your offer."

On weekends, we left high-rise living behind, drove to Miami Shores and pulled onto the grassy area called a swale to visit the house. We brought all four kids to see it. Emmy wasn't impressed—she compared it to the house she grew up in. It didn't measure up. Goldie, who I considered a mini-me because of her passion for work and willingness to take calls at any hour, wasn't shy about saying: "This house is horrible; just tear it down and start over."

Even Noah, who trusted my every word, turned to me and said, "Is this really the best we can do, Kari?"

"Be patient; it will be beautiful, better than any of our other houses." I tried to explain that Dad wanted "a project" and this one would keep him busy for years. Apart from law and gardening, Alan's passion was construction. Only Hannah, our future architect, saw what we did: the oak floors that when stripped and stained could be restored to their original condition, the Chicago brick hearth and the hand-carved florets on the bookshelves reminiscent of the Art Deco era. That was my link to Hannah—she and I saw things through a designer's lens.

"You guys have so much invested in this house. What if you don't get it?" Hannah asked. She was the only woman I knew whose practicality and thriftiness surpassed mine. Her long raven-colored hair began to resemble a bird's nest as she fidgeted with it while her dad and I walked around with legal pads and jotted down ideas. But she and Alan didn't know about the note cards with a sketch of the house. I'd commissioned an artist to draw my Palm Beach house on cards when we first bought it. This was all the evidence I needed to know this house would be ours. In a twist of fate, the same financial crisis that caused my house to linger on the market would make it possible for us to buy this one.

Miami's housing market was improving. At our realtor's suggestion, we upped our offer. With work a far-flung memory, Emmy and I were bonding. She'd forgotten I'd grown up in the Northeast and knew all about puffer jackets, snow boots and fur-lined gloves.

Mid-August to late September is peak season for hurricanes in Florida. Just as we were preparing to meet Emmy in Boston, the news reported a severe one was headed toward Florida. Mona was a wreck. Palm Beach residents were ordered to evacuate. She refused to listen to me or the police officer who knocked on her door and demanded she leave the Island.

"If the house gets washed away, I'm going with it," she said to him.

Alan and I were on vacation in Rhode Island when the eye of the storm turned away from Florida. At the same time, our realtor called to tell us the Miami house was ours—the buyers couldn't close. The bank was in a hurry to get this bad loan off their books. Our trip to visit the historic mansions in Newport would have to wait. And poor Emmy, she'd be faced with moving into her dormitory without parents! But we needed to claim our house. Before our closing, the bank requested a copy of our bank statement. They required proof we had enough funds in our account in case something happened with the mortgage we'd secured. The last two deals fell through due to financing issues. Credit standards tightened after the housing crash, making it harder for borrowers to qualify for loans. Alan suggested we wing it. "We'll tell them we'll transfer the funds and, on closing day, make up an excuse why they're not there."

I didn't want to take any chances. I had lost out on owning a business because I was too shy to ask for help; I wasn't going to lose this house. The timing was perfect, I thought. Mona adored my house. She cared for it as if it were hers. She made each person who came through the door put blue cloth booties over their shoes so the floor wouldn't get scratched. And, conveniently, her lease ended the next month. Surely she'd want to own this house she loved so much, which would give me the cash infusion I needed.

Mona claimed she thought of me as a sister. But it turned out Mona was neither my sibling nor my ally—she was my nemesis. When she got wind I was about to own a second house, it was war. When I asked if she planned to buy my house or renew the lease for another year, she refused to give me an answer.

We became two heiresses battling it out: one desperate to leave Palm Beach, the other to stay. I had no hopes of inheriting family money, but my grandfather was one of the few independent perfume makers of his time. He created the perfume "Jasmine," among others, which he sold from his perfumery off Fifth Avenue in New York. When Grandpa retired, my dad, in addition to his day job as an engineer, continued this business in a mail-order capacity from the basement of our house. When my dad died unexpectedly, so did Michel Pasquier Perfumes, but the legacy of hard work both men instilled in me was the one thing Mona *hadn't* inherited.

The gin she mixed in her tonic must have been toxic. She tried to persuade me to *give* her my house. She acted like she was entitled to it. "Miss Seagram's," it turned out, was the black sheep in her philanthropic family. I gave her a discount on the rent in return for the right to show the house to buyers in Season. She refused to keep up her end of our agreement.

"Now that you're buying a house in Miami, you don't need this one, Kari. There haven't been any offers. I'll give you what you paid for it."

"You must be joking, Mona! I bought this house 14 years ago because I knew it could only go up in value. There are only so many houses between the ocean and the intracoastal. Don't you see what is happening on the Island? People coming here want brand-new homes and there is no place to build. My land alone has quadrupled in value. If you're not buying my property, someone else will. Don't think I don't know you tried to jeopardize every sale."

"You have no proof of that, Kari."

But I did—my Palm Beach realtor, Gary Pohrer, was a former pro golfer. His patience combined with a quiet strength led me to believe he could handle Mona. He replaced Christian as my realtor when Christian moved up to sales in the stratosphere of the double-digit millions.

"Gary told me you made every person who came to see the house feel as if they were in competition with you to buy it. He said you left laundry strewn everywhere, dirty dishes in the sink and refused to unlock the closet in the bedroom. I let you stay when Gary had showings because I thought you *were* my buyer. I sympathized with you for not wanting strangers near your things. I'm not renewing your lease; you can only stay on a month-to-month basis. And if you pull another stunt to sabotage a sale, don't be surprised when an eviction notice arrives in the mail."

When I told Alan about my conversation with Mona, he already knew what transpired. Arthur had called him and said they would look for another rental. Mona begged him to buy the house, but he and Mona were newlyweds. He wasn't ready for that level of commitment. That left us three weeks to come up with the money Alan promised. "There has to be someone we can ask to give us a loan if we pay them interest," I suggested.

Alan thought his brother, a doctor, had the amount of money we needed. If not, I could ask the person I considered a brother, Drew. He was always the first to loan money to family and friends. Alan's brother agreed to help. He knew Alan hated high-rise living. He transferred the money right away. Alan knew his brother was a brilliant doctor; he didn't know he was a compassionate businessperson. He had also loaned money to a neighbor and a nurse in his office, who risked losing their homes to the recession. With the money in our account, the house was ours.

Javier's boxes stood in the living room when the furniture from Alan's apartment arrived. Everything happened so fast, he had never had time to retrieve them. Over Christmas break, Noah and I brought my art and antiques from storage to our "cottage by the sea," as I called it. With the help of Alan's mom, I unpacked the boxes marked "dishes" and placed them in the cabinets crafted from Dade County pine. I was grateful for her help. Housekeeping skills were her specialty.

As we unpacked and settled in, I took in every aspect of our new home with fresh appreciation. This house was smaller than the ones we raised our kids in, but it had character. The floor-to-ceiling glass windows welcomed nature inside like a celebrity guest. The entertainment areas were spacious and airy. The bedrooms weren't big, but if we included the den, there was one for each child if we were ever lucky enough to have them all visit at the same time.

My first house was perfect, even by Palm Beach standards. It shouldn't have surprised me that it was owned by a countess. No wonder I felt like royalty when I lived there. But this "Hansel and Gretel" cottage had better bones. We could turn it into whatever we desired. It just needed some tender loving care. Alan and I had so much love to give. With no kids at home, this house would be our baby. In Judaism, it is said that before a child is born, it chooses who its parents will be. I was certain this house chose us.

One Last Visit With Valerie

Going back to Palm Beach was never a day trip for me. Luckily, there was always an extra bedroom available at Bri's. "the OLD BAGS LUNCHEON" was one of Palm Beach's top five charity events. Don't let the name of it fool you! It has nothing to do with the age of the crowd of women who attended. The name of this luncheon alluded to the gently used bags given to The Center For Family Services by the doyennes of Palm Beach society. Ladies young and old rushed to get an invite in order to snag the designer handbags donated to the silent auction. In honor of Bri's birthday, her friends were hosting a table and invited me as their guest. Before meeting up with the girls at The Breakers, I had to go by my house. Arthur was away and Mona was on lockdown.

Despite her last name, Mona seemed to be without a trust fund. If she did have one, it wouldn't be enough to buy my house. She must have been a "waiter." In Island speak, a "waiter" is a child who must wait for their parents to die before they inherit any money. My lifetime earnings were in this house; I wasn't counting on any inheritance. And no trust-funder or "waiter" was going to prevent me from cashing in on my hard work.

Once she knew her lease could end on a month's notice, Mona became a nuisance. Suddenly, everything in the house needed to be fixed: the dishwasher, the doorbell, a ceiling fan. Every repair was urgent. Before I arrived, she claimed she heard a gunshot in the middle of the night. She needed milk and was afraid to leave the house. She must have been drinking again because Palm

Beach had tighter security than Mar-A-Lago. Local police patrolled the bridges that gave out-of-towners access to the Island, stopping people not for violating the law but for driving a Volkswagen instead of a Bentley. I was sure that news of a shooting would have been all over *The Shiny Sheet*.

Based on Mona's behavior, my realtor thought I'd have a better chance of selling my house without her in it. Gary had a showing the day Mona was holed up inside, and she'd repeated the story of the shooting to his potential buyer. Mistakenly, Mona revealed her cards. She wasn't buying my house and she refused to let anyone else do so either. Mona had overstayed her welcome. A letter from my personal lawyer, Alan, would let her know I was serious; she and Arthur had to move out. The sooner it was sent, the sooner I would be rid of this insanity.

But there was still the question of the gunshot. Was Mona really unhinged enough to make up a story like that? Bri hadn't heard anything, neither had Chip. When I couldn't reach Gary, Alan got the police on the phone. At first, they were reluctant to tell him the truth…when he told them my address and gave them the lowdown on my frightened tenant, they gave him the scoop. Mona wasn't hearing things. A gun had gone off. It was a suicide. My friend Lionel pulled the trigger. Lionel and I shared a friendship that was based on neighborly comradery. Now, I was sorry we hadn't kept in touch. I was sad and in no mood for a charity affair, but I had to appear upbeat because I was a guest. I spotted Sloane, Lionel's ex-girlfriend, in the entranceway trying to find her place card.

"Hi, Sloane, I'm so sorry about Lionel. Did you know he was suffering like this?"

"I had no idea, Kari. He drank a lot, but no more than anyone else in this town. When we were together, he seemed depressed, but I didn't think it was so severe that he'd hurt himself."

"I'm still in shock. He was such a sensitive soul."

ONE LAST VISIT WITH VALERIE

"It's a goddamn waste, Kari—educated, good-looking and all the money in the world."

"You know, Sloane, that may have been the problem. He always teased me about how much I worked. He wished his family never sold their business; he said it would have given him something to do."

"Are you going to the funeral? His sister arranged a reception at The Beach Club afterward," Sloane said.

"I don't know if I can stay for the reception, but I'll see you tomorrow at the funeral."

Before we could finish our conversation, I saw a blonde in a tweed suit carrying a navy alligator handbag—Lana Marks. Of course she would be here since this event was all about purses and the ladies who coveted them. Lori and Bri were placing their bids next to the bags they hoped to acquire. I felt someone brush up against me, and when I turned around, Lana and I were facing each other. I greeted her and said the first thing that came to mind: "How is your business, Lana?" She was eager to explain that it hadn't recovered from the recession, and to my surprise, she asked if I would consider returning to her company. She was determined to rebuild her domestic presence. Under any other circumstances, I would have been flattered, but all I could think about was Lionel. "Let's go," I said to Bri. "I'll be in touch," I said to Lana.

It was nice to reconnect with Lori and the other women, but I couldn't stop thinking about Lionel. Maybe if I hadn't moved, I could have done something to help him. I was relieved when Joan Lunden, the guest speaker, ended her speech. Hearing her talk made me feel worse about not being in touch with Lionel. I was desperate to get out of there.

"Do you mind going to Chanel with me before we go back to my house?" Bri asked. "I need your opinion on a dress I have on hold."

"Not at all. I'm always up for a visit to Madame Coco. And I haven't seen Chanel's spring/summer collection yet."

If I couldn't indulge my longing for fine clothing, I would be glad to help Bri satisfy hers. Drew was the kind of guy who spoiled his wife, so when it came to Bri's wardrobe, money was no object. We parked on County Road near the mom-and-pop stores that whetted shoppers' appetites before arriving on Worth Avenue where designer boutiques served up the main course. I happened to glance inside one, and what I saw was so shocking I had to press my face against the glass for a closer look. It was Valerie, standing behind a vinyl card table with a display of her sweaters on it. Propped on an easel was an ad from *The Shiny Sheet*. It announced "Designer, Valerie Louthan/Personal Appearance at J. McLaughlin."

I'd heard her business had not survived the Great Recession. Nonetheless, it was not like her to be peddling her goods solo in somebody else's shop. To see her in this position, at this stage of her life, made me feel sad and sorry for her at the same time.

"Do you want to go in and say hi?" Bri asked.

I thought back to the summer when I was in Los Angeles with Alan. When I pointed out the mustard-colored façade of the Bijan flagship store, Alan tried to persuade me to go in. He wanted to see the store, the setting for so many of my stories, and meet the famous designer. I refused, citing embarrassment as an excuse—I was unmarried, unemployed and had nothing redeemable to say to my former boss about his underling, the girl he described as a "beautiful rising star."

Besides, my relationship with Valerie ran deeper than the one I had with Mr. Bijan. Valerie brought me into her world, taught me everything she knew and gave me free rein to build her business as I saw fit. The skills she taught me would stay with me forever, and I was grateful. My feelings about that were still complicated—maybe they always would be—but I'd moved past it. With Bri beside me, I pushed the door open and ran right into her—the store was that small. "Well, well, look who it is!" she said, smiling as she embraced me in a warm hug. There were no customers. We had plenty of time to catch up.

"It's been way too long, Valerie," I said and asked about her family.

"The bottle finally got the best of Ian and he died a year ago," she said. She asked about Emmy and was happy to hear I was engaged and living in Miami. "You were always a city girl, Kari. You would have been bored to tears if you had stayed in Palm Beach." This comment gave me the perfect chance to direct the conversation toward business, mainly hers.

"Raising Emmy and running your business were the only things keeping me here," I said. I couldn't help blurting my next question: "What are you doing here, Valerie? Why aren't you in the Bahamas?"

"I was there all season. I'm trying to sell off some inventory before I return to England for the summer. I had a going-out-of-business sale when I closed, but there is still so much left. It's silly for me to keep paying storage fees."

"Inventory," I whispered under my breath. It was Valerie's Achille's heel. She suffered from the ego that affects many designers. Her fear of missing out on sales by not having enough merchandise left excess goods on our shelves. Maybe that's what did her in. At the risk of seeming rude, I had to ask the question that was burning in my mind: "What made you close the business, Valerie?"

She didn't answer right away. When she did, she seemed sincere. "I had problems finding responsible staff. When Ian and I moved to the Bahamas, it was hard to get someone to run the business while we were absentee owners. After the financial crisis, sales fell off. When we were no longer making a profit, we made the decision to close."

"What about the girl who took my place? I heard you were happy with her." She hesitated. I could tell she was choosing her words carefully.

"She wanted the prestige of running a business but underestimated the commitment it took to make it successful. We were told that on many days she didn't even show up to open the shop." I wasn't surprised. I knew what it took to run her business. I had given every part of myself to keep it in the black.

"I'm sorry, Valerie."

"Don't be, Kari. We were ready to retire and spend the rest of our days between the Bahamas and England. We just did it sooner than we expected." Valerie owned a knitwear business in Palm Beach for five years before I came on board. I managed it for five years. Five years later it closed. When I left, we'd amassed a worldwide clientele. It made me sad to think about what had become of our efforts.

If this business were a case study the takeaway would be as follows: You can be a rock star designer and create a brand that resonates with customers. That doesn't mean you're skilled at managing the financial end of the enterprise. I often thought that without Valerie, there would be no business. I was never sure I could be successful on my own without her in the design role. Was it the reverse? That she couldn't carry on without me? Now, I'd never know.

"This has been some day for you, Kari," Bri said. She could see I was shaken up. "Not only did you lose a friend, but you ran into both designers who betrayed you." She grabbed my hand. "Let's go. I want to try on that dress for you." As we walked toward the door, I turned to Valerie and said, "It was so nice to see you."

"Likewise, Kari, don't be a stranger. Ring me up if you're in these parts again and we'll get together."

"I will," I said. I didn't know that would be the last time I saw her.

Back to Sweeping the Chimney

Upon receiving Alan's letter, Mona refused to move out. She begged me to reconsider and even offered to pay more rent. Her gesture wasn't enough to make me change my mind. She lost my trust by trying to discourage a sale. Buyers were returning to the market; I didn't want to miss out.

I thought back to when we first moved to the Island. I never showed Scott the window covered with metal bars in the coral reef. Nor did I tell him that the window belonged to a house where a witch was rumored to live. That story was folklore, but Lionel's suicide was real. So was the Palm Beach Country Club where Mr. Madoff's crimes took place. Add kooky Mona to the mix and there may be enough evidence to convince a buyer my property was cursed.

Meanwhile, I felt oddly thankful that Mona's high standards for my Palm Beach house taught me what needed to be done to my Miami one. With an older home came outdated plumbing and electricity, old appliances and rusted faucets and light fixtures. It was me who oversaw replacing these things. Alan was impressed by the punch list I put together.

"That's some list, Kari. Are you sure you can take care of all this?"

"I hope so; I didn't realize how much work a fixer-upper required. Beth gave me the name of a guy to refinish the floors and a neighbor gave me the number of a handyman. But until we get some minor things done to make the house livable, I can't look for work."

"What do you mean?"

"It'll be hard to arrange job interviews when I need to schedule these workers."

"What job? You have plenty of work to do."

"It is for now, but the longer the gap on my resume, the harder it will be to find work in fashion when I'm ready to get back in."

"Kari, you have a job. You're my wife. You don't need to get a job outside the home."

"But when we were dating, most of the time I worked. You thought I'd just stop?"

"You worked because you were single. It's *my* job to support us. A retail job will mean you'll have to work nights. I don't want to come home to an empty house. We've both been single a long time; I want us to spend our nights together. Make your party favors if you want something to do. You can turn the maid's quarters into a gift-wrapping room, so you feel like you have your own space." I let his words sink in; my mom would be pleased. Wasn't this the role she groomed me for?

But part of me was puzzled. Our circumstances were different from when he asked me to marry him five years ago. Goldie and Hannah lived in other cities now, and Emmy and Noah had flown the coop to college. It would be fun to visit them, but the stay-at-home mom job left when they did. With four kids away, was there really enough to do?

At first, it was hard to tell. The house repairs kept me busy. One evening, I heard a scratching sound coming from the ceiling of my bedroom. When I told Beth, she smelled a rat. She'd had the same problem. These critters crawled in from the bay and entered houses through openings in the stucco if the holes weren't screened off. One walk around my yard showed me we were vulnerable. The company I hired set traps in my attic. When they returned a week later, they said the problem was solved. I paid the technician and asked to be spared the details.

BACK TO SWEEPING THE CHIMNEY

Next, my washing machine and dryer broke. A repair person said they couldn't be fixed. When I told Alan we needed new ones, he asked me to hold off on buying them; he had cash flow issues at work. My mother-in-law suggested a trip to the laundromat. Washing clothes at My Dream Laundry was a nightmare, pun intended! It wasn't the place that was the problem—it wasn't Clorox clean, but it wasn't dirty either. It was the customers; they were rude. While I loaded a washer, a woman took my clothes from a dryer and dumped them on a table while they were still damp. Some machines were broken; when you put your quarters in the slots, the machine didn't start. The regulars knew which machines worked and guarded them like a doorman of a white-glove building in Manhattan. I couldn't compete with these ladies. Trading coins for clean laundry was their skill set. These women were pros, and I was a novice. Instead, I found a store that sold used machines and had two delivered the next day.

I was no longer Cinderella; I'd snagged my prince. But mine came without staff and without funds to hire them. Perla, our housekeeper, came once a week. That should have been enough; I cleaned in between. However, my soon-to-be husband took the homemaker role quite seriously. When he left a scattering of crumbs on the floor after dinner, he requested I sweep it up. The basket of clean laundry that sat in his living room for a week when we dated now had to be folded and put away at once. It might contain a pair of socks he needed to match a certain suit. Laundry, grocery shopping, meal preparation, picking up his dry cleaning and grooming tools and having his tennis racquets restrung were part of my job description. He expected me to know what type of baked goods he liked and learn how to make them or find a bakery that could.

At the end of the day, Alan couldn't wait to come home for supper. He was excited to hear about my day and what I accomplished. Suddenly I felt like Snow White. All he expected of me was to cook and clean and I was supposed to be happy. This work may have been satisfying for a woman when the Disney film came out in 1937, but it seemed outdated now. When he hinted that I should hire a trainer in addition to my boot camp and Pilates classes, I was mad.

"Why not, Kari? You look fantastic. You must have lost 10 pounds since you gave up your business. A trainer will tone you up." Alan thought he was being helpful, but he was missing the point entirely.

"Between my workouts, lugging laundry to and from the garage and walking up the steps with bags of groceries, I'm doing enough physical stuff. I need something to keep my mind from turning to mush."

"Hmm, why don't you see what Celina and Beth do during the day?" Both my college friends lived nearby and were stay-at-home moms. Celina was at her home up north, so I called Beth. After boot camp, Beth agreed to show me the ropes of the three Cs: coupon clipping, cooking and Costco. At Costco, the first thing I noticed was the gigantic carts. Beth was shopping for a household of five. She knew exactly what products to buy. She seemed to linger in the aisles as if she were at a luxury spa, enjoying the free tastings served by different vendors. I approached a trip to the grocery store like a visit to the gynecologist: My goal was to get in and out as soon as possible. That strategy wouldn't cut it here. This Costco was 170,000 square feet.

It was senseless to buy food in bulk for my two-person family. It would go bad by the time we finished it. I stuck to staples like drinks, paper products and detergent. It was forever before we made it to the front of the line to check out. When the cashier asked if I wanted to become a member, I said no. This was one club I had no desire to join.

"Maybe since you don't like cooking, you'll do better with baking," Beth said as she unpacked her groceries."

"Alan does love desserts."

"I'm making a cheesecake for tonight. It's easy; watch me." When she pulled out her Kitchen Aid Artisan mixer, I was scared. To me, a mixer was a small appliance with two beaters you licked. This thing was a beast.

"It can make 10 dozen cookies in a single batch," Beth boasted. I looked on as Beth explained how it whipped the ingredients for the cheesecake. I was glad when she pushed the mixer aside. The only thing I liked was its color—candy-apple red. Beth handed me a rolling pin to roll out dough for the pie crust. She patted it delicately as it formed a circle with scalloped edges. Beth found this to be creative; I was only interested in how it tasted.

"I have a surprise for you, Kari. I booked mani-pedis for us before I have to be at school to pick up the kids. My salon squeezed you in because I have a standing appointment on Fridays. Another plus of this job is never waiting for a beauty service."

I wasn't sold. Beth was a CEO at this job while my skills matched those of an entry-level employee. I had no desire to start at the bottom at this stage of my life, especially when this job offered little growth potential. Beth left her job as the sales manager of a luxury hotel when she was 30 so she could raise her children. I asked her if she missed it.

"Not at all. I love not working. Doug lets me entertain his clients with lavish dinner parties, which is so fun for me. Sure, some of the duties are dull, but no more than administrative stuff at an office. Besides, I'm my own boss. I can volunteer at the kids' school as often as I like and watch them play sports."

"*Kids.*" My closest friends, Celina, Beth and Bri still had theirs at home. Without kids at home to nurture, this housewife job felt like that of an unpaid assistant. I needed to talk to a friend with an empty nest, so I reached out to Gwen. Gwen's son recently left home to attend college at Yale. She wasn't surprised when I relayed my dilemma of getting a fancy meal on the table five nights a week.

"Kari, I've been doing that for Reed for 25 years, and you know I hate to cook. Our husbands are older. It's something men from their generation expect. I'm sure Alan gets home at a decent hour. Reed expects dinner on the table even after late-night rounds at the hospital."

"Geez, Gwen. Does he ever help clean up?"

"Are you kidding, Kari? My Ivy-educated husband doesn't even know how to turn on the dishwasher." The gendered division of responsibilities was a common structure for baby boomers—it's certainly how they grew up and how life continued through the earlier part of their adulthood. But this was 2012—things were different. Or were they? Gwen was on track to be a professional ice skater, then a partner at a law firm before she gave up both roles to be a surgeon's wife and then a mother.

"I can't believe I've known you this long and we never talked about it."

"It's not an exciting topic; that's why I indulge in pottery and travel whenever I get the chance." No wonder she and my other friends vacationed so often. They needed a break from this drudgery. Fashion was a demanding field, but compared to this work, it was easy. I loved to travel, but I never "needed" to get away like they did.

"I'm no longer Cinderella, Gwen, I'm Snow White. My days are spent catering to a man."

"Mine too, Kari. Reed is the dwarf named Doc." Before I could decide which one to call Alan, he was calling me, probably to tell me what he wanted for dinner.

"I need to go. If I don't get to the grocery store, I'll be dealing with a dwarf named Grumpy. Heigh-ho, heigh-ho, Gwen!"

As I drove home, I let Gwen's words sink in. I was glad I wasn't the only one who felt like Snow White. But at least Gwen had a hobby. That might make this job less tedious. Of all the Disney princesses, the one I related to most was Belle from *Beauty and*

BACK TO SWEEPING THE CHIMNEY

the Beast. Like me, she loved to read and knew how to set a proper table. Each day, when my chores were complete, I found solace in the stacks of books at the local library.

The library in Miami Shores had the same feeling of community as The Fours Arts in Palm Beach. It was nice to be around people who enriched themselves through books. But I had too much energy to spend my days reading and concluded that the only way out of this job was to find another one.

Once I began researching fashion jobs, I learned that apparel manufacturers or wholesale companies never had a presence in Miami. The two I found—Eberjey, a lingerie company, and Perry Ellis, a company that sold menswear apparel, didn't have any open positions. The only fashion jobs that existed were in retail sales or management. I refused to go back to retail sales without the creative component. I hated the job when the economy was flush. It would be miserable trying to sell luxury goods to customers who had become accustomed to buying on sale since the recession.

After sending out several resumes for management positions, Domenico Vacca, a menswear company, responded. The brand was familiar to me; they had a boutique in Palm Beach. They made and sold their own products. I'd be able to create again! My concern was the location. The boutique was in the lobby of the Setai hotel in Miami Beach. Would customers drive there to shop? I decided to worry about that if I got the offer.

My first interview went well, but at the next interview, it came up that the manager was required to work evenings and weekends. The hiring manager refused to believe that the company wouldn't lose money if I worked on weekdays. My skills were of no value unless I committed to this schedule. This was sure to put a strain on my relationship. I did that once; I wasn't making the same mistake twice. I politely declined the job offer.

As if I had another fairy godmother, a new opportunity presented itself: one at Alan's office. When the tenants that rented space in Alan's building moved out, they took the receptionist with them. Alan needed someone to answer the phones, greet clients and find another tenant for the vacant space—luckily for him, I had experience in all three areas.

Alan chose the criminal defense area of law because he wanted to help the underdog, the people who had no one to stand up for them. He believed everyone deserves a second chance. He made sure they got one. I'd spent my career catering to the uber-rich. Once I was exposed to the downtrodden, I discovered my desire to give back could be put to better use here than in the luxury goods sector. Even though my title was now "receptionist and leasing agent," I was about to gain exposure to a case that would change both my perspective on the legal system and Alan's perspective on me.

Trial Separation (Not the Kind You Think)

When Noah was 16, I took him to see his father defend a client, Bam, who was charged with first-degree murder. Alan held the record in Florida for getting people acquitted of these charges. When he lost, I was surprised. Alan had successfully poked holes in the prosecutor's case! They appealed the decision, and the retrial was set for this June. Alan didn't want to defend this case again; he was angry that the judge didn't allow him to present a key piece of evidence in the first trial five years ago, and he worried this would be a repeat failure.

Only certain lawyers are qualified to take serious cases like this one, and because this was a state-appointed case (Bam couldn't afford a lawyer), Alan would be paid $100 an hour for his efforts. The complicated nature of the case meant Alan wouldn't be able to take on any other clients at the same time, and $100 an hour hardly covered the cost of running an office, let alone our household.

This case resonated with me. I didn't want Bam's young girls to grow up without a father like I had. I volunteered to work for free while Alan worked on this case. I told Alan we'd need to postpone our wedding until the trial was over.

"Are you sure, Kari? You wanted a summer wedding so it would coincide with the kids' vacations. You've already postponed the wedding from March to June because Emmy was bringing friends home for spring break. You sent out save-the-dates."

"I waited seven years for you to decide to marry me; I can wait a few more months. Someone's life and the well-being of these girls is much more important than our wedding. I'm familiar with the case; I can help you sort through the boxes of discovery. I'll send out another save-the-date."

For the next few months, I worked alongside Alan on the case. I went back over the details of the day of the crime to make sure we didn't miss anything. I told Alan which witnesses I thought he should talk to again, and I organized boxes and boxes of files so no details slipped through the cracks. As we got closer to the trial, Alan practiced his opening remarks on me and I gave feedback on how to make them even stronger.

In the weeks leading up to the trial, Alan couldn't locate one of his witnesses—Bam's cousin. Her testimony was paramount to Alan's defense—she was with Bam the night of the murder. A week and a half into the trial, she called the office and said she had a standby subpoena for that day, which meant she didn't necessarily have to go in person, she thought. Alan's paralegal was in court with him, and I didn't know for certain if the subpoena required her to testify today. She said her car broke down, so it would be hard for her to get there, but she had a friend who could take her to the courthouse if it was necessary. I had a gut feeling that she should be there in the flesh, that it would make a difference to the case.

"Get there right away, courtroom five-two, Judge Glick," I commanded with a tone of authority. "I'll text you the address." She made it.

The trial itself lasted for two weeks. I came every day. When it was time for the closing arguments, I arrived at the courthouse dressed in a dark brown Valentino pantsuit with a silk blouse in the same color as my nail polish and the stripes in the suit. Except for a watch, I wore no jewelry. This outfit was a stark contrast to the image of Bam's siblings—short denim skirts and long acrylic

TRIAL SEPARATION (NOT THE KIND YOU THINK)

nails with glitter adornments for the women and sweatpants, hoodies and gold chains that gleamed beneath the harsh lights of the courtroom on the men. But fashion wasn't the focus today. We were all there for the same reason: to witness justice being served. I was moved by the emotion of Bam's mother, a churchgoing woman studying for her college degree. She swore her son was innocent. The sun set behind the courthouse as we all waited for the jury to reach a decision.

"Kari, it's been a long day; you should go home," Alan said.

"Are you kidding, and miss hearing the verdict? Not a chance. Your closing argument was amazing. You really connected with the jury."

"We have a 'V,'" the bailiff said, summoning us back to the courtroom for the verdict. I had a habit of twirling my hair with my fingers when I was nervous. After doing this for hours my coiffed hair was all matted. It must have only been a couple of minutes between when we filed back into the courtroom and the foreperson reading the verdict, but it felt like hours.

"How do you find the defendant?" the judge asked.

I held my breath. I looked over at Alan, but his face was inscrutable.

"Not guilty," on the first count.

My heart jumped. There was hope. Then another "not guilty" and another. Bam was acquitted of all eight charges. He was a free man.

I wanted to remember this win. I took a picture of Alan with Bam and his family. We were having a celebratory dinner when Bam called. He was crying as he thanked Alan for giving him his freedom. The patrons of the restaurant were looking our way—they could tell something important had happened. I told the entire place about the case and Alan's victory. They broke out in applause.

"Go have a nice dinner, and not a bologna sandwich," Alan joked to Bam.

"You really helped, Kari; you knew Bam's cousin was the key to winning the case. How did you know her testimony was so valuable?"

"Her story made sense to me. When Bam came to her house the night of the murder, she was already awake. She had just given birth and was nursing her baby on a feeding schedule. That's why she knew that it was *exactly* 2 am when Bam banged on her door. And he couldn't have been at her house and committing a murder at the same time. I nursed Emmy; I know about this stuff."

Alan gazed at me so intently it was uncomfortable. I averted my gaze and my eyes were drawn to his charcoal suit. His neatly arranged tie played off the stripes in his blue dress shirt. It was a shade deeper than the one I ironed and gave Bam to wear for the trial. I had dressed Alan carefully that morning. Now, I couldn't wait to undress him. There was something so sexy about seeing my guy give his heart and soul to save another man's life. I called David Ovalle, a reporter at the *Miami Herald*, to write an article about the case and Alan's win. I made sure to save his number. I had a feeling I'd be calling him again. At this moment, I'd never admired any man as much as my husband.

At Christmas, Bam's mother invited us to spend the holiday with her family at their home in Miami Gardens. She placed Alan in an armchair at the head of the crowded table. Bam's grandmother said grace before the meal and made a blessing over Alan and me. For dessert, Bam's grandmother served the most delicious apple pie I ever tasted. She baked it herself and told us to expect one each year as a thank-you for saving her grandson's life. That pie was worth more to me than any paycheck. And each year at Christmas, when we go back to that house to pick up our pie, I remember how this tradition began.

Second Time's the Charm

For girls without fathers, wedding dreams become nightmares. It didn't matter that this was my second time getting married; the grief of knowing my father wouldn't be there took away the fun of wedding planning. For my mom—who valued marriage above all else—the nightmare was that my sister Michele was still single, my sister Leslie was "having issues with her husband" and my sister Jenn, who had just left her husband, was living with Mom. Mom called it "a temporary arrangement," but I had a feeling there was no set exit date, as Jenn had been spared from learning any basic survival skills, not to her benefit.

My mom spent the whole day looking like she was mourning over her unwed daughters rather than celebrating the one under the Chuppah. Michele, meanwhile, didn't come at all. She made up some excuse, but I had a feeling that she too was not pleased I was having a second wedding when she had not yet found a husband. A nice guy had given her a daughter, but neither she nor he could commit to "ever-after." Luckily I didn't have to worry about being the center of attention—Leslie solved that problem when she waltzed in late alongside my mother, wearing a sheer cream blouse with a black bra—hardly appropriate for a ceremony at an Orthodox synagogue. All this only added to the apprehension I felt that somehow something would go south. Leslie knew better. Her own wedding was held at a synagogue just like this one.

I took slow, deep breaths. Thankfully, Alan helped me with the planning. He'd hired the string quartet, chose the menu for our

75 guests and, most importantly, he was here. He was about to be my husband, finally, after eight years. I glanced at all four kids seated in the front row. We'd been through so much together—proms, graduations, moves to dormitories and apartments in so many cities for internships and career opportunities. They were all single and their adventures and misadventures in the dating world may be more bookworthy than mine, but those are their stories to tell. And finally, the fashions, which started with my dress.

Luckily the designer I favored in the 90s, Azzedine Alaia, moved away from the bodycon minidresses that once filled my closet and created a new collection of full-skirted dresses that clung to the upper part of my body then jutted out from the hips, the kind an Olympic skater wore. The style I chose was ivory with small chiffon ruffles in the same color that ran in vertical lines from the neckline to the knee-length hem. This finale was earned, and I was determined to look chic but timeless—even if that meant my dress cost more than the catering bill. To cover my shoulders in synagogue, I wore a faux fur shrug that I thrifted, and on my head I wore a small hat with netting that sat like a halo against my hair. Even my mom remarked that I looked prettier than I did at my first wedding, and that was two decades earlier.

Alan's rabbi insisted the ceremony take place outside, despite the heat, because it's considered more holy to be closer to God outdoors. Perhaps even more holy was that we had two rabbis instead of one—we each wanted the rabbi that had been instrumental to our spiritual growth by our side. But better than that was that I had someone special to walk me down the aisle: Noah. The actual moment of exchanging rings was a blur, but I recalled the simple bands we chose; even mine had no embellishments or rich stones to symbolize our everlasting bond.

As is tradition, Alan smashed a wine glass at the end of the ceremony to symbolize the fragility of relationships and all we hold dear. The symbolism isn't sad, however. It's a reminder to cherish

SECOND TIME'S THE CHARM

what's important and to nurture and care for your relationship. Everyone cheered, "Mazel tov!" I floated through the reception, making sure to thank each guest for spending the afternoon with us. The love from our friends and family made me glow with warmth. I wished I could remove the fur shrug, but I was self-conscious about my upper arms. Everything was so perfect, I wanted the pictures to reflect that. In the end, we couldn't add the raspberries to the champagne for color as I intended (the caterer let us know they weren't kosher), and I—Little Miss Party Planner—left the handcrafted resin coasters made from wildflowers behind. Our guests took home the floral centerpieces instead, and my prince and I departed for our castle.

Pumpkin Carriage or Prince?

After the wedding, Alan and I slowly settled into our life as husband and wife. Bam's "not-guilty" verdict was a professional milestone for Alan, but it was a new beginning for me, too. Not only did I help with the case, but I secured a long-term lease for the firm's vacant offices at a premium price. For me, helping at the law firm was more exciting than the housewife role. I hoped my old-fashioned husband would see that my talents would be of better use at the office than in the kitchen. How could I make my case?

When we got married, Alan added me to his bank account and gave me two credit cards, one for business expenses and one for personal things. He said he'd take care of the bills. I didn't question him—he'd run a business for over 30 years. But when three "past due" notices came across my desk, I was furious. Late fees ate into profits. I stormed into Alan's office and confronted him.

"Where is your accounts payable file?" I asked, trying to hide my anger. I could tell by the expression on his face that he did not want to share this information with me. When he could see I wasn't going to let up, he opened the bottom drawer of his desk. I walked over to it and found myself looking down at a stack of bills that hadn't even been opened. I put aside my surprise that his accounts payable file was 1. not on the computer, 2. not even really a "file" and 3. definitely not getting paid. I went into investigation mode.

PUMPKIN CARRIAGE OR PRINCE?

"Alan, why haven't you opened these bills?" He was looking sheepish at this point. I could tell I was not going to like his answer.

"Business hasn't been good, Kari. There's no money to pay them, that's why." I knew there had been a drop in the criminal defense business since the recession. Fewer and fewer criminal cases came in. Clients who could afford to pay Alan's fees were even more scarce. Often, when a potential client came in for an interview, they complained his fee was too high. When Alan offered to lower the fee, they said they didn't have any money.

We were back where Scott and I had been fifteen years earlier. But Scott worked for a large company. They paid him a salary until he was able to build a client base. Alan was a sole practitioner; no clients meant no fees. No fees meant no money. This wasn't the "happily-ever-after" I imagined. Had I been fooled? I thought Alan was my prince. Was he really the pumpkin carriage all along? When I relayed the situation to Matt, he was shocked.

"This guy's a disaster. Good thing you still own your house in Palm Beach. Now you have a reason to go back."

"You know me better, Matt. I'm not a quitter. I'm not walking away." I'd waited a long time for my glass slipper. It was fragile. What if it broke?

I remembered Rabbi Moshe's lecture on performing mitzvot. "Mitzvah" is the Hebrew word for a good deed. Moshe asked our group who benefits more from a good deed, the person who performs it or the one who receives it? Everyone replied, "The one who receives it." We all got it wrong. It's the one who performs it. *Why?* Because if that person didn't ask for help, we wouldn't be given the opportunity to do the mitzvah. Alan hadn't asked, but he was in a bind; this was my chance to help. Making businesses better was my strength. I'd thought about returning to private equity; now I had an opening. I relayed my thoughts to Alan. "Doesn't that require putting money in?" he asked jokingly.

"I may have no liquid powder, but I bring things that are more important: vision, work ethic and hands-on experience. I've done this at every company I ever worked for and helped my ex-husband do it too." The field of fashion is different from law or finance, but the art of building a business is the same. I was ready to dig in.

"How do you get your cases?"

"From former clients."

"That's it? You don't advertise or have anyone who can refer business to you?"

"No, advertising is too expensive; only former clients and friends send me cases."

Scott had lawyers and accountants who sent him clients, in addition to the people we'd met at charity affairs and parents from Emmy's school. This was a different game. Alan explained to me how fresh out of law school he worked for a lawyer who was a sole practitioner. Shortly after, the lawyer became a judge and passed the firm to him. Since then, he'd run his firm as a practice, not a business. He never thought about where his next case or client was coming from. He worked on the cases, lived off the fees and assumed another case would come in before the last fee ran out. If money ran out before he could sign a new client, he lived off a line of credit he secured against his business. When the financial crisis hit, his clients had no funds to hire lawyers. They could no longer use their houses or boats as piggy banks. His fees dropped so much that Alan's dad had him take a loan against the office building. His dad passed away, but the loan was still on the books. Alan was paying it back in the form of a mortgage payment.

I asked more questions and got the necessary answers to create a plan. In law, unlike fashion or finance, you cannot solicit a client for your services, but you can have other lawyers refer cases to you. It's legal to charge a fee for this. Only lawyers could have conjured this up. And there was someone called a bondsman. Alan never used one, but his friend Lenny did. He explained to me why they were excellent referral sources. I contacted Alan's former paralegal, who was new to the field. Her firm was glad to send clients to the lawyer who held the record for acquittals on first-degree murder cases in Florida. Now we needed mentors.

We met Ron, another defense attorney, at a law conference. He was reserved and had a big following in Miami Beach. A well-known defense lawyer named Steve sat next to us at the Hurricanes football games. His tough-guy demeanor made it easy to believe him when he quoted the seven-figure fees he charged in the good old days. Both men were sole practitioners like Alan and had an alpha, lone wolf vibe.

I felt an immediate rapport with Elissa and Maggie, Ron and Steve's wives. They were practical in the way second wives tend to be. Our kids were the same age. Elissa wasn't practicing, but she had a law degree. Maggie was Steve's paralegal. What began as the guys asking me to outfit their ladies for a party led to lasting relationships. By nature, wolves enjoy social behavior. Steadily, the six of us, along with our offspring, formed our own pack.

Ron and Steve had the foresight to see that the criminal defense field had changed. Steve was older and had invested his earnings wisely. He decided to semi-retire and take only federal cases. Ron transitioned from criminal cases to civil ones. He tried to convince Alan to do the same. Alan resisted. He loved criminal defense work. But civil work was where the money was now. If Alan wanted a paycheck, he needed to add civil work to his practice. I let on to Ron and Steve that Alan's business was slow and that he would take any case that wasn't big enough for them.

Another strategy was to be available at any time. When we dated, Alan was impressed I took every call, whether it was for my sales position at Valentino, my merchandising gig or my own business. Previously, he thought it was disrespectful for clients to call after business hours and on weekends. I tried to change his mindset. Every call could turn into a client.

Our household became like a convenience store—we were open 24/7. This work was exciting to me. Instead of "talking clothes," we were "talking cases." Alan treated the first call as a consultation. If the case piqued his interest, he set up an interview. If the case was in an area he didn't practice, he could refer it to another lawyer and collect a referral fee. Through this network, Alan also got feedback on his fees and strategy. Meanwhile, I took pictures of Alan with his clients and uploaded them to the website. Now, Alan understood how I supported a house and a daughter on a retail girl's salary. I was relentless when it came to bringing in new business. No one got away.

The civil work was a perfect fit for my background. Most of these cases came from high-net-worth individuals. And that is how Alan's practice transitioned to a boutique law firm. The legal part was up to Alan. The strategy to market our brand and run the business was on me.

It took discipline. In the beginning, there was no luxury shopping or vacations. Alan was sad to give up traveling. The hardest part for me was not being able to give back. How was it that the girl in Palm Beach who supported the ballet each season couldn't afford a ticket to a single performance? I told myself it was temporary. We'd sacrifice now and reap the rewards later. We lived modestly until we built a steady client base and created referral sources to keep the cases coming in. When couples we socialized with spoke about the exotic places they visited, we listened. When they asked if we had any trips planned, Alan was embarrassed to say we didn't.

"Don't be," I said. "That's silly; just say something funny."

"You ladies like going to foreign lands," he started saying to the wives, "Kari likes going to the bank."

It was true. I didn't need to be in Rome or Paris. My greatest pleasure came from building something and seeing it grow. I liked seeing our bank balance get bigger each time I made a deposit.

PUMPKIN CARRIAGE OR PRINCE?

It made me feel safe. I'd lived with my nails scraping off the edge of a cliff so long, I savored the security of knowing I had the resources to pull myself up by my bootstraps—preferably ones attached to Manolos.

It wasn't long before Alan was complaining about my visits to Palm Beach. I was still crafting my favors for my charities, dragging Alan to fundraisers there midweek and supporting the Saint Andrew's dance team at the basketball games even though Emmy was away at college.

"You left the Island physically, Kari, but you're not feeling that Miami is your home. I'm sure there's plenty of charities here that could use favors. Call up Ron; he's on the board of some good ones."

Alan was right: Miami was our home now. We should support local groups, and hitting the Miami social circuit might make our business grow. Giving at the level I wanted doesn't come cheap. That's why what happened next couldn't have come at a more perfect time.

Another Door Closes

Working with Alan gave me the work-life balance I desired at this stage of my life. Now I was able to visit Emmy and Noah at college as often as I wished, not just on parents' weekend. I could also network with clients and the other lawyers' wives at my convenience. To keep my creativity flowing, I made party favors for the hundreds of guests in attendance at charities I supported.

I was browsing magazine titles in the checkout line at the market when one jumped out and pushed me over. It was called *Palm Beach/The Island.* I had never seen this magazine when I lived there. How or why this glossy publication got to the grocery store in suburban Miami Shores, I'll never know. The cover shot of Worth Avenue invited me in like a friendly neighbor. As I flipped through pages of past clients and friends at society balls, one photo reached out from the page and almost knocked me over. It was a color photograph of Bitsy and Chip, my former neighbors, at The Coconuts Ball, an invitation-only party held every New Year's Eve.

I smiled, thinking of all the years I'd lived on the Island, not just owned property there. It was longer than I had lived anywhere else. Was I ever really part of this world? Did I ever fit in? Did I ever fully want to? Whatever way I chose to look at it, this Island changed me in ways I never imagined. I came there with the hope of making a life and a living for my family. Now that our finances were on track, I was thinking more toward the future. This most unlikely place and its people had taught me about faith, family and creating a life I could be proud of. Part of me clung to the notion that if I left for good, I would leave these lessons behind too. My Palm Beach house was proof of this. After seven years of realtors, renters and continuous upkeep, there was an all-cash buyer knocking on the door. Until now, I'd been reluctant to answer.

In Miami, Alan had transitioned from handling mostly criminal cases to civil cases. The fee structure for civil work was different. Instead of clients paying the full fee in advance, the procedure for criminal cases, fees for this type of work were billed by the hour. Managing this practice required rainmaking, marketing and attention to detail. My efforts added more to the firm's revenue than any money I could earn in the current fashion landscape.

All our resources went to building our business and supporting Emmy and Noah, who were in college. Gary had yet to find a buyer for my house. A young family rented it for the Season, but there was no guarantee they would renew their lease next year. With three mortgages to pay, there was no extra money to restore the house we lived in. It was time to turn our neglected house into a home. The profit from my Palm Beach house would give us the funds to make the Miami house our dream house. It was time to crack open my nest egg. I reached out to Gary to list the house for sale.

Emmy called to talk about her plans for the summer. She'd applied for an internship at a TV studio in Los Angeles. If she got it, she would be heading west at the end of the semester. "There's an offer on our house; I think I'm going to take it. Are you okay with that? Since I've held out this long, I thought about keeping it as an investment property in case we ever want to live there again."

"That's silly, Mom, I'm going to work in TV; I'll need to be in New York or LA for that. You can sell it." Emmy was a junior in college and majoring in broadcast journalism. She was thinking ahead and about where her life would take her, but still, I would never make a decision like this without checking with her first. The house had been on the market for two years following the storm Mona left. When she finally made an exit, the carpeting in the bedroom had dirty footprints all over it and there were holes in the walls where the TVs had been. I'd fixed her damage and, luckily, found new tenants—a young couple with a baby and another one on the way who were overjoyed to have so much space.

I'd hoped to spend the summer in the Palm Beach house with Emmy, but she got bored after a month. Her friends weren't in town. She returned to Boston to intern at the school's TV station and take summer classes. I said I wanted to be done with this house, but secretly, all along part of me hoped it wouldn't sell. Gary contacted the buyer. They accepted my counteroffer, contingent on an inspection. The amount we agreed on was close to the asking price.

I knew the house would only go up in value, but it was time for me to close this chapter of my life. The buyers lived in the neighborhood. They were heirs to one of Palm Beach's legacy families. They intended to preserve the house, not demolish it to put up a McMansion—the sad fate of so many Island homes. They planned to use it as a guesthouse for out-of-town relatives. I loved this proposed use. My favorite memories were of times spent with family there. They agreed to a delayed closing, so Emmy and I could have one last weekend there. We never got that weekend. Emmy landed the internship out west. She left straight for Los Angeles from Boston and I flew out to get her settled in her apartment.

One Last Sweater Sighting

Crafting favors for local charities and clients gave me a sense of belonging in Miami. However, I received tragic news from Palm Beach that pulled me back there. Drew's blood sugar was low and his pain had gotten worse. Despite adjusting to life in Miami, my community ties and friendships in Palm Beach ran deep. I began visiting Drew more often as his condition declined. One day, while out shopping, I got the dreaded call from Bri.

"Drew's condition took a bad turn. We've called hospice."

"I'm on my way."

"Good," Bri said, and I could tell by the tone of her voice she was glad I was coming. When Alan and I arrived at her house, the shopping bags in Bri's living room made it seem she'd cleaned up at a sale on Worth Avenue. But it was March; sales didn't take place until the Season was over. And what was she doing shopping while her husband was so ill? I peeked inside one of the bags and was shocked to see what was inside. There were at least a dozen of vintage Valerie Louthan cashmere sweaters.

Palm Beach is small. Word spreads quickly, and of course there's *The Shiny Sheet*. That's where Bri saw the ad. Valerie's heirs were having a "Final Sale" to get rid of her inventory. I'd wondered what happened to all the sweaters when the company closed. I'd been so focused on Alan's law practice, I wasn't aware Valerie passed away last year.

"I recognized your handwriting on the tickets," Bri said. She was referring to the white hang tag on each sweater that identified it by a male or female name. At first, I was reluctant to go to the sale. I'd closed the book on that part of my life. When Bri mentioned Valerie's daughter Laura was there, I changed my mind. Laura was Valerie's youngest child and the only one of Valerie's kids who grew up in the States. She had the same quirky charm as Valerie. She was an orphan now, and I wanted to make sure she was okay. And I needed some new sweaters. Nothing on the market matched Valerie's in quality or craftsmanship. The ones I bought to replace hers had pilled after a few wears.

When we pulled up to the Ballet Florida building for the sale, four-foot-tall cardboard boxes were strewn everywhere. For the annual sale at Stubbs & Wootton, Island residents lined up on Worth Avenue from the wee hours of the morning to get the first pick of shoes. Here, everyone scrambled in at once like shoppers rushing through the doors of a department store on Black Friday.

Shoppers, many who had been clients, ravaged through the boxes as they grabbed sweaters in bunches. Mona was there. Rumor had it she and Arthur divorced when they moved from my house. I would have said hello (I harbored no ill feelings toward her), but she was chasing the cute guy from my street with the King Charles Spaniel. I wished her luck. He was prince material. Surely there was a glass slipper in his closet waiting for the right woman. In the five years I ran Valerie Louthan Designs, we never held a sale. The collection was priced from $200 to $1,500 per item. Now, each sweater was marked down to $50. It would take hours to search through each box and find a style in a color I liked.

Nonetheless, I wanted some for nostalgic reasons. The ones I designed were gone. However, I found two fitted mock turtlenecks, one in black, another in petal pink. They would be timeless paired with a pencil skirt. A roomy cowl-neck, in a sapphire blue, would be chic to wear with jeans and boots up north. I greeted Laura and showed her the items I was buying.

ONE LAST SWEATER SIGHTING

"Hi, Laura. Do you remember me? I used to run the business for your mom."

"Kari, of course. You and Mummy had such fun together," she said in an accent that always made me feel like I was sipping tea with Catherine at her family's farmhouse in Emily Brontë's *Wuthering Heights*. "I saw your mom at a trunk show in May a few years ago. We spoke about getting together. I'm sorry we never did; I never got to say goodbye."

"Hm...yes. That was her last season in Palm Beach. She fell ill when she returned to England and never came back to the States again. She passed away a year later." As I pulled out my checkbook, Laura said, "For you, it's $90. That came to only $30 per sweater. I was tempted to buy more, but Alan was anxious to leave. None of the classic men's styles were his size. I asked Laura where she lived. I wasn't surprised when she said Silicon Valley as she worked in technology—family businesses often end this way.

"Mum spoke so fondly of you, Kari. I miss her so much."

"Can I take your number, in case I'm ever in California? We can share 'Valerieisms' together. The thing I loved most about her was her wit—she always made me laugh."

"Of course," she said. I was sad to see what had become of the business. I wondered if I'd bought an equity stake when I had the chance, it would still be up and running. I'd gotten over blaming Valerie for my missed opportunity. Valerie was no villain, and I was no victim. It was just business. She made a decision based on what she thought was best at the time.

When I used to question Valerie about why she wanted to leave the business to me she would say, "Because it's my legacy, Kari. Why should my designs not be enjoyed when I can no longer work or I'm no longer living, if there's someone like you who can carry on what I started? There's an old proverb that says 'people die twice: the first time when their heart stops beating, the second when someone speaks their name for the last time.' I don't want to be forgotten."

I was young and naïve then, but now I understood. Valerie's work lasted a single lifetime. Seeing how fast her life's work disappeared and Drew's premature death made me reflect on my mortality. What was my true purpose? What would I leave behind when I was no longer here? Something inside me sensed that it had nothing to do with cashmere or the law. Perhaps what worked for me and Alan—using our passions to do work we loved and inspiring our kids to do the same—was where our legacy lay. Maybe, as a family, we could help others to see that purpose is the key to self-esteem and living a happy life.

Emmy was about to finish college and venture into the real world. I was so proud that she insisted on leaving the Bahamas, where she was on break, to fly back to attend the funeral. "Mom, I would never not be there," she said as I gave her details of the flight I had booked for her. "Drew is Dad's best friend; he's an uncle to me, and Chloe, Bri and Jordan are my family."

We all knew it was coming, but that day, standing at the cemetery, it seemed the heavy rain was sent from God to wash away the tears most of us couldn't hold back. Drew gave so much to so many. I glanced at Dave, his childhood friend, who was back to practicing law after a long battle with drugs. What would have become of him or his daughter if Drew hadn't paid for his rehab when everyone else gave up on him? Passover was approaching. This was the holiday where the Jewish people escaped bondage by making a bold choice to leave Egypt. This year, I promised myself to break away from the thoughts that enslaved me and live more like Drew, who always saw the positive side of everything. When I cried to him about my sister Jenn still sponging off my mom, he said, "Isn't it nice that your mom has company and they're both not alone?" At first I laughed, but when his words sank in, they made sense. Drew pointed out what I wasn't able to see.

ONE LAST SWEATER SIGHTING

On Passover, those of the Jewish faith are forbidden from eating leavened bread (called *chametz* in Hebrew) during the eight days of the holiday. This reminds us that our forebearers had to flee Egypt quickly to escape slavery, and the bread they baked didn't have time to rise.

The first step in preparing for the Passover holiday is the house cleaning process. Although this holiday coincides with spring, the kind of cleaning it requires is different from typical seasonal cleaning. You must methodically inspect and rid every part of your home of any trace of *chametz*. *Chametz* includes any product made from grain, so not just bread, but also cookies, cakes and crunchy chocolate. You search every corner, nook and cranny to get rid of even crumbs so as to abide by the rules. Pre-Passover, no food may leave the kitchen. After eating, clothes must be brushed off and hands thoroughly washed. Despite these rules, I loved Passover because any holiday that got me excited about cleaning was worth celebrating! And this year I had a lot to be thankful for.

The past year had been rough for Allie and me. Renovating a house and working together isn't easy, especially because we were living in a rundown cottage on our property that had no kitchen. Before we called this cottage home, all four kids refused to stay in it when they visited. But I didn't mind. It gave me an excuse not to cook. We ate out every night. Our breakfast came from a dorm-room-sized refrigerator and a coffee maker set up near the bathroom sink. This sink doubled as our kitchen sink. When Noah visited, he was shocked to see us living under these conditions.

"Kari, you're a rich woman now," he said, referring to the profit from the Palm Beach house. "Why don't you and Dad drive over to the beach and check into the St. Regis while the house is being renovated?" I laughed. I told him I needed to be at the house because the construction business was unpredictable. The general contractor isn't always at the job site. The subcontractors, plumbers, electricians and tile layers seemed to show up when it was convenient, not when they were supposed to. Someone needed to manage the project, and that someone was me.

"But how do you know what to do? Why isn't Dad supervising the workers?"

"Dad has a heavy caseload at work. He doesn't have time. I did projects at my other house; this one's just bigger. And you know what I learned?"

"What?"

"That a good contractor is like a good seamstress. A seamstress tailors the clothes to fit the customer. A contractor does the same with a house for a homeowner. In fashion, it was me who instructed the seamstress how the customer wanted the clothes to look. I'm doing the same here with our contractor. If you're detail-oriented, the two trades are similar." Then I had another thought I wanted to share with Noah. "Living like this will make us appreciate it so much more when it's done." Noah gave me a puzzled look.

"If you say so, Kari, but be careful. I don't want you to get hurt again." He was referring to the scar on my hairline. The first week on the job, I wasn't outfitted in the proper gear. An outdoor light fell on my head and blood gushed from my scalp. Instead of racing to the hospital, I cleaned and bandaged the cut, donned a hard hat, hunkered down and got back to work.

"Don't worry, that scar taught me to never rush to a construction site unprepared. Thankfully, the light fell on my head and not my face. The scar looks like it's from a brow lift." I was determined to host the Passover holiday despite my unfinished kitchen. Bri declined my invite. She was still in mourning and having a small dinner with her parents and the kids. It was time to share my hospitality with my blended family and new friends.

My glazed blue backsplash tiles were stuck in a warehouse. There were no pulls on the white wood custom cabinets. The gas line to the Wolf cooktop wasn't connected. This wasn't going to stop me. I had a sink, two ovens and a dishwasher. All three of our girls and my niece, Nicole, were coming. Noah was bringing two friends. To surprise him, Alan borrowed a sports car from a client. Both men in my life loved foreigns. Steve picked up the soup and side dishes I ordered from Epicure Market. Beth gave me some recipes that didn't require stovetop cooking. I laid out my best linens and set the table with Baccarat crystal stemware and sterling silver flatware given to me by my mother. How could anyone not love a religion that instructs you to set a table with fine things?

The dinner was more than I hoped for. When the telling of the Passover story was complete, the 20-somethings took the wine outside to the loggia. It wasn't the food or the design details but the laughter of children that turned this house into a home. It was just how I imagined it when I first fell in love with this house—all of our children home, together. No one left before midnight. I woke up the next morning to find a note from Noah on the kitchen table.

Dear Dad and Kari,

I didn't want to wake you, but I had to get back to school. Thank you for your amazing hospitality and entertaining me and my friends. They had the best time. They finally understand what I mean when I say, "I need to go to Miami. I need to go home."

P.S. The red Ferrari rocked.

When I closed the sale of my Palm Beach home, I wasn't sure if I sold a house or "sold out." After reading the note, I was certain I had made the right decision. We didn't live in Palm Beach. That house was no longer our home. It was just an expensive piece of real estate. A new chapter was beginning and the more real it became, the more unreal it seemed.

Hip-Hoppin' and Rockin'

When you're in building mode, one thing leads to another. As it turned out, we didn't need to sponsor charity events or donate favors to make the law practice grow. Surprisingly, it was a former client that gave us our next big break. This client sent us a new group of clients and that took our business to a completely different level.

I left the office early each day to prepare dinner for Alan. The shopping part was more fun now that Whole Foods opened nearby—at least they had small carts. I still didn't enjoy cooking. I liked to serve a simple meal during the week, not a feast. However, my new husband was obsessed with food. I never understood the term "fine dining." To me, "fine" was an adjective best reserved for jewelry or art, not dinner.

Each afternoon, Alan decided what he was in the mood to eat. I had the staples, but if he wanted fish, it had to be fresh. That meant a trip to the fishmonger. If it was meat that got his mouth watering, the butcher shop. Salad, side dishes and dessert were nonnegotiable. He insisted all three courses be presented on serving pieces. As we dined on my attempts at *Top Chef*-quality cuisine, I told him he should have been born Christian; to him, every meal was the last supper. For me, the best part of these meals was the conversation. During one of these dinners, Alan turned to me and said, "Hey, have you ever heard of Rick James?"

"The singer?" I asked.

"Yes," he responded.

HIP-HOPPIN' AND ROCKIN'

"Of course. Why?"

"Because I am representing him. He came to the office today."

"That's impossible." I loved the music of Rick James, but I knew he was dead. I thought about it and realized he must be talking about a different artist from Miami who was trending right now. "Do you mean Rick Ross?" I asked. I pulled up an image of Rick Ross on my phone and showed it to Alan.

"I can't tell; this guy had dark glasses on when he came in and never took them off." Rick Ross was known for wearing sunglasses, at night. I found another picture of Rick with sunglasses on. "Yeah, that's him. Rick Ross is my new client." Rick Ross was a hip-hop artist. Alan didn't even know what hip-hop was. But hip-hop was the soundtrack to my life story. When Rick's songs played on XM radio, his deep, throaty voice made me smile no matter what crisis was happening at work or with our kids.

"Why didn't you tell me Rick Ross was at the office? I would have come back. I can't believe I was waiting in line at a butcher shop while you were with our hometown king of hip-hop."

"Kari, I had no clue who he was. I got the call and a few hours later the guy was sitting across from me." The prospect of my husband representing Rick Ross was exciting. I was already thinking how good it would look to list him as a client on our website.

"Who referred him to you?"

"You'll never believe it—it was Bam. Bam grew up with Rick in Carol City. When Bam told Rick how I beat those murder charges for him, Rick knew I was the guy for him. What a coincidence, huh?"

"It's no coincidence. Aren't all criminal defense clients aspiring hip-hop artists?"

Rick's case was a civil matter. Alan worked his magic and won. Shortly after, Rick moved to Atlanta; his case was a one and done. But the friend *he* referred to the practice was on the verge of becoming a household name. This time, I made sure I accompanied Alan when he went to this client's house to be interviewed.

"Give me your first name," Alan said.

"Khaled."

"And your last."

"Khaled."

"You gave me that already. I said your last name."

"It's Khaled."

"So, you're telling me your name's Khaled Khaled."

"Yes. Khaled Mohamed Khaled." Khaled was of Palestinian descent. In the Arab world it is common for people to have the same first and last name. I learned this from my Saudi clients when I worked for Bijan. It was time for me to step in.

"Khaled, I'm Kari. I think we've already met. You were the DJ at my friend Lori's son LJ's bar mitzvah in Palm Beach."

"Yeah, I was. I liked that Lori. You guys were there?"

"Yes; you made the party a hit." This broke the ice. The conversation flowed easily from then on. When it came time to discuss the details of the case, I left the room to join Khaled's fiancé, Nicole, in the kitchen where she was preparing a salad for Khaled. Alan was hired, and this was only the first of many cases this client would bring.

When a client named "Baby" called, Alan didn't need me to tell him this baby was no infant. An interior designer Alan represented had referred him. She'd decorated his mansion on Biscayne Bay. The place looked more like a palace for a Saudi prince than a crib for a rapper from New Orleans. Universal Music signed this baby at age 28. His other rap name was "Birdman," although his given name was Bryan. Bryan Williams was the cofounder and face of Cash Money Records, the label that discovered Lil Wayne, who brought Drake and Nicki Minaj on board.

"When this guy gives you a bird call, you better whistle back," I told Alan.

HIP-HOPPIN' AND ROCKIN'

The results Alan got for Baby gained his trust. When Alan didn't understand the references in Baby's texts, he didn't need to consult Urban Dictionary; I translated them. But it was how Baby behaved on the set of a music video that gained my respect. He was surrounded by a crew that were dressed in all black. Each guy wore a nameplate with the letters "RG" spelled out in diamonds. RG stood for the supergroup "Rich Gang" that released a studio album produced by Cash Money and Young Money Records. It was easy to figure out that the bigger the letters, the higher up in status the person was. Baby was quick to correct a female dancer who asked a member of his crew if he was a security guard. "He's not security. He's been with me since I started," Baby told her.

This man was loyal. It made me feel a connection with him. If you're wondering what a white girl from the suburbs has in common with a Black man who grew up in boys' homes and the streets, it's this: We both grew up without fathers. The loss of a dad transcends barriers of race, income and social class. This kind of pain causes more harm to a kid's heart than a gunshot wound from a Glock.

"Give this guy Baby a chance to get to know you," I told Alan. "Don't ask for a retainer to get started. Being raised in a world without a father teaches you not to trust. Even if he doesn't know it, you're all he's got. He has lawyers to negotiate his music deals, but no one to protect him from people trying to take a piece of what he's built."

Over time, our relationship rose to the level where we attended hip-hop industry celebrations as Baby's guest. It was me who found nothing more exciting than to be present at these events. Alan felt proud his clout with these guys was the reason these invites were extended. And that's how, on my birthday, I had my own private meet-and-greet with Lil Wayne. As a favor, Alan had asked Baby to introduce the two of us.

It was just before midnight when Lil Wayne finally arrived at the set of M3 Studios. I was excited to point him out to Alan. Shockingly, Alan started off in the direction where Lil Wayne was standing with his entourage. Lil Wayne was wearing headphones, and it was obvious he was absorbed in a creative process. This was not the time to disturb him. The studio was heavily guarded. We had to show ID and leave our phones when we pulled up. I ran after Alan and tried to stop him from approaching Lil Wayne, but I wasn't fast enough. Thankfully, from across the room someone else saw what was about to go down and got there just in time—Baby.

"Yo man, what are you doing? You can't just walk up to Lil Wayne! That's not dope. You need me to introduce you. He's like a son to me. He's been with me since he was a kid." I promised Baby we'd wait until after the song was recorded to meet Lil Wayne.

I spent the rest of the night hiding behind a screen as the video was recorded. I was so absorbed seeing Wayne perform that I almost missed my chance to meet him. By the time the shoot ended, Wayne was heading out and it was Baby who said to Alan, "Where's your wife? She needs to meet Wayne." Baby motioned for me to come and join him and Alan. I walked over and was in disbelief he knew just what to say to Wayne before introducing us.

"This is my lawyer and his wife Kari. they're big fans; they went to your concert in West Palm Beach." *That is exactly how I would have prefaced it.* Wayne put his arm around me and said "Oh yeh, then you must be the one celebrating a birthday." And all I can recall from the conversation after was how I told him how much his lyrics and metaphors inspired me, and to please not retire because his words were what got me through so many tough days. Then, he turned toward me and hugged me! Alan had no idea this was my best birthday gift ever and even though I'd never tell him, it would be okay if he never gave me one again!

HIP-HOPPIN' AND ROCKIN'

From that moment on, Alan made sure he was one call away. If his phone rang late at night, which was often, I woke him up. In the past decade, hip-hop had become the most listened to genre of music in the nation. And it wasn't just the music I marveled at; it was the culture behind it. Hip-hop is reminiscent of the greatest American rags-to-riches stories. My grandfather came to this country with nothing and founded a perfume business that catered to socialites and celebrities. My father lost his chance to run it when his life ended abruptly.

The verses these artists put to beats referenced pop culture. Their lyrics resonated with millennials and Gen Z the way Springsteen's did with kids from my generation. And how could a fashionista like me not love these guys? They recreated the high-low fashion trend. They paired Dior and Balenciaga with Hanes T-shirts and Timberlands. With our accountant's okay, I bought birthday and Christmas gifts for their families. Only a girl from the luxury sector knew what designers they liked. Thankfully, Gucci and Burberry made kids' clothes.

These gestures made a connection; Alan's results kept these guys coming back. Among their employees, sound engineers and artist friends, we had plenty of new cases in this part of the practice. Alan wasn't defending clients just to earn a fee, just as I didn't sell anyone a product just to collect a commission. He cared first and foremost that justice was served. I cared too, which made Alan care even more. He wanted to impress me. Other cases came from contractors and interior designers, and the clients who used their services. The kids of affluent parents added another demographic to the firm. There was no longer a need to seek out referrals.

Alan's product became a service for a new breed of luxury consumer. Fortunately, his wife knew the level of attention these types demanded. When a skill comes naturally to someone, they think it's easy. Alan found it tedious to communicate with clients by phone, text and email. In the past, clients paid their fee up front and trusted him to deliver a not guilty verdict. Alan was shy, except when he was making arguments before a judge and jury—then his theatrical nature shined. Discussing cases with clients on a day-to-day basis was stressful for him. And why wouldn't I want to help with his firm? I didn't need to purchase an equity stake in this business; my status as a wife made me an owner. Titles never meant much to me, but Alan insisted on naming me chief operating officer.

My position at Alan's firm gave me proximity to the cases involving the hip-hop crowd. I was glad to be of service to these men who contributed so much to our city. The South Florida economy of my youth was based on tourism; these guys brought the music to Miami! Their product was different from the ones I represented in the past, but it was exciting and relevant.

My pastime of driving around listening to hip-hop music now equated to revenue for the firm. When a new song by a client played, I immediately called Alan. It gave him a good lead-in when he needed them to discuss their case. When Nicki Minaj rapped about the jeweler to the hip-hop stars in a song called "Plain Jane Remix," I couldn't wait to tell Alan. Her lyric "Queen is the name, Rafaello did the chain" made me chuckle. This cat Rafaello was in litigation with an artist we had on retainer. My husband was the lawyer on the case. *And* he was favored to win.

These clients were colorful characters. They brought me to the front lines of the hip-hop universe. I would much rather be invited to watch Khaled shoot a music video in Malibu with Lil Wayne and Justin Bieber than be a guest at someone's table at a gala in Palm Beach. No hedge fund husband could make that happen for me. Khaled told everyone he knew, which was a lot, considering he had 16 million Instagram followers, "If you get in trouble in Miami, this is the guy to call." We couldn't pay for that kind of advertising.

HIP-HOPPIN' AND ROCKIN'

And I wasn't the only one who liked having an in with these guys. Suddenly, Alan was a celebrity in the circle we ran in. At parties, parents gathered around him, hoping to secure music internships for their kids. Now we were given prime seating at their parties. And how about the up-and-coming artists who needed his services? All they had to do was read his website to know they were getting the best. We hired two additional lawyers so Alan could concentrate on the cases he enjoyed. One morning, I could tell Alan was in a bad mood. "What's the matter?" I asked him.

"Khaled had the nerve to ask me for a discount on his bill because of the amount of work he's given me. And on top of that he wants me to take on a new case for him."

"Let me look through QuickBooks and I'll get back to you," I said. I dutifully did the research and came back to Alan.

"Khaled's fees were 20 percent of the firm's income last year. Khaled is right; he deserves a discount. He's not just talented—he's a businessman too. You can learn from him," I told my husband.

"What the hell is there to learn from a guy who isn't even an artist?"

"You're wrong. Just because he doesn't sing doesn't mean he's not an artist. Hip-hop is known for its culture of collaboration. Khaled is a producer; he brings the best artists together to make music." Alan was beginning to get it, so I continued. "Alan, Khaled was nominated for a Grammy Award for 'I'm on One,' the song he did with Drake, Rick Ross and Lil Wayne. Bringing the best talent together to create hit songs and albums is a tremendous art." I was on a roll.

"But Kari, he wants me to defend him in a personal injury case that was brought against him. I've never done personal injury."

"Take a page from his playbook and do the same with his case. Bring in a lawyer who has experience in personal injury, but you stay the lead lawyer on the case. Khaled's happy with your results so far. If this case goes to trial, he trusts you'll win." As with a line of luxury products, we created a strategy to produce different streams of income: criminal defense, civil defense, interior design law, construction law and, thanks to Khaled, personal injury law.

Our lawyer friends told us if we wanted to make big money, Alan should stop taking pro bono and court-appointed cases. But Alan couldn't give up this work; he loved the action. And it was his way to give back. Alan's skills were as a trial lawyer. The same creative thinking that allowed him to formulate brilliant defenses didn't translate to bringing in cases, but it didn't need to. His chief operating officer was also a marketing maven. She knew how publicity and customer loyalty led to profits for a business.

I'd learned from Scott to let a professional turn our money into more money. We invested our riches with Adam, the financial advisor I chose to manage the seven-figure profit from the sale of my Palm Beach house. I had reason to trust him. When I asked where he'd received his training, he named a firm called "Magnum Securities." He was sure I'd never heard of it. I had; it was Seth's firm. Adam reviewed the monthly statements that told me how much the account was up. It was equal to what I earned in a month as a salesgirl.

We put the rest of our resources back into the economy by giving people work and small business loans. We didn't charge interest. We supported causes we believed in—literacy, the arts, social justice and upward mobility for all.

It was fun when other lawyers came to court to watch Alan in action. He became known as "the one to beat." The respect judges showed him was impressive. I was proud to play Lois Lane to his Superman. It felt good to be part of the squad that sought justice for the city. I liked being the girl at the salon known for my generous tips or the one my personal shopper could count on when he needed a commission. I knew how far those extra dollars went; I'd been there. Starting a college fund for my housekeeper's son was a given. She helped me with my holiday entertaining. She was part of our family now.

It had been a hectic week at work interviewing law clerks and paralegals. Like me, many of them worshipped the artists we represented. They were eager to join our flock, but this weekend my presence was required at a completely different place of worship.

A Valuable Lesson From Lana

It was an honor to be invited to the bar mitzvah of Rabbi Moshe's son. I didn't want to miss it. The temple had grown from its humble origins to a cultural center serving more than 500 members. Many of my friends and former clients from Palm Beach would be at this event, but the first person I bumped into wasn't anyone I expected to see.

After the service, I left the sanctuary to return my prayer book. There she was, right in front of me, the reason I came to this town 21 years ago: Lana Marks. Her style of dressing hadn't changed: a pastel-colored skirt suit in a tweed bouclé fabric that resembled those designed by Karl Lagerfeld. I knew hers were custom-made to ensure a better fit. The Chanel buttons were sewn on afterward. Her shoes were the same, Manolo Blahnik pumps, with just a bit less heel height, probably to account for her age, which by now must be north of 60. She seemed as shocked to see me as I was to see her.

"Kari," she said in her charming South African accent, "how are you? And what are you doing with yourself these days?" I was glad I'd chosen the red lace Dolce and Gabbana skirt and fitted long-sleeved top with hand-embroidered pink and red rosettes. I was overdressed; this outfit read more "charity luncheon" than morning service in a temple. However, it gave me the confidence necessary to address Lana. I explained I had remarried, moved to Miami and managed my husband's business. Alan reached for my

A VALUABLE LESSON FROM LANA

hand as he made his way through the crowd to stand near me. I introduced him to Lana and her husband.

"Lana, glad to finally put a face to your name. Kari's told me such good things about you over the years." Her eyes came back to mine, as if she were trying to see if what he said was true. It was during this quick lapse in conversation that I summoned the courage to ask her what I wanted to know for a long time.

"Funny, I was just thinking about you, Lana," I said, trying to soften my tone before hitting hard with my questions.

"Oh, really. Why is that?" she asked.

"I live near Saks Fifth Avenue in Bal Harbour. The only exotic skin handbags they carry are those by Nancy Gonzalez. I was curious why her brand is there and not yours." Bal Harbour was one of 10 Saks Fifth Avenue locations that carried Lana's bags during the year I worked there. Together, she and I made certain we not only met but exceeded the sales plan given to us by each store that bought her collection. After New York, this branch netted the highest sales. Shortly after I left the company, Lana's bags were no longer carried by any Saks Fifth Avenue or Neiman Marcus stores. I needed to know why.

"Whenever I'm shopping with Kari, she points out the Nancy Gonzalez bags and tells me how Lana's, the line she represented, are so much prettier and a much better quality. Kari can't believe that Saks carries Nancy Gonzalez's collection instead of yours," Alan said. I was glad he remembered. It sounded more credible coming from him than me. Lana started to allude to something about Nancy Gonzalez having a son who was "in with the buyers." When she could tell I wasn't buying it, she changed her tune.

"Kari was the best I ever had," she said, looking at Alan.

"No one who's worked for me since has had the work ethic or the ability to connect with store buyers and customers the way she did. Despite the success of my boutiques, I have not been able to get my collection back into Saks or Neiman Marcus, but I refuse to give up. My collection will be in those stores again." She pressed her business card in the palm of my hand. "Please come back to work, Kari; we will make this happen. Call me after the holidays."

Alan and I made our way to the social hall, which was overflowing with guests. We didn't see Lana again. On the way back to Bri's, I took the card from my clutch and saw that it listed all the cities that sold her product: Palm Beach first, followed by London, Macau, Shanghai, Singapore, Beijing and Qatar. I had to give her credit for finding other markets to sell her goods when the stores in the States said no to her. I wasn't surprised. This was a woman who called the accessories buyer at Saks Fifth Avenue 25 times before they agreed to carry her collection in just one store.

It would be tempting to try to do something no one else could. The economy had improved since I ran into her at "the OLD BAGS LUNCHEON" years ago. I no longer considered the time I worked at her company as something she took from me. I was a new mother when I'd flown to New York four times a year to show her collection during market week. I'd dropped everything to travel for trunk shows, anytime she deemed it necessary to make our sales goal. My ambition got the best of me. Twenty years had passed since I left her company. I couldn't recall the details of the dispute that led her to fire me. I don't think she did either. It wasn't important. I knew why she wanted me back now.

We spent the night at Bri's so I could edit Jordan's college essays. The mint tea Bri served at breakfast wasn't strong enough for Alan. He needed caffeine; that meant a trip to Starbucks on Worth Avenue, which, conveniently, was right by Lana's shop. It was Sunday and most stores were closed, but hopefully I could get a glimpse of her merchandise from the window of the shop. Surprisingly, when we arrived, her shop was open. When we walked in, a salesperson asked if she could help us.

"I'm Lana's former sales director," I said. "I was hoping to see her new collection."

A VALUABLE LESSON FROM LANA

"Well, you're in luck; she's here. Let me go get her." Lana walked to the front of the boutique. We reminisced about the fun times we had traveling across the country doing trunk shows together.

"Come work with me again, Kari. I'll make it worth your while."

"She can't; she's too valuable to me," Alan piped up. Lana's eyes veered toward me to gauge my reaction. But I didn't want to reveal my hand just yet. Unbeknownst to Lana, I'd moved on from selling handbags with a beginning price point of five figures. Representing high-end accessories was exciting to me at age 30. My priorities had changed since then. The six-figure salary she dangled didn't tempt me. The only interest I had in Lana's bags now was to own one, preferably at the wholesale price.

Lana's eyes sparkled when I said I was there to buy a purse. When she remembered the style I requested was on loan to a magazine, she led me to her private office. "I wouldn't let anyone but you see these, Kari. It's my latest collection of evening bags. I know you'll appreciate their beauty." I gasped when she showed me a few. The Kelly green clutch in baby alligator was embellished with real emeralds at the clasp. In my day she designed bags for many a Hollywood star, but this one could only be worn by royalty or the bride of a czar.

Alan doubted me when I told him Valerie's business went under because I left. He laughed when I said Lana may have lost the department store accounts for the same reason. Now he thought otherwise.

"Their loss is my gain," he said, smiling at me.

In December, our bookkeeper did the firm's year-end accounting. The business had the highest revenue and profits in 37 years. Many of the fees came from hip-hop stars and their entourages, but most of the income came from high-net-worth individuals who suffered an injustice. Alan had underestimated the reach of hip-hop. It seemed that even the ultra-rich heard of the artists he represented. All it took was a look at his client roster for them to sign on the dotted line. Most cases he settled. In the ones that went to trial, he hadn't lost one since we got engaged.

After he overcame his shyness, Alan found the courage he needed to talk to clients. In time, these clients understood how important his service was to them. His wife knew how to keep clients engaged and run a business on a shoestring budget.

"Maybe we can relax a little now—let's go on vacation. We deserve it."

"I don't think so," I said, not knowing if he was joking or not. "You have a big trial coming up. But as a belated birthday gift to you, I planned a trip to New York. We leave next weekend."

To surprise Alan, I splurged and booked a suite at The Bryant Park Hotel, a boutique hotel with a view of The New York Public Library and a winter village where we could watch skaters as they crisscrossed on the ice. I reserved a table at Campagnola, his favorite restaurant. Campagnola made me nostalgic for the Italian countryside. Small tables nestled close to each other like new lovers. People who dine there know one another by name. At dinner, I toasted my handsome husband and told him we were here to celebrate what he'd accomplished this past year: winning his first personal injury case; adding a roster of recording artists, interior designers and civil clients to the practice; hiring more staff and completing the first stage of the restoration project on our house.

He leaned in toward me and said, "The person we should be celebrating is you, Kari. You're the reason everything's turned around. No one works harder than you. Nothing gets in your way. And if you hadn't made me do that murder trial, we would've never gotten the hip-hop clients. Gaining their trust gave me the confidence to deal with other people with big money."

"It was a team effort, Allie. We did it together." I liked it when he complimented me on my brains instead of my beauty. My looks came from my parents. My business sense was my own making.

A VALUABLE LESSON FROM LANA

I mentioned to Alan that the hedge fund manager Steve Cohen, who owned a piece of the Mets, was seated nearby. He never got over my ability to recognize faces. He knew it was helping him now.

Two gentlemen dined at a table nearby. One of them questioned the waiter about the identity of the man and his much younger wife, seated nearby. The waiter said he didn't know us.

"Can you check the name on the reservation?" one gentleman asked the waiter, not knowing I'd overheard. The waiter went to the front of the restaurant to check the reservation list and then came back to the man and whispered our last name in his ear. The waiter shrugged his shoulders, showing the name meant nothing to him. We could tell the name didn't ring a bell to the man at the table either.

To my amusement, the man continued to look our way the entire evening. Alan was sure he was staring at the seven-carat fancy yellow diamond ring he gave me for our anniversary. "One carat for each year you waited for me," he said when he placed it on my finger. It wasn't the ring. Women notice things like that, not men. Alan carried himself with a strength and charisma that drew people in. I noticed it on our first date, the first few minutes after meeting him.

I would be forever grateful to my father-in-law for telling Alan to forget the garment industry and go to law school instead. His dad, Morris, paid Alan's tuition, despite having four younger children to educate. Morris paid for all five of his kids' college and professional degrees. He was the son of Polish immigrants to this country. His parents had no formal education and couldn't afford to give their only son one. Morris wanted something better for his children. He owned a single Chevron gas station in North Miami Beach. I wished he were here to see his son now. My guy got a late start in the money-making game, but he was catching up.

Once Upon a Time in Palm Beach

Late fall, just before the city skipped into winter, was my favorite season. I couldn't wait to walk in Central Park and see the leaves as they changed colors. I scored orchestra seats to see *Hamilton* on Broadway. We were meeting our girls at Sant Ambroeus for brunch. Goldie found a place for her passion for logistics as a producer for television. Emmy landed a job in publicity, a perfect fit for a girl who had been photographed by society magazines and local newspapers since childhood. Hannah was employed by a design consulting firm based in California, but she was able to work from their offices here. Noah couldn't be with us; he started a new job in Tampa. A car took us from the hotel to DJ Khaled's penthouse on the West Side. We brought a gift for his baby boy. Nicole, Khaled's fiancé, was grateful for the outfits from Bergdorf's. The baby's room was full of expensive jewelry and sneakers given by other rappers, but the poor little guy had nothing to wear.

"How did you know to get clothes?" Alan asked.

"Babies can't go outside until they get their shots. New moms are overwhelmed; they aren't thinking about clothes. I certainly wasn't. And Nicole's a New Yorker. She has great fashion sense—I knew she'd appreciate a gift from Bergdorf's."

Emmy was a fall baby, too. It was colder than usual that year. After she was born, I didn't venture outside for months. I never liked receiving gifts, but when packages were delivered each day, I couldn't wait to see what my friends and colleagues picked out for my girl. My favorites were the doll-sized designer outfits, chosen with so much love.

We arrived in SoHo before the girls. We stepped into an art gallery where an exhibition was taking place. Well-groomed men and their wives were buying up pieces like bubble gum.

"Kari, look at the price on this one," Alan said. "How can such young guys afford this?"

"It's finance money. They buy art as an investment, not just for pleasure. That's Jean-Michel Basquiat; his work is hot right now." Hedge fund couples in New York are as common as the trust fund pairs found in Palm Beach. The difference was their attire: Supreme hoodies and Nikes for the former, Vineyard Vines button-downs and Stubbs & Wootton loafers adorned the latter. The wives of both were the same: blond, super thin and the kind who carried a Birkin bag in a signature shade on a Sunday.

"Sometimes I feel bad for you, Kari," Alan said.

"Why?" I asked as I read the providence of a painting I liked.

"You'd have a better life with a finance guy instead of a lawyer."

Alan always led me onto the dance floor with this song. Unlike most men, money was never a high priority for him. In our culture, women wield beauty to secure the affection of wealthy men. If you were blessed with looks and brains, as he felt I was, guys with fortunes were a given. It was a constant struggle for me to convince my husband that I came out the winner when I married him. Fitting in with any group was never for me. I had my own goals. I longed for family, love and purpose. I had all three. I rested my case.

"It depends how you define 'better.' I would much rather hang out with the MCs in the music world than the masters of the universe in the finance orbit any day. We have much more in common with them."

"Really? How do you figure?" Alan asked.

"We're artists, like them. They make music, you come up with strategies to defend them and I reinvent luxury businesses. Wall Street has plenty of guys making money who aren't building anything."

"But they're building businesses," Alan said. I shook my head.

"They make a living by trading off companies other people create. They're not selling a product that is tangible or that contributes anything to society. If they use their fortunes to give back, great. But many of them place so much value on their houses, cars and art collections because that's the only thing they have to show for their work. That's not us. Our work is original; it comes from our hearts." Creativity is fueled by passion. Lana reminded me of that when I saw her in her shop. Her enthusiasm for her product was no less than when we first met.

Alan wouldn't let up. Once he veered off onto this road, it was hard for him to turn back. "You'd have better seats at the Heat games if you married a hedge fund guy." Seats at basketball games are for Miamians what seating at charity events is to Palm Beachers. There is a social hierarchy determined by status. Hip-hop artists and finance guys sit on the floor at center court. The next rows up are reserved for corporate business owners and their families. These seats come with staff to serve you; there's no need to fight the crowds at the concession stands to get a beverage or a burger. Above them sit professionals, or if they can't attend, their staff.

At galas on the Island, folks who buy tables are seated in the center, just the right distance from the band. You will find the biggest patrons on the outskirts of the dance floor, a short distance from the ballroom doors. This way, they can exit quietly without being noticed if something more important comes up, which is often. Those who bought tickets at face value are seated toward the back of the room, far from the entertainment. Guests given gratis tickets are placed at their tables.

"Let the hedge fund guys sit there. If we had floor seats, I'd be afraid a player would fall on me. A share of season tickets, 12 rows up from center court, is good enough for me. From our seats, I have a view of Gucci Mane, Rick Ross, Lil Wayne and Khaled. I can see who they're with and what designers they're wearing. Remember, when we get back, there's a home game against Oklahoma, and then we have the art shows—one in Miami and one in Palm Beach. We may be priced out of the art market in SoHo," I added, "but we've picked up some amazing pieces at the fundraiser for Young at Art." I said this to boost his ego.

A VALUABLE LESSON FROM LANA

Once a year, this museum asks artists to donate artwork and sculptures. Apart from the cost to attend, raffle tickets were sold. When your number was drawn from a glass bowl, you got to choose one of the donated pieces. For a few years, we scrimped to buy a raffle ticket, but that year we bought two, which meant we'd go home with two pieces of art. We were happy to support our friend Mindy, an artist and the founder of the museum.

I was more excited about the show in Palm Beach. It was an event I never missed. In past years, I went to look. That year I was coming to buy. Alan promised me a year-end bonus for my work. I requested a gift from the show instead. Like your favorite store, where you know you will always find something you like, the show's display of jewelry, art and decorative objects reflected my style. Finally, my finances matched my taste level.

But before I could think about art, I had business to take care of in Miami. The charitable foundation that occupied a wing of our office building wasn't renewing their lease. They were moving north to Miami Gardens, closer to the at-risk youth they served.

"I thought you said the broker that got us the nonprofit didn't want the listing, Kari."

"He didn't. I did some research and found a broker from another company who does. She seems like a go-getter." Rubi had shown the space twice. Already, she had an offer. She said she needed to discuss it with me in person and made me promise not to tell Alan about it. Something was up—I needed to get home and find out what exactly was going on.

Once Upon a Time in Miami

The Monday after we got back, I raced from boot camp to meet Rubi at the office. I was so excited I almost forgot to bring the pastries I'd brought from my car.

"The group that's interested in the building is a plastic surgeon's office," she said as she dipped a croissant into her coffee.

"Wow, that's fabulous. How long a lease do they want?"

"That's why I wanted to talk to you in person, Kari. They're not interested in a lease. They want to buy the building. Their offer is double what Zillow says it's worth. Those ideas you gave me to present the space worked." She was referring to a floor plan I mocked up with the intention to help close a deal. I included dimensions of each office, research of what similar spaces were renting for and improvements we made to the building.

The number she threw out was worth considering. We could find another space to house the law firm. But I knew my husband. He designed this building and rebuilt it when it was destroyed by a fire. It was his second home. He was 66, but he wasn't ready to retire. If he was still working, he wasn't leaving his building.

"Let me run it by the boss, Rubi. When do you need an answer?"

"As soon as possible. It's a cash offer; they want to close in three weeks." Secretly, I hoped Alan would pass. I didn't want to sell an asset that was going up in value if we didn't have to. When we discussed it at dinner, I tried not to sway his decision.

"Wow, Kari! That's a sizable number. I didn't think the property was worth anything near that. If we put the profit in the stock market, the return would be more than a rent check."

"Don't think about the money; it's irrelevant. We own the building free and clear. I paid off the mortgage. Rubi will find us another tenant. If we sell it, we'll have to find another space to work from. This office building is like a second home to you."

"How'd you pay off the mortgage?"

"With the profits from the law firm."

"We're not selling, Kari. As far as I'm concerned, I'm just getting started."

"I hoped you'd say that. In that case, I'm going to remove the foundation's name from the outside of the building and design a different logo for us, if that's okay with you." When the final proof for the new signage was ready, the shop owner called me to come in and approve it. I looked carefully at the font and the wording I'd chosen: "Alan R. Soven & Associates: Boutique Law Firm."

"What's the R stand for?" the owner asked.

"Robert. Why?"

"Just curious."

The name may not have meant much to him, but it meant everything to me. Robert was my father's name. How was it that I never made the connection between his name and Alan's middle name? A father is the first guy a girl falls in love with. Suddenly, my mind was filled with memories of mine: the way he showed me how to swing a hammer when he built a playhouse in our yard, the countless times he tried to teach me tennis, the endless rides in his red sports car. No wonder I fell for Alan; they were alike. He'd be proud of how I turned around Alan's firm. He used to tell me since he had no sons, his legacy would live on in his daughters.

"It's fine; please deliver it tomorrow," I said as I wiped a tear from my eye.

I was excited for the party at the museum in Miami tonight. Mindy gave me the scoop about an up-and-coming artist she thought I'd like. She wouldn't tell me her name, just a hint. "She's young and she's donated two pieces. I hope your number is one of the first to be called, so you have a better shot at getting one of her pieces. This artist is so you, Kari."

The night of the auction I put on the same red lace skirt and fitted top I'd worn to the bar mitzvah. This outfit brought me luck that day, so perhaps it would again. Alan and I arrived early, so we could get a close look at the donated artwork displayed throughout the museum. As we walked up and down the aisles, I saw a piece that resembled a photograph. It was a girl with long blond hair in a pale blue dress with a white apron tied around her waist, sweeping a glass slipper underneath a rug that looked like grass. This piece was titled "Cinderella." It was part of a collection the artist called "The Once Upon A Time Series." Only five had been made. This had to be the piece Mindy meant. She was privy to how challenging the housewife role was to me when Alan and I first married. Alan laughed when I showed him the piece. "You can get it, Kari, but it's not my taste; you'll need to hang it somewhere I won't see it."

"Of course. It'll go in Emmy's room." We walked to the bar to get cocktails and continued browsing. Alan saw a glazed ceramic sculpture of a brown paper bag, the kind you put your lunch in and brought to school when you were a kid. That would be his pick. We glimpsed Mindy from a distance. She was engaged in a conversation with one of the sponsors. This wasn't the time to pull her away. When we spotted her again, I asked if the Cinderella piece was what she had in mind for me.

"Actually, no, but the one I had in mind is by the same artist. It's called 'Sleeping Beauty.' It's of a girl with long hair dressed in a pink princess costume in bed with a silk mask over her eyes. Next to her is a nightstand with alarm clocks piled on it. It reminded me of Emmy because you always said you could never get her up in the morning until she discovered Starbucks."

"That sounds adorable. I can't believe I didn't see it. Where is it?" Mindy walked me to the wall where the piece was displayed. She was right. It made me think of my girl. And it was so clever, a modern version of Sleeping Beauty. This piece and the "Cinderella" one would look great side by side in Emmy's room, which doubled as my study now that she lived in New York. "Allie, I hate to tell you this, but you're not getting that brown bag sculpture for your office. The pieces I want look much better as a pair; I need both."

"Let's decide when our numbers are called. If the one you want is still available, you can have both picks." That's how it worked with us. We had a deal. He got to choose hotels and restaurants. I was in charge when it came to furnishings and art. The red lace outfit brought me luck again. Our two raffle numbers were called early in the auction. We went home with my two fairy princesses.

Once Upon a Time in Palm Beach

After work, I drove to Bal Harbour Shops. Work was super busy, and I needed therapy—the retail kind. Valentine's Day was a week away and I was shopping for a new dress for "The Vernissage," the preview party held opening night of The Jewelry, Art and Antique Show. The lucky Islanders who had received a VIP pass would be lined up to get first dibs on the goods. Alan and I left for Palm Beach before rush hour to avoid traffic. We planned to meet Bri on the red carpet. She was bringing a new beau. I didn't want to make a bad impression.

We left our car with the valet and caught up with Bri. It never surprised me how small Palm Beach was. The boyfriend she introduced us to was someone I already knew. His daughter had taken gymnastics with Emmy. He set off to get us drinks from the bar. We walked through the show admiring the artwork, furniture and jewelry. It was that last item on the list that made the women in this town go wild. The lavish display of rubies, emeralds, sapphires and diamonds all under one roof had to be one of the best in the world. Alan glanced at my hand and said, "I think you need another ring to balance out that rock on your left hand." This event called for fine jewelry. I was wearing my yellow diamond.

"Let's see if there's something I like. But this ring makes such a statement, it might be too much to wear another large gem on my other hand."

"Oh, Kari," Bri said as she gave me a hug. "Who'd have ever guessed these would be the kind of problems you had?"

"Not me, and certainly not from this guy." As we turned a corner, I was drawn to a booth that resembled someone's home library. The sign read "Imperial Fine Books." As I browsed through leatherbound first editions and classics, I stumbled upon *A Thousand and One Nights,* which included the story of *Aladdin.* The proprietor of the shop introduced herself as Bibi and said, "Are you aware that the story of *Aladdin and the Magic Lamp* is one of the most well-known and retold fairy tales?" I laughed, remembering that this story is where Alan's nickname came from. And there had to have been a bit of magic that turned him into a prince.

"I wasn't, but the story has always been a favorite of mine," I replied. I continued searching until I saw *The Wizard of Oz.* Something about this story spoke to me. Growing up, my sisters and I watched the movie every Thanksgiving, but I couldn't remember ever reading the book. Bibi directed me toward a cozy club chair in the corner of her booth and handed me both books so I could leaf through them.

"I want to pick the story that's most inspiring to me," I said. Bibi could tell it was hard for me to decide between the two.

"If you look at your shoes, I think you'll find your answer," she said. I glanced down at my feet. I was wearing the red satin crystal-embellished high heels I'd worn to my first ball on the Island. Suddenly, it hit me. Mine was no Cinderella story; I never aspired to be a princess. And unlike Jasmine, I wasn't born into royalty. Like Dorothy, I was a girl from a small town who journeyed to a magical place. I handed Bibi the copy of *The Wizard of Oz.* I didn't ask the price.

"I'll take this one."

"Are you sure that's what you want, Kari?" Alan asked. I nodded. Alan placed his credit card on the small table. Bibi had been patient with me; I was happy to give her a sale. She had a lot of competition. This crowd wasn't here to buy books. We caught up with Bri, who was trying on rings in a jewelry booth. She winked at me as she flashed her left hand. An oval-shaped diamond solitaire stretched up to the knuckle of her ring finger. Then she saw my shopping bag and said, "What did you get, Kari?" I pulled the book out to show it to her.

"Your husband was willing to buy you jewelry and you got a book...are you insane?"

"It's a limited edition, exactly what I wanted." I kissed Bri goodbye and explained we had a dinner reservation. "Give the kids a hug for me. It was nice to see you again," I said to Bri's beau. "Let's get together again soon." As we exited, I saw Arthur, my former tenant, accompanied by an attractive blonde with a tiny waist in a pearly blue dress. I wasn't surprised. It was never hard for a man to find a date in a town filled with Cinderellas. As we waited for our car, Alan asked, "Are you sure the book is enough, Kari? You know I planned to spend more."

"It's more than enough," I replied. Then I had a thought. I called Sarah, the artist who made my two princess pieces.

"Hi Sarah, it's Kari, Mindy's friend. I know it's late, but I was wondering if you had any other pieces from your 'Once Upon a Time' series?"

"I do; would you like to come to the studio and see them?"

"I'm not in town, but can you email them to me, so I can look at them on my phone?"

"Yes," she said.

"Kari, who are you talking to? Can't it wait?" Alan asked.

"No." Alan knew me. When an idea popped into my head, I had to see it through. When we got to Chez Jean-Pierre, Alan stopped at a table to greet David Roth, the famous criminal defense attorney. I slid into the banquet and looked at the images Sarah sent me. The first one was "Rapunzel." It wasn't what I was after. My hair was never my strength. The next one was "Snow White," standing in front of a kitchen sink surrounded by dishes. I had no desire to relive that stage of my life. Then I glimpsed the last one. It was a young girl with brown pigtails, dressed in a white puff-sleeved blouse and a blue and white gingham skirt. You could only see her from the back. She was sitting on the floor in her closet staring at her collection of shoes. In the bottom right-hand corner was a red crystal high heel. *Bingo!*

"I'll take Dorothy," I wrote back to Sarah.

"Is everything okay?" Alan asked as he watched me slip my phone into my handbag.

"More than okay. The artist who did the princess pieces made one of Dorothy from *The Wizard of Oz*. She's holding it for me. Now I have a rare book and a piece of art."

"I'm so glad you can finally lead the life you deserve."

"What life is that?"

"The princess's life—collecting art, attending charity events, lunching with the lawyers' wives, shopping. Maybe you can schedule more beauty treatments and hire a personal trainer?"

"Really, Allie, you think that's what makes me happy?"

"Sure, why not?"

"I've spent the last five years revamping your law practice. You know what? I'm not interested in running a business. After the first few months of steady income, I got bored. I miss the adventure of something new. You have a plan in place. We have staff who can take over my responsibilities. As for the princess's life, I didn't do all this so my nails could look pretty. My manicure is too perfect. I need to go hang from another cliff."

"But if you're not going to work or live the princess' life, what are you going to do?"

"The princesses you're reminiscing about are from stories that took place long ago. A modern-day princess gets down off her throne and does something to help people. I don't know what my next move is, but I look forward to taking some time to find out." Alan paid the bill and we left. As the valet brought our car around, I asked Alan if he could drive by my old house. Usually, he complained when I made this request. This time he didn't. As we approached the house, I could see my chandelier hanging in the entranceway. The toucans etched on the glass doors looked up to the lights as they danced with the crystals. I'd called the new owner, Chip, to see if I could take it; he said it would be okay. I'm glad I never found the time. This way, when I came to town, I could see it. Part of me was still there.

If you happen to be in Palm Beach and take North Lake Way to the end where it winds around to the water, you may see the window where the witch is rumored to live. Don't be scared. You see, this witch isn't wicked, like the one from the west in *The Wizard of Oz*. She is more like Glinda, the good witch, from the same story. All along, she was there to guide me.

It was dark, but a streetlight lit up that window in the coral reef. For the first time, I saw the brim of a witch's hat and the silhouette of her face against the metal bars of the window. The moon's shadow made it seem as if her lips were moving. I imagined she whispered to me the same words she said to Dorothy: "You had the power all along, my dear. You just had to find it for yourself."

"Kari, you look sad; are you okay?" Alan asked.

"I'm fine. I was just thinking how magical Palm Beach seemed when I first came here. But when my marriage fell apart, the hurricanes struck and the recession hit—the magic wore off."

"Palm Beach will always be magical, Kari. And you took a piece of that magic with you when you left. Just look at everything that's happened to us! What more proof do you need to see it working? I'm tired; can we turn around and head back now?"

"Yes, I want to go home."

So that's how I paved a Yellow Brick Road: starting in New York, stopping in Palm Beach and commencing again in Miami. Along the way, I met some phony wizards, a few fairy godmothers and many potential princes. I never needed them to save me. By following my heart, I found my own version of happily ever after. It happened to me, and it can happen to you—right here, right now, in any place you call home. Click your heels together, wish big and write your own story.

Acknowledgments

I am blessed to have had the support of so many people during my writing journey. First and foremost I need to thank my extraordinary editors Alice Peck and Kate Cavanaugh, who believed in my story from the beginning. Alice—working with you was equivalent to getting a master's degree in creative writing; what more can I say? Kate—you read my book word for word and weren't shy about telling me which parts needed to go, which were worth keeping and all the while giving me carefully constructed line edits.

To the authors who came before me: Candace Bushnell, Lauren Weisberger and Curtis Sittenfeld. Writing a book while the world was on lockdown and socialization was prohibited was challenging. To stay inspired, I named key characters after you three. Curtis, I'm sorry I named you after a man and in a sex scene no less, but the way you described teen romance in your novel, *Prep*, made me want to go back and endure the drama of high school all over again just to have a relationship like your characters Lee Fiora and Cross Sugarman did.

To my coterie of fairy godmothers who gave me the courage to push forward and keep writing, I'm forever grateful: Melissa Fields, Nicole Nicholas, Marla and Nina Scherer, Cynthia and Monterey McEachern, Perla Trejo, Cindy Mirapol, Morgan Williams, Barbara Pozo, Bianca and Marissa Zingales, Miles Rote and Scott Gershon.

Bryan Williams—a girl couldn't conjure up a better fairy godfather than you. When you told me that my writing was really strong and this is what I should be doing, there was no turning back. How could I not trust the advice of the guy who discovered Lil Wayne, the greatest rapper and wordsmith alive? The world may know you as Birdman or Baby, but you will always be my #1 Stunna.

Big hugs to my dazzling daughter, my disciplined stepson Noah and my brave nephew Brandon. You are my heart, my soul, my everything, and watching you three grow up has been a joy and a privilege.

My deepest thanks to my amazing publisher, Anna David, and her talented team at Legacy Launch Pad Publishing who turned my dream of publishing this story into a reality.

Special thanks to the denizens of Palm Beach who graciously welcomed me from the moment I first stepped foot on the Island and treated me like family; without all of you there would be no story to tell.

And lastly, to the fictional character Dorothy Gale, for showing me the way home.

About the Author

Karen Soven spent three decades in the luxury fashion industry before repurposing her skills to help grow a boutique law firm. She holds a BA in mass media studies with a minor in marketing from the University of Miami, though she's quick to note that she's not really a "credentials person." Born on Manhattan's Upper East Side, Karen now divides her time between Miami and Palm Beach. For fun, she enjoys crafting party favors, entertaining at home, practicing yoga and mentoring youth. *Once Upon a Time in Palm Beach* is her first book.

For more information about Karen Soven and *Once Upon a Time in Palm Beach*, scan the QR code below:

About the Publisher

Legacy Launch Pad is a boutique publishing company that works with entrepreneurs from all over the world.

For more information about Legacy Launch Pad Publishing, go to: www.legacylaunchpadpub.com.